DIVINE REVELATIONS

The Essence of All Things

A Treatise on Perception, Reality, Absolute Truths,
Language, Nuclear Structures, the Yi Jing, the Kabbalah
& the Universal Human Mind

by

W. R. Hohenberger

Second Edition, First Printing
ISBN-13: 978-1522735076
ISBN-10: 1522735070
Library of Congress Control Number: 2016901803
CreateSpace Independent Publishing Platform, North Charleston, SC

Book Cover by Weible Design, Inc.
Printed and Distributed by CreateSpace - an Amazon Company
Printed in the United States of America

Table of Contents

Acknowledgements

I would like to thank God, for the honor and privilege;

my mother and father, for their exemplary love;

my wife, for her support and understanding;

*my daughter, for helping me on the graphics and
for being all that a father could ask;*

*my family and my friends,
for being there when I needed them most;*

*Fu Hsi and King Wen,
for without the Yi Jing, the OWS would not be possible;*

*Rabbi Yitzhak Saggi Nehor and the ancient Hebrew culture,
for without the Kabbalah, the OWS could not be proven;*

*Briddell, Lockyer, Volk & my other CNPS friends,
for without their works and their help,
the OHF would have never been found;*

*and all scientists & philosophers, great and small,
for helping me to find my part of the truth.*

iii

Joshua

What a fine young man,
everyone his friend.
He was so young and fragile,
yet so bright and strong.

His operation, too long and too hard,
his physical heart, too weak.
He fought a valiant effort,
but earthly life was not God's plan.

Disbelief, anger and fear were felt,
with loneliness and sorrow to come.
Searching for answers, looking for reasons,
trying to understand the good for us all.

Knowing God, secure in our faith,
only doubting ourselves.
Waiting for the day we shall see him again
in the Promised Land.

Prologue

It has now been forty-one years since I conceived the first ideas for this book during the month of January in 1975, thirty-two years since my son died in 1984 when I committed myself to writing it all down, and twenty-four years since I published the first edition of this book in 1992 titled *Perceptions - A Symphony of Words*. So here it is now in 2016, and I am finally publishing this new and greatly expanded second edition and with a new title, *Divine Revelations*. I decided to write this prologue to the new book, and then to include the original 1992 introduction from the old book with only minor amendments in its entirety immediately following this prologue, as it is still as applicable today as it was in 1992. The fundamental premises of this book are a growing and expanding Earth, another world that exists beyond the world that we perceive, out of body experiences including life after death, an Organized Word Structure (OWS) that details and defines the mental processes functioning with the human brain, and simplified mathematics and understandable structures for sub-nuclear forces. It includes an absolute derivation for the meaning of 666 from the Book of Revelation within the Bible, and absolute proof that truth is the essence of the true spirit of the real living God. In other words, this book includes delineated descriptions for how it all works, and provides a basic foundation for a true theory for the basic fundamentals of everything.

Accordingly, my book has grown substantially, has a new and more reflective title, and is now twice as long as the original book. Pictorial renditions have been added to Chapter One for the imaginative and picturesque descriptions for the world beyond our human perceptions. I visualized these images in the 1980's, described them in my book in the 1990's, published images on-line in the 2000's, and now see others duplicating my techniques in television ads in 2015. I have also added a new Chapter Two that delineates and illustrates the reasons why the visual images that we perceive exist solely within our minds. Accordingly, it is clearly shown that the world as we see it, exists solely within our minds, and that there actually exits another world beyond our human perceptions. As hard as it is to believe, both the objects of our physical world, as well as the invisible forces of the supernatural world, each have their own existence independent of our own human perceptual and visual imagery, just as was described in the first chapter of the original 1992 version of the book. A greatly expanded Chapter Three includes the psychological origins for both the Yi Jing (Yijing or I Ching) and the Kabbalah, as well as, a more detailed OWS for the human brain. This newly integrated OWS, Yi Jing, and Kabbalah along with an additionally integrated Lüscher's Color Test provides volumes of detailed information about the organizational structure of the fundamental processes functioning within the human brain.

For those of you who have seen the movie *The Matrix*, after reading the first three chapters in this book, you will understand both the origins of the matrix and the basic concepts behind the matrix as presented in the movie. Much of the movie was based upon my 1992 book, which was published, not so coincidentally, just a few years before the ideas for the script of the movie were conceived. The script was originally to be a comic, but was expanded into a full length movie and then released in 1999 without my knowledge or consent. When Marvel Comics contacted me in 1993, I told them they could use some of the ideas from my book in a comic, but not to reference my work as I did not consider comics a proper venue for my works. I never saw the movie until just a few months ago as my main interest in life is uncovering the real truth and I have little to no interest in science fiction. However, at conferences I attended, other attendees kept telling me of the similarities between my works and the movie *The Matrix*. So I watched the movie and it was only then that I realized what had happened. For those of you who are familiar with both the movie and the Yi Jing, I believe the Yi Jing to be the oracle that is referenced in the movie, since it is an integral part of the matrix as was originally proposed in my 1992 book and as is suggested in the movie. Furthermore, the ideas for the Red Pill and the Blue Pill were clearly taken directly from the Red Symmetry and the Blue Symmetry within the Yi Jing, as was again detailed and presented in my 1992 book. I also believe that some of the fundamental ideas for the movie Avatar were probably also derived from my writings in my 1992 book.

I have also included a greatly expanded analysis of sub-nuclear forces in Chapter Four, presenting both mathematical proofs and structural diagrams and drawings for the overall and internal structures of both the electron and the proton, which are of primary importance since they are the basic mathematical building blocks of matter. Although the math may be ancillary and somewhat exhausting, it is the ideas behind the math that is essential in understanding the various juxtapositions that exist between our world and the real world that exists beyond our human perceptions. Accordingly, any theory of everything must include mathematical proofs, as well as real and understandable descriptions for both the visible and the invisible forces of nature.

There is still much work that needs to be done, but the basic ideas are all there. So if you stick with it and study my book, you will learn a lot about a lot of things. Hopefully, it will make you stop and think about yourself, your life, those around you who you love, the world that surrounds you, but most importantly your relationship with God and His Eternal Truths.

The Original 1992 Introduction

I began this book when I was just a boy, staring out my bedroom window and peering in wonder at the stars in the night sky. That is not much different from most of us at some point in our lives, as we are each searching for our own individual truth. Somewhere along the way, I even decided with my youthful ignorance that God did not exist and that this world of mine was the only world. Never did I realize that others saw a different part of the world than I did; and never could I have realized that there are actually other worlds completely different from the one any of us saw.

While I was watching things, others watched people. When I saw people laugh and cry, others laughed and knew why they cried. I stumbled and fell within the confusions of my mind, as I simply could not understand why others would not do as I would have done. I unknowingly hurt many people along the way, as well as myself, while others also hurt me. The irony of this life is that while it should be simple, it is instead difficult; and while it should be a celebration of being, it instead ends in a procession of death. It was during just such a procession for my son, that I committed myself to completing my task and to recording my ideas with pen and ink to paper. Little did I realize the magnitude of my challenge or the hardships of my undertaking.

The fundamental ideas, which are the basis for this book, were initially conceived in January 1975, and subsequently grew within my mind for the next nine years. I tried many times to share them with others, but it was difficult to get nonprofessionals to understand because of their seemingly abstract nature, and almost impossible to get the professional person to listen because of my lack of formal training in each of the respective disciplines being discussed. Then in 1984, from the grief of losing my son, I wrote the poem of dedication and realized that I must similarly record my ideas from my heart, as well as my mind.

Accordingly, this book represents my search for the absolute truth and is presented to you in the form of metaphysical images, philosophical reasoning, and psychological and spiritual insights. Its purpose is to unite the disciplines of metaphysics, philosophy, meta-psychology and religion into a single integrated whole. Many people say there is no absolute truth, but my heart disagrees. We just haven't found or recognized that truth. According to Tze-Sze, grandson of Confucius, "the absolute truth is indestructible. Being indestructible, it is eternal. Being eternal, it is self-existent. Being self-existent, it is infinite. Being infinite, it is vast and deep. Being vast and deep, it is transcendental and intelligent." Truth is reality; it is the way things really are; it is never telling a lie; and it can only be found in the honesty and sincerity within our hearts. Only when we are honest with our selves and those around us, can we hope to find the real truth; and only when we know the truth can we hope to make those decisions that will positively affect our lives.

I had a friend who told me a story about going hunting with three other men in the Colorado Mountains when he was a young man. Somehow he managed to become separated from his friends and hopelessly lost in the mountainous woods. He had no idea of where he was, which direction to travel, or how to find his way back to camp. Eventually, without food or water, he apprehensively nestled down under a tree for three very long days, until a search party finally found him. Such is the case with the human race, as we, too, are lost and our only hope is to be rescued by the eternal truths of an omniscient and omnipotent God. Currently, we seem to be so perplexed and bewildered by the confusions of our minds and so far from the truth, that the real truth is no longer even visible. We have become blind to both our own errant ways and to God's eternal truths. We either hold on steadfastly to ancient and antiquated beliefs, or we completely discard them in favor of our own beliefs, by which we can conduct our lives in almost any way we deem necessary or practical.

Contrasting these innate tendencies toward both deaf and blind human nature, are the honest remarks of honorable men, within which can be found the essence of all truth. Most of us seem to have difficulty accepting those truths, especially when they do not fit into our own limited perspectives. However, unless the person professing the truth is judged to be dishonest or insane, we must at the minimum, accept it as at least a symbol of the truth. Symbolism itself appears repetitively throughout human history in our writings and our religions, as well as in our visions and our dreams. In each case, it is the direct result of our unlimited and unconscious potential to understand the truth, speaking out through our limited and conscious knowledge of the truth. Symbolism, therefore, represents through the limited vocabulary of our conscious intellect, our only method for describing our innate and unconscious knowledge of the truth. Accordingly, our various religions become an almost unlimited source of insight into the absolute truth. An example quotes St. John the Divine from the Book of Revelations in the Bible: "...and before the throne was a sea of glass like unto crystal."

Within this book you will find the basis for understanding that truth as well as many other truths, thereby establishing a more complete truth within your own mind. You will be able to say to agnostics, "Absolutely yes," when asked, "Does God exist?" You will know that because we are here, He is there. You will be able to say to atheists, "Absolutely yes," when asked, "Is there a Hell?" You will know that there is a bottomless pit engulfed by a lake of burning fire. You will be able to say to the philosopher, "Absolutely not," when asked, "Does sound exist on an uninhabited island?" You will know that sound, as well as our visions are mere functions of the mind. You will also be able to say to troubled friends, "Absolutely yes," when asked, "Is there a Heaven?" You will know that there is another world made from the crystalline energy of liquid light interspersed by a fabric of waves of the stellar mist.

Within this book you will take a journey of the imagination through the realities of the universe. You will see and understand in picturesque detail the birth of a crystalline star, the heartbeat of inter-spatial waves, and the angelic images of spiritual life. You will learn that the earth was created from the seemingly nothingness of the universe, was only half its current size in the childhood of its life, and today is still growing and expanding from the forces of creation within its center. Within this book you will learn about, and understand, the spirit of the soul, the eternity of life, the origin of the ego and the self, and the constructs of good and evil. You will learn about the truth of the God of Abraham, the wisdom of the Chinese culture, and the origin of good and evil within the religions and the civilizations of man. You will have the opportunity to open your heart, to meet God, and to become a child of God if you so choose.

Before you discount these claims as incredulous, please allow me to share with you the parable of the woodsmen. There once was a woodsman who became an expert at felling the great trees of the forest within a few inches of where he wanted them to fall. A fellow woodsman was very impressed by his skills and asked him how he developed such a talent. He answered, "Come with me tomorrow and I will show you." The next day they went together into the woods and the expert woodsman taught his new friend his skills. They would walk completely around the tree, viewing its lean and its shape from various positions. They would then make the precise cuts and fell the tree within an inch of their mark. As they were resting on the stump of a tree, they noticed another woodsman felling a nearby tree. The second woodsman asked the expert woodsman which way the tree would fall. The expert woodsman answered saying, "I do not know for sure. I only know that it will not fall this way." Such is the case with our own lives, as we each see only our own point of view, and unless we walk the path of the other man, we cannot know the wisdom of his point of view. Therefore, I ask you each to come with me on a journey of both imagination and enlightenment, and then to try to understand my point of view.

However, we must first develop a few fundamental insights before we begin our journey. For instance, we must first realize that all of the images, sensations, and sounds perceived by the human being exist solely within the apparatus of the human mind. That is, as we look around and observe our surroundings, the objects that we perceive as existing outside of our body are actually images existing within the substance of our mind. This does not mean that the objects themselves do not exist outside of our body, but only that their reflected images exist within our mind; and that instead, their true existence is actually much different from those reflected images that we perceive within our mind.

When this innate truth is finally realized, it becomes apparent that there actually exists another world outside of our perceived world. It is comprised of the combined substance of the physical world and the forces of the spiritual world and can be visualized through the powers of our imagination into a single integrated whole. For instance, if an atom is seen as a phosphorescent bubble as if it were a single spark aglow in the dark, then structures of atoms could be seen as phosphorescent objects glowing in the dark. Accordingly, objects such as tables, chairs, and even our bodies could be described as structures of crystal emanating with light or as phosphorescent fabrics woven from radiant strands of crystalline light. Then imagine a single atom supernaturally dissolved into a translucent vapor, faintly permeating the whole of the darkness and gently enveloping the other atoms. Add to it the forces of the spiritual world as ghosting images of various shades of dark and light magically suspended as superimposed images within this universal substance of translucent light.

Applying these descriptions to our everyday world, see a handful of children at a camp meeting outing, as imaginary ghosts sitting around a brightly-lit campfire and surrounded by a glowing halo of fire-lit mist. See the trees around them as phosphorescent crystals glistening from the reflections of the fire-lit mist, and projecting interlaced auras throughout surrounding halos of a glowing and radiant mist. Then, add geometric images of transparent lights hovering over each of the children as a band of Guardian Angels in the night. And finally, see within each of the children's minds paralleled images of colored versions of their camp meeting scene, as they mysteriously yet ironically discuss the improbable existence of other worlds filled with ghosts, goblins, and angels. It is from this perspective that all of the fundamental forces within the universe, and hence the true reality of both ourselves and the universe, can be perceived.

In support of these claims, I offer this one additional piece of evidence. That is, one of the original ideas conceived back in 1975 was the theory for an expanding earth. In fact, it was the second idea to be conceived in the long chain of ideas, which are presented within this book, and it was conceived solely from a philosophical and metaphysi-

cal point of view. It was almost seven years later and with great satisfaction and contentment that I discovered geological evidence presented
by progressive geologists in support of that theory. As incredible as a
growing and expanding earth may seem, after reading the metaphysical
insights presented within this book, along with the geological evidence
presented in other books, it is almost impossible to deny. For those in-
terested in that evidence I have included excerpts of it along with other
quotes from selected authors in support of the basic premises contained
within this book in Chapter Seven.

The theories and philosophies presented in this book are then proposed not as the complete truth, but as the foundation for a comprehensive and absolute truth. It is also understood that it will take many
years of additional study, clarification, and correction to achieve that
goal. However, due to its broad perspective and the nature of its content, even though it may still contain some errors, it is presented in the
sincere hope that it will help others to seek and to find God, and to
thereby establish a firm foundation for the conquest of their lives.

The Circle of Truth

The first chapter in this book is about the visual world beyond, the
second - the visual world within, the third - the mind, the fourth - the
scientific world, the fifth - divinity, the sixth - emotions, and the seventh - other's insights into the truth, and which together collectively
represent a circle of truth. Circular logic, circular reasoning, and circular arguments have long been discounted as pragmatically useless since
the original premise that justifies the conclusions are then used to justify the original premise. However, I propose that when a circle of truth
is large enough to encompass all things that are known to exist or that
can ever exist, and to prove and to explain all data that has ever been
collected or that can be collected, then it is argued that circular reasoning is not only valid, but then becomes *a great circle of everlasting
truth*. Accordingly, no matter which chapter a person starts reading in
this book, there will always be questions that can only be answered
from a perspective presented in one of the other chapters. Therefore,
each reader must decide for themselves the best order in which to read
the book depending upon their own expertise, knowledge and interests.
Enjoy reading.

Chapter One

Enlightened Mysteries

*"We shall some day catch an abstract truth by the tail,
then we shall have our religion and our immortality."*
- Henry Adams (1838-1918)

Introduction

Henry Adams was born in Boston, the grandson of John Quincy Adams and the great-grandson of John Adams, the sixth and the second presidents of the United States, respectively. He graduated from Harvard in 1858 and then toured Europe just prior to the outbreak of the civil war. During the war, he served in London England as private secretary to his father, who had been appointed by Abraham Lincoln as ambassador to the United Kingdom. He was an author, journalist, professor and historian and wrote several novels. The above quote concerning abstract truths is from Ernest Samuels, *Henry Adams: The Middle Years* (1958).

The explanations and descriptions presented in this chapter were originally conceived as an abstract truth; in that I realized very early that there were two worlds, the perceptual world that we see and the conceptual world that we draw as a model for the real world that surrounds us. I like most human beings just assumed that the world that we see is the real world and that the conceptual world was just another way of looking at our perceived world. It was years later that I realized that the conceptual world was just as real as our perceived world; and then even more years, before I realized that I had it all reversed, and that our perceived world is actually the illusion and it is instead the conceived world that is the real world.

Heaven & Earth

Our World

It seems at times that there is a great abyss between the knowledge of our minds and the feelings found within our hearts. However, along with most of our seemingly inherent deficiencies there is usually found a force with the ability to bridge these irreconcilable chasms within our psychological being. As such, curiosity is the outward response to the inner need for fulfillment within living beings. Nowhere on earth is this force manifested greater than in the human being. At birth, we were each given a mind with the natural instinct to search for newness in life.

As children, we established values and priorities, which represented the culmination of those early years of learning. As adults, we are each involved in a constant struggle to find the remaining solutions to the unanswered questions, which developed during those fragile years.

This unquenchable thirst for the knowledge of whom and what we are can be most easily seen in the natural curiosity we exhibit toward the world in which we live. In its name, we have explored the earth's lands and seas, peered into the distance of the universe and the smallest of the atoms, and studied the creatures of life for a definition of life. During this journey, we have amassed great volumes of information about our universe. While at the same time, we have failed to develop a common perception of the universe; and probably, only when we develop this common perception will be able to find those answers about ourselves that we are so earnestly seeking.

The Mysteries of Nature

Currently, we are proposing theories for the structure of the universe based on the thought that the universe is comprised of a small amount of real substance and that the remaining space is empty and void. The following theory is based on the thought that the universe is comprised entirely of substance, and that physical matter, as we know it, is but a small amount of that substance. Furthermore, it is proposed that physical matter is merely a single form of energy, of which many other forms are not only possible but also probable; and that the grandeur of the universe is far greater than previously imagined.

Champs-Elysees - Paris

The entire basis for scientific study is cause and effect. If we see a cause and know it to be real, then the effect must also be real. More importantly, if we see an effect and know it to be real, then the cause must also be real. This is a truth, which cannot be violated and cannot fail. It is only its application that fails, and that is a failure of ourselves to understand. Through science and technology, we continue to increase our knowledge and understanding at an ever-increasing pace, and although our accomplishments are impressive, we have failed to understand some of the most basic fundamental happenings around us. Therefore, it seems almost necessary that there exist a deeper, yet simpler and clearer reality for the universe that we perceive.

In order to develop this new perspective, we must rethink the very basis for the existence of ourselves, and our universe. It must include reasonable and comprehensible explanations for currently unexplained phenomena such as magnetic, gravitational, and nuclear forces; while at the same time, it must be accepted by the more holistic nonscientific human mind. Two different perceptions of our universe: the first, an abstract form called science, and the second, an innate feeling created within the boundaries of our mind. Accordingly, thoughts of reason and their respective descriptions will be presented based on two assumptions: first, the absolute totality of a universal substance; and second, that matter and energy are merely different manifestations of that same universal substance. I propose that from this foundation a new level of unified acceptance can be achieved.

City Streets - Hof, Bavaria

The first assumption dictates that everything and all things are made of a single fundamental substance and that this substance completely fills our universe. Temporal descriptions for this substance are meaningless, since these descriptions are merely perceptions within our minds describing variations in the substance. For example, its sensations are the contact of its particles of matter with its particles of our bodies, its color is the frequency with which its waves interact with its particles of our eyes, and its taste is the chemical interaction between its particles of matter and its particles of our taste buds. Accordingly, it is everything and everywhere, and it is the size of the universe, and its composition is of itself. However, we must remember that it is just as real as we are, and with that we must be satisfied.

The second assumption dictates that the universal substance possesses the ability for variations of itself, that is, a substance, which can change its form or its density and is fluid in nature. The first law of thermodynamics is the law of conservation of energy. It states that energy cannot be created, nor destroyed, but must always remain the same. An even more basic revelation of this law is the recognition of the existence of energy, and that the total energy present in the universe is a constant. Again, a description for energy is also meaningless, since energy is simply a potential to cause change and is only as real as its ability to exist and as its effects that we perceive. Although neither the universal substance nor the energy of change can be directly perceived, their effects can be heard, felt, and seen. Hence, it must be possible for their own real existence within the heavens, to be understood by our intellectual being, to be visualized by our mental being, and, finally, to be felt within our spiritual being. Instead of using the historical name of aether for the universal substance, from this point on, it will be referred to as the stellar air, stellar winds, stellar clouds, stellar sea, cosmic mist or liquid light.

Star Struck

Imagine a sea of stellar air dispersed throughout the universe, filling all the space between the stars and the planets and also being in the stars and the planets. It is as though the heavens are suspended by, and within, the stellar air. See waves of all sizes rippling through the stellar air, as waves on a quiet river caused by children skipping rocks across the surface of the water. Look back at the physical bodies of our world and see glowing liquids of light, as the limbs of a tree are covered with the beauty of shining ice on the morning after a winter storm. See each of these bodies as ghosts, sparkling with complex patterns of motions within themselves, as millions of phosphorescent balls bouncing wildly in the spaces of a cube or a majestic cloud forming in a summer sky. See them each disturbing the evenness of the stellar air as they travel to and fro, just as a boat makes gentle waves of water as it travels across the stilled surface of a morning lake. Imagine all of these things from another world, and let your imagination loose to its limitless possibilities, but mellowed by the realities of our everyday world. With the spirit of inquiring minds, let us visit the very existence of ourselves, and the world within which we live.

However, before we can begin our journey, we must first rethink the mystery of the weight of our body. Each of us feels the sensation of our body being attracted to our mother earth. Regardless of where we are on this earth, how we position ourselves, or whether we work or play, we feel a constant force of considerable proportions tugging within our body and pulling us each towards the earth. At times the muscles of our legs are barely strong enough to keep our bodies erect. There must be a real, but simple explanation for such a constant and repetitive sensation. It must not violate the rules of cause and effect, and yet must exist in harmony with the other occurrences that we perceive within the world. The cause is a mysterious force invisible to our five senses, but forever acting on each particle within our body. The effects are objects falling freely through the air, but always toward the earth, and the sensation of a force, acting within our body propelling our inner self toward the earth. It is as though our body is a dead weight to our soul, our burden of life, on our journey of life through the relentless corridors of earthly time.

The Earth

The earth was born from our universe, just as we were each born from our earth. It had a physical beginning and has grown through many seasons of change, just as we each have, until today it shares a part of its existence with us; two different forms of life having in common a short period of overlapping space and time. During its life, the earth has developed beautiful mountains and plains, gigantic oceans, and numerous rivers and lakes, while at the same time the forces of nature have been constantly eroding at their very existence. As the forces of the rain and the wind work to dissolve the mountains and to fill the oceans, there must be an even greater force at work replenishing the earth with these beautiful creations. Two effects, the weight of our body and the growth of our earth, and a cause that must be as real as its effects and as simple as its absolute existence, yet hidden by the windows of our minds.

Picture the earth as a crystalline ball,
glowing and glittering and sparkling so bright.
See deep in its middle, a core that is empty
a dark dreary dungeon, without any light.

Its center is growing, increasing in fury,
absorbing black balls, in a molten slurry.
Imagine this cauldron, as froth for new atoms,
just as their source, was the life for our earth.

Imagine small waves, joining together,
producing more balls, but this time of light.
As David and Goliath, the light balls do capture
the dark balls, while making new matter.

To make this new matter, stellar air is required,
to come from the heavens that surround us.
See great stellar winds flowing like rivers,
through a spherical cone, and becoming our earth.

The force of its wind, as it blows through our bodies,
is the weight that we feel of ourselves
As the air that we breathe, as it blows up a storm,
is the force that can push us around.

See the physical bodies of the world as crystalline formations formed from glowing balls of liquid light. As you walk through the main street of your local city or town, imagine the streets, the storefronts, the signs, and everything that you see as translucent sculptures carved from the beauty of shining ice. It is as though you are traveling through a tunnel of whiteness, and all that you see is glistening like sculptures of ice. See the streets and walkways as sheets of ice as on a frozen mountain-lake. See the storefronts as whitened facades plastered with a mixture of water and ice, the windows as a glaze of frozen water, and the displays behind the windows as glittering sculptures shaped and molded from carvings of ice. See a light pole as a single icicle towering from the streets, and see its wires as silver strands spun from threads of frozen water and gently draped across its arms. See the dirt beside the streets as flakes from a newly fallen snow, the pebbles on the streets as balls of sleet, and the gravel within the streets as diamonds sparkling in the snow. Imagine the living creatures scurrying through the streets as ghosts cast from liquid vapor, and then empowered by an animated light into a sparkling silhouette. If only for a moment, capture a brief glimpse of the real existence of our physical world, as if it were a shining city perched atop a diamond hill, glistening from an all-intrusive lining of semi-translucent ice, and then gently accented by ultra light coverings of frozen sleet and snow.

Diamond Hills

See each of the forms within this city as complex creations made from billions of glowing balls of liquid light. Look inside their majestic forms, and see miniature balls of varying sizes interconnected in myriads of loosely packed arrangements. See some fastened rigidly as the legs of a triangle, some able to move and to cause movement as lever arms on a machine, and some moving freely among unknown forces as driftwood floating down an ever-changing stream. See gaping holes within these miniature structures, just as there are spaces between the structural members of an old steel bridge. And finally, see the stellar wind flowing down from the heavens and into the earth, as it blows through their perforated forms holding their bodies against their mother earth. With this vision in your mind, see and feel within yourself the force of the stellar wind blowing through the spaces of your body, just as the forest feels the force of a gentle breeze blowing between, and caressing, the branches of its trees.

It seems at times we get so entrenched in the thought patterns, which are needed to live in our everyday world that it is difficult to accept reasoning, which has little direct application to that world. At other times we seem willing to accept almost any explanation, as long as it fulfills even a small part of our inner needs. Somewhere in the middle there exists the real world hidden by the limited perceptions of our mind. Just as we can see the trees sway on a windy day or feel the chilling effects of a winter wind, we also can perceive in our mind the realness of the air that we breathe. What is this air and its wind? Is it a perception, which exists solely within our minds, or does it have an existence of its own? Likewise, what is the stellar air - a mere perception or something as real as we are, but hidden by the windows of our mind?

The focusing or bringing together of perception and reality has been for human kind an immensely difficult task. And then, we have added confusion to this task by failing to clearly differentiate between the meanings of the two words. For example, what is real to the magician is but an illusion of perception to the person observing the magician. This prestidigitation is both a part of reality, as well as, an illusion of perception; legerdemains or slights of hand of the magician. This confusion is then transferred to our other thought processes, as we further confuse reality with perception. We sometimes see images of strange occurrences which we later convince ourselves never occurred; or vice versa, we may at a later time fabricate an entire event which actually never occurred only to believe in our minds that it actually happened. We as human beings cannot always be sure that the images we perceive are truly representative of the actual occurrence. The only way to resolve this apparent conflict is to dissociate the meanings of the two words within our minds, so that reality is defined in absolute terms only, and perception is then limited to a lesser or partial derivative of that absolute.

It is then the inner development of both of these perspectives, which is required in order to understand the world around us. For example, think of our minds as existing within a shrouded enclosure, our five senses as differently shaped openings allowing only limited information into that enclosure, and our mental imagery as inner reflections of the messages sent to us from another space and another time. It is as though we are puppets on a string controlled by the complexity of the forces within and around us. From this removed and remote perspective, what we see and feel are really mental responses to the interaction of our bodies with our immediate surroundings. When seeing an object painted blue, the real world is stellar waves smaller than the size of dust, a structure of atoms and molecules reflecting waves the size of blue, and a body with an eye, a mind, and the ability to perceive. Do we really see an object painted blue, or do we perceive an image in our minds from the messages of waves sent through space and time? Two different perspectives of the same event: the first, the inner feeling of our own earthly being, and the second, a remote perspective from the knowledge within our mind of our earthly being.

Furthermore, what is meant by the phrase *space and time?* We can locate any point on earth or in the heavens by giving three dimensions the length, width, and height relative to our current location. But if we are asked to locate an airplane in flight, we must ask at what time. Similarly, everything in the universe is in motion; the stars in the sky, our earth and its matter, and the atoms and molecules, which are all in constant motion. It is meaningless to locate a point in space, unless we include the fourth dimension of time, describing the event occurring at that point. Just as distance is a variable and can be described in three dimensions, time is also a variable and can be described as a fourth dimension. Likewise, just as we can be taught to think of space in three dimensions, so also can we be taught to think of space and time in a fourth dimension. At times we attempt to draw images representing these four dimensions; however, this tends to only confuse our perceptions since we are trying to illustrate the fourth dimension of time using a distorted image of the first three dimensions of space. This confusion becomes even more apparent as the meanings for dimension and length are interchanged within our minds. Length is the measurement of distance, whereas dimension is simply the representation of a variable. Just as the first three dimensions of distance represent the variation of space, the fourth dimension of change represents the variation of time. Universal space and time is simply a description for three-dimensional space in motion.

> See the earth agrowing, expanding in its size,
> and its core dissolving, until the day it dies.
> Imagine at its birth, a black ball lit with fire,
> as a soul awaiting for a body to admire.
>
> See the earth aglowing, as bright spots do occur,
> as tiny floating islands in a sea of burning fire.
> See its fire die, as its islands win the fight,
> to form a glowing skin, as a ball of liquid light.
>
> See the earth agrowing, expanding in its size,
> and its skin distorting, forming patterns in its skies,
> See its islands crack and crumble as they drift apart,
> forever building new creations, as a work of art.
>
> See the earth aslowing in the autumn of its age,
> adorned with beauty's majesty, for man a living stage.
> See its life course altered by ever changing fates,
> as it's growing but decaying into other energy states.

Imagine the entire life of the earth compacted into a short episode of space and time. Create in your mind a vision of a spark born from the darkness of the universe, growing in size as a ball of fire, and through generations of change developing into the earth on which we live. Imagine the complexity of the forces at work within the earth and the multiplicity of changes, which have occurred during the life of the earth. See seemingly minor changes at an early time develop into glorified creations as the earth's body continues to unfold. See rivers of stellar air flowing into the earth, holding the matter of the earth together, while at the same time feeding the fire of its internal growth. See the body of the earth continue to grow in size, as its surface constantly changes to fit its newly created size. See the emergence of its lands and its oceans; see its mountains rise from the distortions of its lands; see its rivers build roadways from its mountains to its lakes; and see its rolling hills carved by its winds and its waters on its lands. See this as a vision of space and time, an inner movie of the imagination, shown in accelerated time.

Crystalline Valleys

Visit this land called Earth, and see its true existence as a palace made of crystal. See its plains and its valleys as sheets of shimmering glass and a floor for us to stand upon. See its mountains as snow-covered glaciers forming walls for us to gaze upon. See its trees as inverted chandeliers, its grass as rigid strands of silk, and its fields of wheat and rye as cloaks of white satin covering its naked lands. See its flowers as delicate laces assembled from snowflakes, its grassy knolls as spindles of cotton, and its horizons as crystal protrusions beckoning its skies. See its rivers and its oceans as crystalline pools of beads and pearls, its vapors as miniature silver balloons jittering through its skies, and its clouds as luminous shadows floating in its skies. See its cities as edifices of ice, its highways as pavements of silver gold, and its living creatures as ghosts transposed from another land. See the earth as a fragile sphere of crystal, its mountains and valleys etched from its surface by the forces of time, its life forms individually hand-carved from pieces of ivory, and it all gently wrapped in a glowing halo from heaven.

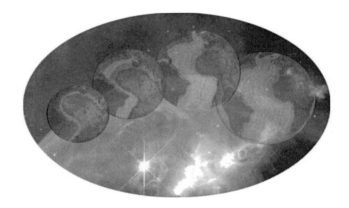

A Growing & Expanding Earth

As the earth continues to expand and to grow, other forces are at work erasing these footprints of history from the earth. These forces are normally considered to be forces of decay, and can be thought of as the processes of energy transformation or the physical change of energy from one form to another. In contrast, the forms of creation are highly integrated forces, which at times seem to transcend the laws of physics. However, according to contemporary physics, both forms of energy transformations must occur within the two laws of thermodynamics, or what could be more appropriately called the two laws of energy change. The first law was the law of conservation of energy as previously discussed and fixes the total amount of energy present in the universe to an absolute level. The second law is the law of entropy. It states that all energy transformations must proceed toward a more even distribution of energy.

For example, pile salt in the middle of a saucer and then shake the saucer. The salt will more evenly distribute itself across the bottom of the saucer. Regardless of how long you continue shaking the saucer, the salt will never pile up again in the center of the saucer. Likewise, the energy of the universe is on a one-way course toward a more even distribution throughout the universe. However, this law seems to contradict some of the more common, everyday energy transformations presently occurring on the surface of the earth. For example, air pressure variations cause water vapor to condense in the air and fall to the earth as rain; gravity causes the rain to flow into the rivers, lakes, and oceans; and the sun's heat evaporates the water back into the air as water vapor. This recurring cycle, composed of three nonreversible energy changes, will continue for a long as the sun, the water, and the earth continue to exist in their present form. However, it is still a cycle driven by the process of entropy, since the changes occurring at the surface of the sun and in the center of the earth are each progressing on their own nonreversible course toward a more even distribution of energy throughout the universe. It is proposed that entropy is likewise but one step in an even greater, universal, recurring cycle; and that furthermore, it is the direction of this cycle, which defines the direction of time.

The Universe

If we are to ever truly understand this energy-dynamic universe, and hence get a glimpse of its true reality, we must learn to divorce the perceptions created within our minds from their absolute existence. We must transcend the five senses of our minds, and instead enter the sixth sense within our minds. We must discard the notions of mass, temperature, touch, color, sound, and the other definitions of our physical world; and instead visualize the various energy formations found within the universal world. The basic techniques required to accomplish this task are simply three; that is, first by imagining two phases of energy, the stellar air and the liquid light. The second technique is by imagining two shades of energy, the light and the dark. Finally, the third technique is by imagining two motions of energy, flow and spin. By utilizing these fundamental descriptions, mental pictures of all the energy formations within the universe can be visually drawn, including both the objects of our physical world and the invisible forces of the heavenly world. There are then three numerical methods for quantifying the size or intensity of each of these energy formations. They are pressure or density, velocity or flow, and angular momentum or spin.

Pressure energy is simply a differential in density between any two points in the stellar air. At the lower end of the pressure scale is the energy of darkness. Just as it takes energy to remove air from a bell jar, so does it also take energy to create holes in the stellar air. Midway in the pressure scale is the energy of lightness. Just as waves on the ocean can be seen in height, so also can stellar waves be seen as various shades of darkness and brightness. The upper end of the pressure scale represents the energy of liquid light. Just as oxygen can be compressed into a liquid gas, so also can stellar air be compressed into liquid light. Therefore, within the boundaries of the energy of pressure, both phases as well as both shades of energy are described.

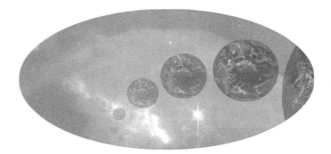

Space and Time

The only remaining descriptions are the two motions of energy, flow, and spin; and they can be seen to exist at any point along the pressure scale. That is, the energy of darkness can flow or can spin; the energy of the stellar air can flow or can spin; and the energy of the liquid light can flow or can spin. The energy of flow is measured in terms of velocity and the energy of spin is measured in terms of angular momentum. There is one special form of angular momentum, which requires an individual description. That is when one object revolves around another object as the earth orbits the Sun. This form of energy is actually a unique combination of both flow and spin. Also, additional minor variations in the structures of energy formations can be visualized by adding words such as jiggle or wobble to each of our descriptions. All of the energy formations within the universe can be seen by combining these basic descriptions; that is, a view of matter not as mass, nor a view of energy as an invisible force, but instead as a unified perception of the universe.

> See a heavenly ocean afloat in our skies,
> very great and immense, as of infinite size.
> A world of beauty and eternity time,
> and a haven for life of another kind.
>
> See a dark storm abrewing, deep in its center,
> two energy forms opposing each other.
> A struggle of life, to establish what's right,
> and to forever control the dark and the light.
>
> See an emptiness center, surrounded by light,
> and its sudden explosion into a showering flight.
> As millions of balls fight for their lives,
> for their food of existence, in the stellar skies.
>
> Some grow glowing skin so incredibly fast,
> that nothing escapes, and a shadow is cast.
> Others slow down and let their light shine,
> while others speed on 'til the end of their time.
>
> See more millions of balls, except smaller in size,
> as the life for our Earth and the stars in our skies.
> See its splendor and glory, and its beauty unfold,
> as the story of life in the heavens is told.

If you are to hear this story, you must be a curious soul and have in your possession an open and imagining mind. Awake as from a sleepless night and stroll from the harshness of your earthly dreams, to ponder and reflect upon the true nature of the world that surrounds you. Believe not that the world you perceive is the only world, but only your present world. Leave the confines of your earthly dwelling and climb aboard the spaceship of imagination on a journey of enlightened images throughout the heavens. Instead of the emptiness and the darkness of space, behold in your midst an endless ocean of stellar light, an eternal sea of space and time larger than the limits of your human mind. See its dimensions as differing shades of darkness and lightness intermingled with harmonic motions of droplets of light, and its firmaments as billions of holes encased within crystal and sprinkled throughout its glowing halo of light. See its liquid energy leaping and splashing about as it plays melodies of science on its heavenly lute. Hear these songs as minstrels of history sung by a heavenly choir to the universal amphitheater of spiritual life.

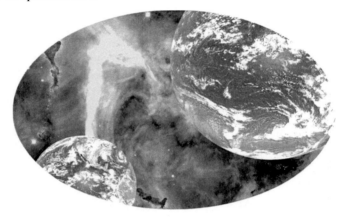

Heavenly Dances

Alongside this heavenly choir, see a heavenly cast performing with splendor their choreographed show from the unwritten pages of the script of eternal life. See each of these performers display his wares as projections upon a domed stage of heavenly mist. Look about you and see the majesty of the universal suns radiating their waves through the stellar sea, as they create myriads of spherical patterns interlaced with echoes from their celestial friends. See the galaxies as crystalline snowflakes tumbling ever so gently through a transparent fog of luminous light, and see their stars appearing and disappearing as magical flashes of sparkling light, adding to it the dimension of celestial life. See some stars so small that if they stood in the place of our sun they would be but a pinpoint in our sky, and see others so large that they would appear as a silver and gold rainbow stretching halfway across the sky. See the most intense stars growing so fast they cast a shadow of darkness throughout the sky, and see yet other stars circling in pairs and pulsating as if their bodies were a stellar heart. See some stars as only made of darkness, or still others as only glittering mists of light, but see all of the stars magically suspended within the universal ball of the energy of light.

Heavenly
Spires

See both the galaxies and the stars born from the energy of the heavens just as a hurricane is born from the energy of our winds. See their bodies as three-dimensional whirlwinds spinning a web of liquid light as they effortlessly hover in the sky. See the stellar air flowing out of the heavens and into the stars, as it is magically transformed into liquid light and becomes the bodies of the stars. See each star grow from its birth into a superstar and then, in a giant flash, instantly transform into a miniature white dwarf as its energy returns into the heavens from whence it came. Peer into one of the stars and see its core of darkness engulfed by a boiling ocean of molten light; then see within this ocean, swirling waves transforming light into matter as effervescent bubbles and vertical plumes emanate from eruptions deep within the star.

See the space surrounding each star as a three-dimensional checkerboard, alternately glittering and sparkling in the various shades of silvery charcoal and bright silver-gray. See these patterns as fingerprints of the stars, as though each star clothed itself in its own kaleidoscope of style. See the stars forever changing these garments of glitter as they reflect the life within the star. See high above the stars, the stellar air standing almost still as it provides yet another home for life within the heavens; and see living souls born into the heavens as spirit-filled balloons rising to meet the stars. See the energy of the heavens and the energy of stars dancing together, as if the universe itself were alive.

Electrified Lights

Since the total amount of energy in the universe is constant, all change within the universe is neither the creation nor the destruction of energy, but simply a rearrangement of the distribution of energy. The process of entropy dictates that the universe shall continue to change until all energy is evenly distributed throughout the universe; that is, energy captured in a structure without change. However, this seems to be a conflict of words, since energy was described as the potential to cause change. It would therefore seem necessary to expect either a limit to the process of entropy or to develop a concept in which the energy of the universe changes in a never-ending cycle. In order to accomplish either of these goals, a better understanding of energy transformations must be developed. Energy transformations, by definition, are the natural or supernatural changes, which occur to the various structures or formations of energy. They can be visualized as mechanical processes and are controlled both by the law of conservation of energy, and the law of entropy. That is, any time a change occurs, not only must the total amount of energy be conserved, but also each of the three types of energy must be conserved. This rule is best summarized by the scientific adage, "for every action there is an equal but opposite reaction." In addition and according to the law of entropy, the change can only occur as long as the end result is a greater dispersion of energy throughout the universe. It is these limitations, which govern the formation and transformations of matter and energy, and therefore, the course of life within the universe.

Before an attempt is made to piece together a possible life for the universe, some basic definitions should be reviewed. First, the effective universe is that area of space filled with the stellar air and with the matter of our physical world. Since beyond this there is nothing, there is no reason to discuss its existence or nonexistence. Also, the total amount of energy in the universe is constant and exists solely within the boundaries of a finite universe. The size of the universe could either be contracting, remaining the same, or expanding. If the universe were contracting, one would expect the energy of the heavens, the stellar air, to be transformed or compressed into the energy of matter, the liquid light. If the size of the universe were constant, then one would expect either energy transformations to occur in both directions or for no energy transformations to occur at all. If the universe were expanding, one would expect the energy of matter, the liquid light, to be transformed or released into the energy of the heavens, the stellar air. There are many examples of the latter case, such as a light bulb producing light waves, or the energy released by a nuclear reaction. But then, how can one explain a beginning and an ending to a continuously expanding cycle, and does this expansion cycle continue forever or must there not be a limit to that process?

Think instead of a universe made of two worlds; that is, the heavens fashioned from the energy of the stellar air and the physical world fashioned from the energy of liquid light. Think of the heavenly world as maintaining a constant size and its energy transformations occurring in both directions. The previous examples illustrate the energy of matter changing into the stellar air, and the birth of a star or a planet is an example of the energy of the stellar air changing into liquid light. Then think of the physical world as another world, distributed within and throughout the heavenly world and constantly expanding in size, thereby establishing the effect of entropy and the direction of time.

From our limited perspective within the physical world, only the dissolution of energy into the stellar air would be easily seen.

Imagine yourself in another space and another time, at the center of
the beginning of time. See yourself, surrounded by oceans of stellar
light and see the heavens move in perfect motions as multitudes of
voices singing songs in perfect harmony. See darkness growing about
you as inconspicuous as other areas of darkness within the heavens, but
as unique as your position in space and time. It is as though this moment were chosen from the seas of eternity to fulfill the destiny of eternity itself. A moment in time, engulfed by its own existence and growing in the dimensions of its own brief time, until it transforms the energy of the universal light into an accelerating explosion of newly-
formed life. With a unique yet personal inquisition, you have just wit-
nessed the birth of the first stars within the universe, their short-lived
existence, and their subsequent explosion into billions of more stars as
the beginning of the physical world. It is a spherical wave of subtle
darkness growing from its seemingly insignificant size, until it transforms into billions of balls of darkness speeding outward through the
universal ball of light.   And then, as each of these stars journeyed outward through the universal ball of light, you saw them explode in a
heavenly cadence into glorious bursts of newly formed life as they were
transformed into the galaxies within the heavens, and then the stars
within the galaxies. It is as though the entire universe were resting in
the palm of your hands, as real as a glowing crystal, but as elusive as a
soft and gentle halo of light; and within it you saw miniature cascading
explosions of darkness turn into fire and become light.

See a heavenly rain of fire coating the physical world with a crust of
liquid light. And upon this crust of crystal, see the histories of our earth
and our lives inscribed by the laws of physics and written in the language of science. See our futures written within the seas of the heavens
by the laws of eternity in a language that can only be found within our
hearts. See our physical world travel outward through this heavenly
ocean of stellar light, while its liquid body dissolves back into the stellar vapor of aethereal light. As it approaches the farthest edges of the
heavens, its rate of decay accelerates until the matter of substance is
gone and the energy of darkness disappears outside the universal world
of space and time. However, since it is the energy of nothing, not only
can it travel through space and time to nowhere, but it can also be recre-

ated in an instant at a distant location from nothing. Could it be that as the energy of darkness journeys outward through the universal ball of light and leaves the confines of the heavens that another point in space and time is chosen to fulfill the eternal destiny of life and time?

It was then the instructions for the universe that were holistically present at the center of the universe, at the beginning of creation and at the beginning of time, and not necessarily the substance, which was instead distributed throughout the universe. As the present physical universe with its self-contained instruction set expands throughout heavens, a new instruction set is being developed at its center for the next grand cycle of universal creation.

The Cosmos

For many years there has been a philosophical discussion, especially for those within the scientific community, concerning the potential existence of a supernatural substance, the aether, in the vast open spaces of the universe. It is readily accepted that energy travels from the sun to our earth in the form of light waves and heat waves, and also that we can send radio signals to space vehicles traveling through space. It is also recognized that the only difference between these various communications signals and the sun's natural heat and light waves, is frequency or size of the wave. However, since there has been no previous theory, which could establish a common basis for developing comprehensive answers to these mysteries, the existence of this substance has been seriously doubted.

Adding to these concerns are the somewhat confusing characteristics of light. That is, light sometimes has characteristics which resemble a wave such as a radio signal or a heat wave; while at other times it characteristics are similar to those of a particle, such as an x-ray or a gamma ray. This confusion can even be seen in the descriptions we have given light. For example, we refer to light as light waves as well as light rays and have given the name photon to each of the individual waves light, as though each wave was a separate particle of light. Referring back to the descriptions given for the various shades and phases of energy, could it be that light is merely a single point on that continuous spectrum of energy? Could it be that as spin and velocity are added to the energy of lightness and darkness, a new dimension of energy formed?

Could it be that light is merely the boundary for this new dimension, and that on one side is the energy of waves and on the other side is the energy of the particles of liquid light?

Look at the air, at a sky of the day;
see space colored blue, as a water-filled bay.
Look toward the heavens, at a sky of the night;
see a blanket of black, but sparkling with light.

Look into your mind, and see heavenly oceans
of space made alive with eternal motions.
See great stellar waves speeding through time,
and waves standing still, so meek and sublime.

See radio waves, as big as a mountain;
the sun's light waves appear as a bubbly fountain.
See crisscrossing patterns filling the skies,
as stacked figure eight's, all different in size.

See video waves that you hold in your hands,
and the sun's heat waves are sized, as the desert sands.
But when you imagine a wave that's too small,
a new creation occurs, a bright glowing ball.

If we are to see these bright glowing balls, we must embark upon the next leg of our journey, the transformation from the world of the astronomically large towards the realm of the microscopically small. As we begin, we see subtle variations in the brightness of the stellar sea as spherical halos, some dark and some light, floating in a crystal sea. They appear as glowing spheres of soft light, marching in rank and file, half black and half white, throughout their cosmic sea. Suddenly, one befriends us, instantly appearing as a point of bright light, first spiraling outward as a halo of light and then spiraling backwards to another point of bright light. Rebounding from the force of its light, we continue onward through the choppy waves in the crystal sea.

We then zoom on in our Milky Way Galaxy and see a preponderance of snowflakes as in a spiraling wintertime storm. The smallest dimensions are snowflakes, and when visually interconnected they form repetitive images of larger snowflakes, and when further interconnected even greater images of even greater snowflakes - an overlapping and delicately interlaced fractal structure, such that each snowflake is an image of a million snowflakes. And then we see this inter-tangled menagerie of snowflakes gently hung within a preponderance of echoing bubbles constructed from transparent, yet visible, light. Next, we zoom in on our sun, and to our astonishment, see a jiggling and quivering body, which is magically spewing spherical balls of liquefied fire and blasting our skies with tracers of light. These bright flashes appear collectively jittering as winds made from sparks, and are leaping yet splashing outward through a sunlit halo of simmering mist. The brilliance of this solar wind pierces the softness of the stellar wind as these sparkles of crystal emanate in radial patterns against the in-flowing universal mist.

Cosmic Rays

We now continue our journey towards our earthly home, where we see the glowing spheres becoming smaller and brighter, still spiraling inward and outward as they pulsate through their cosmic sea. As waves on our ocean, they rise up from the forces within the stellar sea, grow and diminish, and collide with the shores of our earth, just as waves on the ocean collide with the shores of our lands. And finally, with visual surprise we see others as ghosting white sands penetrating our hands, as we feel their radiant warmth gently grow within the skin of our body.

The Atomic World

The dilemma caused by the confusing characteristics of light is then solved, by the bringing together of the descriptions used for waves and particles. That is, they are both products of the stellar air and are only different by their relative energy forms. The simplest form, the stellar waves, exists in many sizes from very much larger than our earth to very much smaller than a speck of dust. When spin and velocity are added to the smallest of waves, the energy of pressure becomes particles of liquid light, and their opposites become antiparticles of liquid light. At point where the waves and the particles meet, the photon or light wave is created. A more complete understanding of the forces at work within both waves and particles is presented in Chapter Four. These four basic forms of energy: stellar waves, light waves, particles of liquid light, and antiparticles of liquid light, represent the fundamental forms of energy found within the heavens.

> See a ball of liquid light, as a pinpoint in the sky,
> shining very brightly like the twinkle of an eye.
> See its birth and death, as points in space and time,
> and its life between, as a drawing in the sky.
>
> See it wandering through the heavens, as a roaming star,
> and gentle waves rippling outward from its trip afar.
> See it growing fragile wings, as a butterfly,
> or the petals of a rose, as a picture in the sky.
>
> See it speeding through the heavens, as a streak of light,
> or as a falling star, in the dark sky of the night.
> See it form an image, as a mountain standing high,
> suspended in the heavens, as a sculpture in the sky.

As we continue our journey into the realm of the infinitely small, we see miniature waves of misty light magically transform into spinning droplets interspersed between halos of light. We see them formed from the energy of the heavens just as a droplet of rain is formed from the energy of the clouds in our skies. We see the energy of pressure compressed into a tiny wave of eclectic light, set into a spinning rotation as a ball of liquid light and then hurled through the cosmos at the speed of light. They appear as miniature three-dimensional hurricanes, half-dark and half-bright, pulsating within their cosmic sea. As we complete our transformation into the domain of the twinkling lights, the subtle waves can no longer be seen, but are instead replaced by a choreographed dance of micro-miniature balls of liquefied light.

We watch this eclectic dance with amazement, as tiny balls of liquid light slip serendipitously through hollowed rings of seething fire. We see one flauntingly don this gown of fire as a hallowed satin negligee. It stands admiringly within a hall of mirrors and dances collectively among its peers to group induced fantasies of holographic lights. We see them grasp with eternal hands, waltz to spiritual bands, twirl in ecliptic flights, and prance to psychedelic flashes of lights. We see their footsteps as fainthearted echoes spiraling through the essence of time, as they magically perform their transcendental dance of enlightened mysteries, both within and upon the universal stage that is built from the cosmic mist.

It is simply simplicity, which is an inherent property of most happenings when there is a more, complete understanding. For example, all of the various substances found on the earth are made from approximately one hundred different elements. Originally, it was thought that each element was comprised of a nucleus and a cloud of electrons; however, as we expanded our knowledge, we added protons and neutrons along with the electrons to be the three basic building blocks of matter. But then no one could explain how protons could remain so close together within the nucleus of an atom so new particles were devised, named gluons, to hold the nucleus together. Then from the physics labs their opposites - antiprotons, anti-electrons, antineutrons and new particles mesons, pi mesons, and neutrinos were created. Then to explain gravity, gravitons were devised; and to explain the forces within the atom; quarks, strangeness, and red, blue and green color quarks were introduced.

Could it be that the atom is much simpler, as originally considered, and that instead of discovering new particles within the atom, we are actually creating these particles from the energy contained within the atom? Could it be that the nucleus is actually a simple structure representing a composite of protons and neutrons and that its outside shell of electrons is merely the reflection of that structure? And finally, could it be that the form of an atom resembles that of a bubble, with its composite structure formed from the energy of liquid light?

> Imagine an atom as a ball glowing bright,
> a hard hollow ball with soft shells of light.
> There are billions of each, of identical twins,
> only to be different, by their shapes and their spins.
>
> And their forms are so many, as opposites join,
> as too much and too little simply combine.
> Or as billions of many form complex arrangements,
> like the forms of our world, a creation so fine.

We now begin the final leg of our journey from the realm of the infinitely small, back to the estranged realities of our everyday home. The balls of liquid light fade away into the distance, and as we turn to look away, we see bubbles of liquid light appearing on the opposite horizon. Some are vibrating and some are floating, while others are simply meandering through their micro-miniature cosmic sea. The largest appear as a crystal ball and the smallest appear as a crystalline pea, with each having multiple reflections as if they were in a hall of mirrors. Some have spinning tentacles and appear as floating mines hovering in a stellar sea, while others appear as glass-blown sculptures reflecting the sea. With the radiance of light, they reach out with their magical hands and embrace, as crystalline snowmen and interlocked tripods inter-mingling their hands. See multitudes of atoms telescoping away as they are visually transformed into silvery strands and glowing crystals spun from complex webs of liquid light.

Our Homes within Ourselves

We now must say our farewells, as we must each make our final and solitary journey to our homes within ourselves. We see the fibers of our muscles as atoms spun into threads of silver, and see tissue as phosphorescent fabrics woven from these various strands of silvery light. Our skin appears as tinseled blankets saturated with silvery fluids and lined with a cotton candy coating of translucent light. Muscles are seen as telescoping fibers empowered by the energy of light, cartilage as plastic pads glowing with light, and tendons as glass-fiber cords braided from light. Our lungs appear as garments of silk stuffed with woolen knittings of luminous yarn, and our heart as rubberized tweeds of transparent nylon and Dacron. Our veins appear as stretchable sheaths of elastic glass, and our kidneys as double-knit fabrics filtering pebbles of crystal from glittering, spring waters - the rivers of life. Proteins appear as spiraling ribbons constructed from timbers of glassware; bacteria as chrome-plated robots or machines made from glass; cells as aquatic factories producing crystalline ice flakes, the nutrients of life; and salts and minerals as purified gems of emerald and jasper, dazzling adornments within this tapestry of life.

Electric Gardens

Arriving home we contemplate our strange experiences. We have seen a unique similarity or oneness, which exist within the universe. That is, each of its happenings is a unique combination of the three basic types of energy: pressure, velocity, and angular momentum. Also, they each can be described by the two shades of energy, the dark and the light; the two phases of energy, the stellar air and the liquid light; and the two motions of energy, flow and spin. Radio waves and heat waves were waves of pressure riding within the stellar air and traveling through the heavens. Light rays were spherical waves of pressure spinning their way through the heavens, and the illusion of color was the size of the wave. X-rays and gamma rays were miniature balls of liquid light speeding through the heavens. Atoms were bubbles of energy made from the energies of the dark and the light, and molecules were structures of bubbles of liquid light. Gravity was the pressure of the flowing stellar air pushing against the bubbles of liquid light. When all of the bubbles of a substance were rigidly interconnected, it was a solid; when they were torn apart by their inner vibrations, it was a liquid; and when they accelerated beyond the pressure of gravity, they floated free to become a gas.

Electric Hydrangeas

Although these descriptions are different from those normally used to describe the world around us, they are in fact similar to the ones used almost daily to describe the less tangible forces of our everyday world. For instance, we think of the air pressure in an inflated balloon and the water pressure deep within the sea; we monitor the speed of our airplanes and our automobiles; we watch our children watching their toy tops spinning; and we visualize the earth orbiting the sun. It is then these same descriptions, which describe not only our everyday world, but also both the macros and the micros of the universal world. For example, see electricity as liquid light flowing along the surface of the atoms within a wire, and see static electricity and lightning as pulsating streaks of liquid light. See magnetism and electromagnetism as circular distortions within the stellar air, and see the forces of cohesion as aberrations within the stellar air as it flows from one substance to another. See the atoms in the filaments of a light bulb oscillate violently and cause waves in the stellar air, just as the oars of a boat make waves in the water. See an electrical motor spinning from the stellar winds, just as the blades of a windmill turn, from the winds from the air of the lands. See a computer as a giant abacus, operated by liquid levers and liquid gates, and its electronic logic as liquid light flowing through a maze of metal roadways, just as water flows through a maze of dikes.

See our radio and television broadcasting towers as structures of glowing balls of liquid light; and at their summit, see crystalline wands transforming harmonic vibrations into spherical waves, rippling outward through the stellar sea. See each of these waves as spherical halos, sized ten feet across and speeding outward through the stellar air toward each of our homes at the speed of light. See your television antenna as a skeletal framework of cylindrical art, and see its bubbles of liquid light resonating in unison from the impact of the stellar waves, just as the strings of a guitar vibrate from the impact of the guitar player's hand. See streams of liquid light flow back and forth through channels of wires from the antenna to the insides of your television, a mechanical box. See them funneled and guided through walls and gates in complex patterns as they grow and are shaped. See shining bubbles, in the shape of a cone, vibrate from the force of the stellar winds and cause waves to ride through the air to the sense of our ear, so we can hear our mechanical contraption. See a stream of liquid light colliding in violent explosions with coatings of frost, and see spherical waves ride through the stellar air to the sense of our eye, so we can see our mechanical contraption.

By extending these descriptions to ourselves, we begin to understand that our own touch, taste, and smell are mere mental representations of the pressure of the atoms of the universe pushing against the atoms of our bodies, that sound is the mere mental manifestation of pressure waves traveling through the atoms of the air and transferred into the atoms of our ears, and that vision is a mere mental illusion created within our minds from the pressure of stellar waves pushing against the atoms of our eyes. From our limited perspective within the universe, most of us tend to see only the individuality or superficiality of the events just described, and tend to miss the underlying importance of their shared similarities and oneness. The universe is actually comprised of both individuality and wholeness, and with all of its separately functioning bodies interrelated and dependent upon one another. It is this difference in perception, which accounts for our difficulties in understanding reality. The universe is a paradox within itself, seemingly infinite in size when comprehended by the finite man, but actually a finite size, which is instead filled with a near infinite variation of perception.

Lighthouse by the Sea

We can better understand this paradox by illustrating two different perspectives of the universe. In the first case, we as human beings are limited to where we can go in this four-dimensional space and time by the maximum speed of our bodies. If a friend needs our help in exactly one hour, but is located on the other side of the earth, it would be impossible for us to go to his aid. Without our help the event that occurs may be very unfortunate to him, but it is beyond our ability to be there. Likewise, if our friend is located on a distant planet and needs our advice in exactly one second, it would even be impossible for us to send him a message of help because of the limited speed of light. The limited speed of light becomes the glue of the energy of the universe. Since we are fashioned from that energy, the maximum rate at which we can travel through the universe and maintain our physical form is a critical limit to our access of the unfolding history of the universe.

We sometimes fantasize that we can travel backwards in time; however, this would require the exact reversal of change, which has already occurred, and a feat, which even the most advanced machine would find impossible. As previously discussed, time is simply a method of measuring the rate of change within the universe. However, just as a jogger can run faster in the air than a swimmer can swim in the water, the motions of energy also vary their speeds because of the variations in the density of the stellar air. Therefore, the speed of energy within the universe, or time itself, can speed up or slow down. Also, since our clocks are made of mechanical motions, which are just another form of energy within the stellar air, they too can speed up or slow down. However, in no case can the motions of energy within the heavens be reversed in time. Therefore, our only hope to visit our friends from a bygone era is to meet again in another space and another time, where we have each learned to live in the eternity of its own time.

Contrasting with this massiveness of the universe and our limited ability to control our destiny in it, is the smallness of the subatomic world and the almost unlimited information available in it. If we could freeze all of the motion within the universe, and therefore stop time for just a brief moment, we could visualize the fixed dispersion of the stellar air and the liquid light within the heavens. Each point in space would be different from every other point in space only by its relative density and form. By comparing adjacent points in space to a common point, composite descriptions for a larger scope of the universe could be devised. This is, in fact, what happens as we extend our limited perception of the universe to the entirety of the universe.

For example, if you are in the middle of a room, the area of space occupied by the retina of your eye contains much of the information necessary to describe most of the other objects existing within the room. The portion of the room perceived by the eye is only dependent upon which direction the eye is oriented. It is as though microscopic images of the inside of the room can be found at any point in the room; and that as the point of perception is moved, the apparent image gradually changes detail, representing the various perspectives of the room. A seemingly infinite amount of information is contained in each of the almost infinite images, but all of the images, combine to form a single continuum of energy within the room. Furthermore, within this single continuum exists not only the images formed from light waves; but also all of the images formed from the entire electromagnetic wave spectrum. It is then the complex interaction of these various forces within this single continuum of energy, with the particles of our physical world, which determines the force to be perceived.

A Return to Nature

When viewing the universe from this perspective, the oneness or unity of the universe is much more apparent. For example, place an object, such as a chair, in the room previously described. Then not only would the space occupied by the chair be altered, but also the entire space within the room would be altered, since each of the almost infinite images within the room are now changed to include the image of the chair. Furthermore, if the object chosen were made of metal and the perspective chosen were radio waves, then the radio images outside of the room would also be altered. Just like the stars, all material objects, including our own bodies, are surrounded by an aura of reflected and self-generated energy from the entire wave spectrum.

This unique unity within the universe is an inherent part of the universe, and any change occurring within the universe will automatically become a part of the rest of the universe. Carrying this perspective one more step, if a point of view is chosen in the remoteness of outer space, images of the entire universe and its corresponding descriptions could be envisioned. However, in this case the images would represent a much more limited; and therefore distorted perception of the universe, since the image produced is a composite of many different events at many different times, and is only a partial glimpse of the true reality of the universe. However, from this single point a limited perspective of the entire universe could be devised; and by comparing additional points at various times, this limited perspective could be expanded to more closely approach the true reality of the universe. This is the task the study of science has undertaken, an almost endless task since each time an event is perceived, the perception itself simultaneously alters the event being perceived.

Topic of Discussion

It is the goal of science, and rightly should be, to develop a perspective of the universe upon which we can build our society. However, since science is the study of partial events it alone can never totally describe the entire event. This is not an inherent weakness in science it-self, but instead a limitation to the scope of science. It is only by com-bining the study of science with the other aspects of our total being that we can hope to arrive at a true perception of the universe. It therefore requires a higher step of individual awareness and individual accep-tance to determine the appropriateness of the perceptions presented. These perceptions are therefore submitted to the scrutiny of each per-son's individual knowledge and understanding, realizing that only when everyone is bound in a common agreement can we be reasonably sure that we have developed a true perception of the universe.

Chapter Two

Peering through a Rainbow

*"God offers to every mind
a choice between truth and repose.
Take which you please
you can never have both"*

Ralph Waldo Emerson (1803-1882)

Introduction

Ralph Waldo Emerson was an American essayist, lecturer and poet who formulated the philosophy of Transcendentalism and was a champion of individualism. Although I am not fond of those words that end with ism, it is only through transcendence that a true perspective of the world that surrounds us can be perceived. Whereas transcendentalism

indicates a bias toward the esoteric in disregard for the realities of this
world, transcendence is merely a balanced approach to rise above the
images of our perceived world and instead visualize and understand the
true reality of the real world that surrounds us. Accordingly, in the last
chapter, vivid descriptions and transcendent images were painted for
the realities of the world that surrounds us. While in this chapter, philosophical reasoning and structural understandings will be used to define and describe the world that is within us. However, any discussion
of this world that is within us and within our corresponding human psyche must begin where we left off in the last chapter.

Therefore, we begin first by summarizing these perspectives from
yet other points of view. Accordingly, all of the conclusions presented
in this chapter are based upon the absolute necessity of cause and effect,
through the *a priori* existence of substance, structure, mechanism and
process. It is simply unreasonable to conclude that anything can come
from nothing, that the phenomena of the universe have no cause or that
these phenomena occur by some magical process unknowable to the
human mind. Instead, there is substance and structure for all things that
exist, and furthermore, there is an underlying logic of mechanism and
process, for those things of substance to take on life through the laws of
cause and effect. Moreover, it is simply *simplicity*, which is an inherent
property of most happenings when there is a more complete understanding. Consequently, the following conclusions are offered as a
structural understanding of human physiology, and a solid foundation
for the development of a new understanding of what it is to be human.

Human Perception and the Holographic Mind

As I discussed in the previous chapter, the mechanics of human perception is a phenomenon of the mind and not of the objects being observed. The red flower is not really red, nor is the blue sky really blue,
nor is the green grass really green. In fact, the perception of color is
nothing more than an enhanced representation of the world around us
created within the boundaries of our mind. This is not to say that the
world around us does not exist, but only that it does not exist in the
form in which we perceive it. The true form of the universe is that of a
world of energy, which is built from the forces of the dark and the light
and given life through the motions of change. Whereas, the universe

within us is a world of color carved from those forces, and given a fixed existence within the substance of our mind. An image of color of the world around us is an apparition created by our mind and exists solely within our mind. This is a difficult truth to accept because it is contrary to our perception of being; however, just the same, true it is. Neither the existence of this world around us nor the existence of this image within us is unreal, but instead it is the insistence upon the common identity of these two worlds, which is unreal. And what is this grand illusion within us, but that state of being, that wonderful world of life within which each of us lives.

In order to better understand these phenomena, the mechanism that causes the sensation of color must be first understood. The mechanics of color is normally described by saying that when white light, which contains all of the various colors of light shines on a blue object, the blue light is reflected and the other colors of light are absorbed. Furthermore, when the reflected blue light shines against the pupils of our eyes, we then perceive the existence of the blue object. This description is totally subjective to our own biased perception of being. Bear with me, as this biased description is translated into a more objective point of view.

That is, a wave of light energy propagates through the substance of space and arrives in the near vicinity of an object composed of a structure of atoms. Most of the energy is absorbed as increased vibrations by the atoms within the structure; however, a single wave determined by the spacing between the atoms is reflected back into the substance of space. This reflected wave then propagates through the substance of space and arrives in the near vicinity of the pupils of our eyes. This wave, along with the other waves of energy at this point, collides with the atoms of the receptors within our eyes. The atoms of the receptors of our eyes are mechanically tuned to vibrate only to waves the same size as the reflected wave. Coded signals representative of that wave are then sent to the brain where an image of the structure is created within our mind and perceived by the contents of our mind as *blue*.

Notice that the word *blue* was not used in the second description until after the image had been perceived within our mind. There are dozens of similar examples, including color perception, color blindness, double vision, holographs, 3D movies, virtual reality, dreams, visions, hallucinations, dizziness, color-blindness, the varying perceptions of animals, open triangles which appear closed, pictures which can be seen as a face or a vase but not both, out of body experiences, and near-death experiences. All of these examples add up to the same conclusion that these images can only exist within our minds. Accordingly, only four of the above will be presented as a detailed analysis: first the color of objects, second the mechanics of colors, third holograms, and fourth the varying perceptions of animals. In the first case, the color of objects can be determined by first visualizing the atoms from which they are made; however, in order to accomplish this task, one must first develop a method for visualizing atoms as pure energy. In the last chapter, I described atoms as balls of liquid light, and in Chapter Four, quarks are defined as three-dimensionally shaped charge segments of an electromagnetic wave, which can be visualized as eddy currents or vortices within the aether or the stellar air, and thereby atoms possess no structure or mechanisms for the process of color. Particles, which are saturated composites of those quarks, also possess no color and can be best described as saturated vortices of liquid light. Likewise, atoms, which are made from those particles, also possess no color and can best be described as complex saturated vortices of liquid light. Accordingly, objects, which are made from those atoms, also have no color, but can instead best be described as constructs of complex saturated vortices of liquid light. The bottom line is that atoms by themselves have no color, but are instead pure saturated energy; and therefore the objects they form also possess no color, but are instead constructs of pure saturated energy.

Accordingly, as the spacing between the atoms within an object is changed, the size of the wave reflected by the object also is changed. Since it is the size or the frequency of the wave interacting with our eyes that causes the sensation of color, it is therefore the spacing of the atoms within the structure that determines the color we perceive. That is why substances appear to change color during chemical reactions, because the structures of the atoms within the substances are changed and not because the substances actually change color. For example, imagine each of the atoms as balls on a pool table. Arrange the balls in various patterns, being sure that each ball touches at least one other ball, simulating the bonding of atoms in chemistry. If the balls were all colored red, perceptive descriptions for the various patterns would be as differently shaped structures of red balls. At no time would the red balls change color because they were rearranged. Likewise, when the forces of chemistry rearrange the atoms of liquid light in order to form the various substances of our physical world, they also do not change color. Therefore, if one views a single atom as a glowing bubble of liquid light, one must expect to view their combinations as glowing structures of liquid light. The sensation of temperature is then added to this description by describing it as a glowing structure of vibrating bubbles of liquid light.

Moreover, human color perception is a three-dimensional process and accordingly a three-dimensional spatial continuum, whereas color electromagnetic wave generation is a linear process and accordingly a linear continuum. Our current understanding that white light contains all of the various colors of light as diffused by a prism into the linear rainbow effect red, orange, yellow, green, blue, indigo, and violet (ROYGBIV) of colors, only applies to the generation of light waves and is being misapplied to process of human color perception. Whereas the creation of the rainbow spectrum of colors by a prism is a linear effect, color perception as observed by human beings is a three dimensional spatial effect. For example, one may justify the creation of the intermediate colors of orange or yellow within the color spectrum of ROYGBIV, by mixing the colors green and red; however this same logic then fails when mixing red with blue, for that same linear sequence should thereby create the intermediate colors orange, yellow or green instead of the observed colors of magenta or purple. There are actually three different processes involved in human color perception; the first is Color Electromagnetics, which deals with electromagnetic waves, and which was illustrated in the first chapter of this book. The second is Color Electrodynamics, which deals with the creation of colored images within the mind, and which will be discussed in detail later within this chapter. And third is Color Psychosomatics, which deals with the influence that colors have on the human mind, and which will be discussed in the third chapter of this book.

There are therefore, two realities for the world within which we live: the conceptual world of absolute reality, and the perceptual world of our human conscious reality. Both are real and exist at the same time; however, at different levels of existence. The third example, which goes beyond the illustration of the illusion of color and furthermore supports the argument of the image existing solely within our minds, is the holograph. For those unfamiliar with a holograph, it is an optical machine capable of creating those magical three-dimensional images dancing within the staged display of a haunted house. A closer analysis of this phenomenon will show that the holograph does not create the image at all, but instead creates an aura of reflected energy, which completely fills the room. When our eyes interact with this energy, the dancing image is created by our mind and within our mind, and is then superimposed upon the image of the stage set already found within our mind.

In order to understand this phenomenon, the mechanics of producing a holographic film must be better understood. A beam of laser light is directed toward an object, and the reflected light from the object is allowed to hit the film. The reflected light is not focused on the film as in a normal camera, so that the reflections from the entire object are allowed to hit the film at all points on the film. This would be similar to a double exposure in a normal camera, except that in this case it is a near-infinite and holistic multiple exposure. At the same time, a second beam from the same laser light is allowed to directly hit the film so that only the interference pattern between the second beam and the multiple images is recorded on the film. Needless to say, no recognizable image is visible on the film; however, within the structure of atoms of the film is coded the information of each of the near-infinite number of images.

In order to reproduce the image, all that is needed is another laser beam the same as the original beam, the exposed film, eyes and a mind. In this case, when the laser beam is directed at the film from the same angle as the original beam, the interference pattern is canceled out, and an aura of reflected energy or a pattern of waves is produced and fills the room. When this pattern of wave energy interacts with our eyes, the original image is recreated within our mind. Since the original object has long since been removed from the room, and since no image is visible on either the film or the laser beam, the only place the image can possibly exist is in our mind. To further prove that no single image was on the film, the majority of the film can be destroyed, and by illuminating only a small portion of the film, the entire image is still created within our mind. If you are still filled with disbelief, the next time you have an opportunity to see a holographic display, select an object on the stage set and walk over and touch it. However, try to find and to touch the dancing image and you will find this to be an impossible task, for you would have to reach within the substance of your mind.

Human Perceptions and Parallel Worlds

In order to better understand the innate truths of this organized being that we call ourselves, enhanced methods for describing it must first be developed. In the last chapter, I proposed methods for visualizing both matter and energy in an integrated fashion. Within this chapter, two realities, the perceptual and the conceptual worlds, are introduced. Whereas the conceptual world roughly corresponds to the absolute world of existence, the perceptual world corresponds solely to the images created within our minds. Accordingly, if it were possible to rearrange the physiology of our minds, it would be possible to develop different perceptual worlds. This is exactly the case with the various forms of animal life found on the Earth. For instance, the eagle sees with telescopic vision, the cat sees with night vision and the dog sees in black and white vision. The whale and the dolphin see with sonar, while the bat sees with radar. We humans see in binocular vision, while the deer sees in surround vision. Also, we humans see in color by day and black and white by night. There are actually two different imagery systems within our eyes, one for bright lights and in color, and the other for dim lights and in black and white. Imagine if we were also created with telescopic vision, as is the eagle. It would be like having a telescopic lens from a 35-mm camera contained within the apparatus of our eyes and our mind. Imagine being able to zoom in on a distant object just as naturally as we blink our eyes; or imagine creating three-dimensional images within our mind from the x-ray vision of radar or sonar. Likewise, our own perceptual world is a very highly sophisticated holographic image projected upon and within the substance of our mind.

We are well aware of the differences between our human perceptions and that of the animals, but we naively continue to believe that our perceived world is the only true world and that other vision systems are simply limited or enhanced aberrations of our world. We never really understand that the world we perceive occurs solely within our minds, that the animals have another reality of their own, and that there is even a greater and more absolute reality for the real universe. Our world is

Plato's shadow on the wall, and our world, along with the animals' worlds, are but parallel worlds to the single and true universal world. If there were one hundred people and ten animals together in a room, there would then be one hundred and eleven parallel worlds in that room. They are the one hundred worlds that the people see, the ten worlds that the animals see, and the one true world that none of them see. Solipsistically, we infer that animals change the color of their skin to match their surroundings and escape their predators. But, how on earth do the animals know that their predators even see in color, since color is an aberration of reality, uniquely tailored to the psyche of the other species mind?

Fig. 2-1 − Open Triangle (left) versus
Actual Visual Image Created by the Mind (right)

There are many other examples of optical illusions which can be explained by this separation, or dichotomy, of the absolute world from the perceptible world. For example, dreams, visions and hallucinations can be seen as the ability of the mind to recall and recreate past experiences, or to fabricate and create new and imaginary experiences. During periods of conscious awareness, these images may even be superimposed upon the normal perceptual experiences already being viewed by our mind. Other examples include the illusions of virtual reality and 3D movies, which both create artificial worlds within the boundaries of our mind. Another very unique example of an optical illusion is constructing a triangle with two of its three sides not connected at one corner, but which appears to be connected within our mind when viewed from the direct line of sight of the two open ends as illustrated in Fig. 2-1. In this case, the mind is actually tricked into creating the image of a closed triangle within our mind, when the closed triangle actually in reality does not exist. Other examples are double vision, dizziness, and color-blind vision, all easily explained by malfunctioning holographic displays within the mind. Finally, and of course, one cannot forget the magician who is the prestidigitation master of illusionary tricks.

Other examples are staring at a red image which then becomes an illusionary blue-green image within our minds, as our eyes are turned away from the red image to a plain white surface; or when the color gray is placed next to various other colors and thereby appears to change its own color. The mechanics for this process was discovered in the Polaroid research labs back in the 1950's when it was learned that the mind's visual system actually changes the intensity of all colors based upon the amount of each color being perceived. In other words, the mind has a built in automatic color gain control system where colors are balanced to a predetermined relationship. This phenomenon explains the striped dress picture that was recently reported in the news media, whereas the dress appears to change color when viewed under different lighting conditions as illustrated in Fig. 2-2. Lighting conditions, adjacent colors and their interdependent relationships alter the automatic gain control system built into our minds. Our mind can create only one image at a time and that image is a composite of all the factors both within the mechanics of reality and within the mechanics of our minds. This list of examples goes on and on, such as a cat that appears to go either up or down a flight of steps, colors that appear different but are actually identical as shown in Fig. 2-3a, or a face that appears to be either an old woman or a young woman as shown if Fig. 2-3b, each depending only on how your mind processes the images of the pictures. Accordingly, there are multitudes of unique and exclusive variations of optical illusions that emanate from deep within the biological apparatus of the human mind, and thereof occur only within the occipital lobes of our human brains.

For one final example pick out a dominant object, such as a window or a television, in your field of view, and then push on the outside corner of your right eye with the index finger on your right hand until you have artificially created double vision. Do you now see two televisions or do you see two images of a television? Then, ask yourself which image is the real television. Normally you pick the original image from the left eye as the second image from the right eye may be either skewed or distorted in clarity. Now close your left eye and ask yourself the same question, is the remaining image the real television? The only alternative is that you have created two televisions from the magic within your finger, which obviously is not the case. Accordingly, the only way this sequence of events can happen is if the images are created by and exist solely within the mind.

Brighter Image
Additional
Brightness & Contrast

Original Image
Normal
Brightness & Contrast

Darker Image
Less
Brightness & Contrast

Fig. 2-2 – The Changing Colors of a Dress
(http://www.wired.com/2015/02/science-one-agrees-color-dress/)

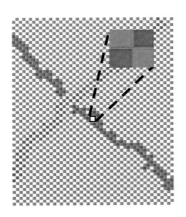 

Fig. 2-3a & 2-3b – Identical Pink Squares (left) and
Old Woman and Young Woman (right)
(http://www.grand-illusions.com)

Human Perception and Color Electrodynamics

As I proposed earlier, there are three separate and individual processes involved in human color perception. The first is Color Electromagnetics, which deals with the generation of electromagnetic waves in the visible light spectrum. The second is Color Electrodynamics, which deals with the creation of color images within the human mind. And the last is Color Psychosomatics, which deals with the effects of colors on the psychology of the human mind. Color Electromagnetics was visualized in the last chapter, briefly discussed earlier in this chapter and will be visualized and defined in Chapter Four in more detail, and color psychosomatics will be discussed in Chapter Three. In this chapter, color electrodynamics, which deals with the creation of color images within the human mind, will be discussed. Accordingly, the red, blue, green (RGB) and cyan, magenta, yellow, black, (CMYK) color wheel in the diagram in Fig. 2-4 can be transposed into a three-dimensional color sphere representing color electrodynamics by the following process.

First, take a normal two-dimensional color wheel as illustrated in the upper left image in Fig. 2-4, and transpose it onto a three-dimensional xyz color axis as illustrated in the upper right image in Fig. 2-4. Second, take the previous 3D color axis and imagine it to be a 3D color ball as shown in the bottom left image in Fig. 2-4. Paint the surface of the ball white on one side and gray on the opposite side of the ball and both at a 45-degree angle to the RGB-CMYK color axis, as illustrated in the lower left image in Fig. 2-4. Then imagine the six primary and secondary colors painted on the surface of the ball at each end of the three polar axes, also as illustrated in the lower left image in Fig. 2-1. Next, imagine all of the other infinite colors from the color wheel transposed to the surface of the ball. Finally, imagine all of the colors, including red, blue, green, gray, cyan, yellow, white and magenta, all fading to black at the center of a 4D transparent sphere as illustrated in the lower right image in Fig. 2-4.

The direction of the xyz 360-degree three-dimensional rotational or spin axis of the color sphere represents both the hue and the saturation of all colors, and the luminosity of the colors is represented by its black center and its bright outer surface. Accordingly, black, white and gray are colors, just as much as the primary and secondary colors are colors. This image could easily be replicated by the structure of a rotating gyroscope with the angle of the axis of the gyroscope determining the hue and the saturation of the color perceived and the rate of spin as the luminosity of the color perceived. All colors are singular and only different by their rotational axis and their rate of spin. This is the structure microbiologists need to be looking for within the human brain in order to duplicate the mechanics of our human perceived colors.

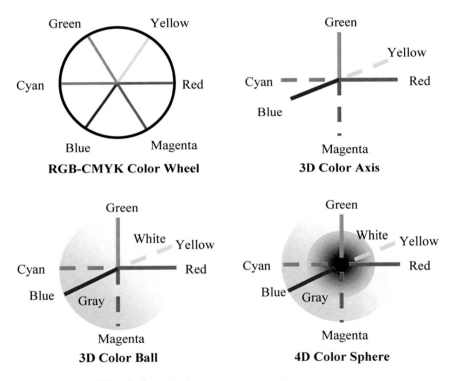

Fig. 2-4 – Color Electrodynamics of a conventional
RGB/CMY Color Wheel (upper left) and proposed actual
Color Wheel Psychosomatics of the Human Mind (lower right)

I therefore propose that the above referenced 4D color sphere is the method by which the illusion of the perception of color is created within the occipital lobes of the human brain. As was indicated earlier, human image perception is a four-dimensional continuum, with three dimensions of color and the fourth dimension of luminosity; and accordingly, color perception is a partial derivative of the universe. The bottom line is that the mechanics that produces the human sensation of color must exactly replicate the actual array of human perceived colors, or the conceived mechanism is the wrong mechanism. Therefore, the RGB-CMYK color wheel may have many practical applications, but replicating the actual process of color generation within the human mind is not one of them. Moreover, regardless of what polar coordinate system is defined for the mechanics of color perception, the coordinate system must have a fixed reference system to work, and therefore must and can only occur within the human mind.

For example, create a three-dimensional polar coordinate model on your lab desk with a moveable ball to indicate the appropriate color, and then include a laser-monitoring device to measure the location of the ball, thereby defining all of the possible colors. Consequently, if you then move the measuring device to the opposite side of the model, the laser-monitoring device would give you the incorrect color, even though nothing changed in the model. Therefore, the colors and the reference system determining the colors must be in a fixed reference system, which can therefore only occur within the human mind. Both the system generating the illusion of color and the system monitoring the illusion of color must be in the same fixed reference system for the structural model to work.

This structural solution will only be found by first defining both the mechanism and the processes within the human brain that create the images that we perceive; and then by defining the molecular structures that create a similar gyroscopic spatial mechanism that replicates our four-dimensional, human perceived color continuum. In a similar fashion, there must be a very sophisticated, color enhanced, visual imaging system functioning within the occipital lobes of the human brain. However, there are a few other peculiar occurrences that can and do occur to those images, such as double vision or spinning images from too much alcohol, hallucinations or false images from LSD, spinning images from going around in circles, vertigo from inner ear problems, or the imagery of our dream world while we are sleeping.

Moreover, when any part of this system malfunctions, diverse imagery and other unintended colors can and do result. For example, it is well known that some people see words in colors with each letter being a different color as they read the sentence. This aberration is easily explained once it is realized that both our imagery and the color of our imagery are strictly phenomena of the mind. Also, how many times after a traffic accident, do you hear someone say that he or she looked but never saw them coming. The mind does not always include all of the details in the imagery that it presents to the person in the accident, maybe because of the length of time the objects were observed or the individual priorities of the person at fault at that moment. Sometimes we just get in too big a hurry, and do not concentrate long enough for a complete image to be presented to us. Uniquely, we each have a front row seat to the inner mechanics of the human visual system. All we need to do is to first realize that the images that we perceive are all occurring within our human brain and then find the biological structures that describe and define those aberrations that we actually see.

The Philosophy of Human Perception

Many of the mysteries of our universe and of our psychological selves can be unlocked from the perspective that our visual images exist solely within the minds. But first, one more theorem, a combination of the law of cause and effect with the theorem, which states that the whole is greater than the sum of its parts, must be introduced. That is, when an effect is discernible at any organized level of existence, an equivalent discernible cause must also be recognizable at that same organized level of existence. It is from this basis that imaginative descriptions can be developed for our human body, our human mind, and our soul; and that pictures can be drawn for such illusive concepts as our state of consciousness and the spirit of our soul.

I propose that this theorem is a self-evident truth; that is, its opposite is obviously incorrect. For example, a man perceives a part of the world around him; however, there exists no cause either within him or within his surroundings to account for his perceptions. This in effect repeals reality, our existence, and the existence of reality itself. Philosophers have long argued the difficulty in proving the differences between the dream world and the real world. Their arguments suggest that all happenings might even occur solely within our minds. However, I suggest that for any organism to possess sufficient knowledge to dream a concert pianist playing the piano, while he cannot play the piano, is impossible, improbable, and impractical. It is impossible because there are insufficient atoms within our minds to project all of the occurrences within our visible and audible worlds; improbable because it represents disintegrated capabilities functioning as an integrated whole; and impractical because it defies the simplicity of common sense. It is totally illogical to suggest that there are no causes for the effects that we perceive, and it is then irrational to suggest that we cannot find those causes. The entire basis for scientific study is cause and effect. If we see a cause and know it to be real, then the effect must also be real. More importantly, if we see an effect and know it to be real, then the cause must also be real. This is a truth, which cannot be violated and cannot fail. It is only its application, which fails and that is a failure of our selves to understand.

The human being is a highly complex organization of overlapping and interconnected systems and subsystems functioning synergistically as a single and integrated whole. It is comprised of billions of atoms arranged into multitudes of differing structures and shapes, forming the various molecules, cells, and organs which acting together promote the continuance of life within our bodies. Its sophistication and almost incomprehensible complexity has become apparent only with the increasing knowledge accumulated from the scientific investigations of our potentials and our capabilities, as well as our limitations and our fallibilities. The diversity of diseases and ailments which we experience are a living testament to the complexities and vulnerabilities of the systems functioning within our bodies. If these very same atoms were rearranged into simpler and more common everyday substances, their equivalent would be approximately a half-barrel of water, about a gallon of a highly complex substance called protein, and about a cupful of salts, minerals and ash. Obviously, this second description does not reflect the description for a human body, and therein lies the difference between the whole and the sum of its parts.

When organization is introduced into any arrangement of atoms or parts; the whole experiences an increase in value, which is directly related to the corresponding level of sophistication existing within the organizational structure. A simple example would be a hammer, a chisel, and a block of steel. When the atoms within a block of steel are forged into the shape of either a hammer or a chisel, the new object is endowed with a greater potential for usefulness than the original block of steel. Many of these simple examples could be given, but due to their primitive nature, they contribute very little toward solving the mysteries existing within the human psyche. However, if the idea of organization is combined with the visualization techniques introduced earlier and expounded upon in the last chapter, enlightened perspectives for both the human body and the human psyche can be developed.

But first the idea of organization, especially in conjunction with cause and effect, must be further explored. All of the thoughts and visualizations presented in this book are based on the absolute certainty of cause and effect, not merely from a deterministic point of view, but also from a more generalized, yet holistic point of view. The law of cause and effect exists not only on the microscopic level but also on the macroscopic level, not only on the differentiated level but also on the integrated level, not only on the materialistic level but also on the spiritualistic level. It exists in each of the infinite perspectives of the universe and permeates the whole of the universe in an absolute fashion. However, it in no way refutes the existence of an organized whole. In fact, the whole being greater than the sum of its parts implies organization or integration of its lesser parts and operates synergistically within the law of cause and effect.

In order to better understand this relationship, we must also look at its opposite; that is, the whole is only greater than the sum of its parts, provided there is an inherent organization. When disorganization exists, there is no whole but only a conglomeration of parts. In this condition, the law of cause and effect is transformed into the random possibilities of uncertainty. The simplicity of macroscopic cause and effect is then replaced by the complexity of the probabilities of microscopic cause and effect. In the first case we have harmony or order and in the latter case, chaos or disorder.

Within the human being is a highly sophisticated complex of individual cause and effect relationships, which together define the organized whole. However, within this complex is an inherent paradox. That is, the being we perceive as the self is not the whole, but only a part of the whole. For example, the reflected images of the outside world, which we now perceive as a part of the apparatus of our mental psyche, are obviously not a part of our self. Another example would be our memory control apparatus, which builds the soul, but is not a part of the soul or the self. Our paradox, either individually or collectively, is then being the part but trying to understand the whole.

Ultimately, we are each involved in a battle between organization and uncertainty. Our lack of understanding of this process, our confusions and our misunderstandings, in no way refutes the existence of that process, but instead is indicative of that process at work within ourselves. When the level of self-organization transcends the level of uncertainty, order reigns; however, when the opposite is the case, chaos reigns. This is the process, which is basically at work within the life cycle of all beings. That is, organisms are born, grow in complexity, are overcome by the maverick forces of disorganization, and then cease to exist. The law of cause and effect has the ability to create, as well as to destroy, and is controlled only by the nature of the organized being within the whole. Since it is our nature to develop both good and bad psychological traits, we must each climb high enough in the tree of self-knowledge, to unerringly see the inherent truths of our good and bad ways, if we as a species are to survive.

Human Consciousness and the Soul

There is, then, an inherent dichotomy, which exists between the outside world and the perceptions of the human mind. For example, we tend to identify ourselves with the entirety of the human body, and this simply is not true. We are not the reproductive system, although we enjoy its fruits. We are not the digestive system, although we sense its pangs of hunger and enjoy its gratification of fulfillment. We are not the skeletal or the muscular systems, although we enjoy the motility they provide. We are not the immune or the hormonal system, although without them we could not exist. We are not the nervous system, but it is there where we reside. The human body is a temple, harboring myriad forms of life, and its nervous system is the tabernacle for our soul.

The nervous system is, therefore, the essence of our human existence, as it is what unites our systems into an integrated whole, as well as provides the differentiation between our bodies and our selves. In order to understand this phenomenon, a broad perspective of this one aspect of our human anatomy must be assimilated. First, the nervous system can be divided into nerves and nerve endings, the spinal cord, and the brain. There are then two types of nerves, sympathetic nerves and parasympathetic nerves. Sympathetic nerves chemically induce the electrical flow of energy and parasympathetic nerve chemically inhibits the electrical flow of energy. Each nerve is a single functioning cell with some, such as those in the spinal cord, as long as three feet. They interconnect electrically at chemical junctions called synapses. The majority of our nerve endings culminate as the sense of pain, touch, heat, and cold in our skin, with the remainder connected to the previously visualized autonomously functioning systems within our bodies.

The spinal cord acts as the communication channel between the nerve endings and the brain. However, it also provides another critical autonomous function; that is, our physical reflexes. Electrical impulses actually short circuit directly from the sensory nerves to the motor control nerves to induce movement. This entire process occurs solely within the spinal cord, and we have only limited abilities to inhibit them. Our body jumps, and our hands recoil from threatening objects as predetermined by our genetic code. This is not a simplified process, either, since if the hand is touched with a hot object, one set of muscles must be activated; however, if the elbow is touched, another set of muscles must be activated.

The brain is then further divided into the brainstem, the midbrain, and the cerebral cortex. The brainstem sits atop and blends into the spinal cord; and through the parasympathetic nerve system, controls the remainder of our autonomous functions such as breathing, heart rate, blood pressure, and the digestive system. The midbrain is divided into the limbic system, the cerebellum, and memory control systems. The limbic system and memory control systems are made up of hundreds of separately functioning organs and are interspersed with ventricles of circulating fluids, which nourish the entire system. They function as complicated chemical-electrical circuits, which interface the nerve endings, the spinal cord, and the brain stem with the cerebral cortex. In addition, they control the development of the living being growing within the cerebral cortex. They are, in fact, the control circuits for the making of a soul. The cerebellum is located behind and below the midbrain and coordinates our physical movements into sequentially smooth actions, and when it does not function properly, we become jittery and clumsy. Similarly, emotions originate in the cerebral cortex and not in the limbic system, which instead simply converts those signals into reflections of our psychological and behavioral characteristics.

The cerebral cortex is a folded or crumpled-up tissue surrounding the midbrain and is composed of six layers of brain cells. If it were unfolded, it would be approximately sixteen inches by twenty inches by one-eighth inch thick. It is symmetrically divided into two halves, the left and the right half, with each half containing four subdivisions, the frontal lobe, temporal lobe, parietal lobe, and occipital lobe. These divisions represent definite chasms, which exist between each of the eight lobes, which are then interconnected by bundles of nerve fibers; for instance, in the case of the left and right brain, it is called the corpus collosum. This is actually barely a beginning at understanding the complexities of the brain, as scientists are still continuing the cataloging process. However, it is unnecessary to attempt a more complicated understanding since end conclusions can be achieved, philosophically.

First allow me to present a simplified visualization of the nervous system. Start by visualizing the nerve endings as a glowing silhouette ghosting the contour of our skin. Our sense of touch is seen as a series of pulses of light journeying from this glowing silhouette through electrified threads and funneled onto braided cords of liquid light. The spinal cord appears as a woven mesh of fibers channeling surges of liquid light into integrated impulses which are leaping, spinning, and jumping about within this inter-tangled mesh. Waves of psychedelic light are then projected as a laser light show of geometric art, upon a crown of cotton candy webbing filled with electrified fibers of saturated light. Sound is seen as harmonically tuned waves resonating through symphonic programs that are orchestrated by and within this saturated light. Finally, vision is a four-dimensional image cast by microscopic gyros spinning shadowed webs of color that are suspended within the fibers of this saturated light. The human being is a composite force of shades of dark and light, which lives and dances as ephemeral images, within the substance of our mind.

Our soul is then the combined memory traces of our physiological and psychological states of consciousness; and whereas the physiological level of consciousness is innate and thereby opposed by nonexistence, the psychological level of consciousness progressively develops throughout our lives and is opposed by the unconscious. The interesting thing about consciousness is that we each have a front row seat to the process of consciousness within our human minds. That is, since the entirety of our soul, as well as all of the images that we perceive of both ourselves and the world that surrounds us, exists within our minds; then all we need to do is to look around at ourselves and the world that surrounds us; and accordingly, integrate those processes that we define as a part of our consciousness into our concept of the human mind. Our spirit is then the harmony or disharmony within the soul, or the level of conscious and unconscious integration within the soul. The soul can be visualized as the light of the conscious intellect, and the spirit as the ghosting images of both dark and light within that intellect. Although the soul and the spirit are normally thought of only in abstract terms, by applying previously developed visualization techniques to the human mind, substance can be added to the perception of the soul, and therefore, the soul and the spirit, as well as consciousness, have the potential to exist outside of the brain.

The overwhelming abundance of well-documented near-death experiences reveals hints of the potential for life of another kind. Also, since human beings can only perceive the images created within our minds by our minds, it would seem reasonable that outside of our minds almost anything is possible. It must be remembered that there are two realities for the world within which we live, the absolute reality and the perceptible reality, and that they are separate but parallel worlds. That is, they are both congruent and interconnected, and what happens in the one world similarly also happens in the other world. This explains exactly how the human being separates the objective from the subjective worlds. For both the objective and the subjective worlds exist within both the visual and the sensual worlds within the mind, and it is then through the processes of consciousness, self-awareness and self-knowledge that the two worlds are individually defined and that the soul is created. The physical world of the universe is the real world, that is, it is the one that is really out there, and it includes both the world of matter made from the liquid light and the world of electromagnetic energy made from the stellar air. Whereas the metaphysical world is the world that we perceive within the human mind, and that exists and only exists within the human mind, and which is but a reflection of the true world that is really out there. This definition is just reversed from the way most contemporary disciplines view reality, for in truth this humanly observed world is the illusion and what a grand and wonderful illusion it is, and the world beyond the mental imagery of our minds is in fact the real world.

Fig. 2-5 – An Illustration of the Human World and the Real World

Similarly, human beings actually have two bodies, as illustrated in Fig. 2-5. The first are the real physical bodies of the real people in the real physical scene, that exists outside of our minds, and as illustrated in the large picture by the black and white overall image. The second is the reflected metaphysical images of the same black and white scene, which is visualized in color by and within the observers mind, and which is illustrated in the drawing by the oval colored image in the lower left portion of the picture. Accordingly each of the observers within this scene would have their own color version of the entire scene, along with a color vision of their own body in their own mind and within their own mentally created holographic world. In addition to this visual image of their own body, their real physical body would still exist outside of their minds and within the real universe. The meta-physical body actually has four aspects, 1) sensual, 2) visual, 3) spatial, and 4) motional, which together form the complex energy field within the mind that we each identify as our self. This then provides a mecha-nism for near-death experiences. That is, when the physical body dies, the energy complex of the intellectual body and of the human soul transmigrates out of the brain and into the heavenly world. For this brief moment, the consciousness of the intellect is in the unique position to view both the physical body that had always been misidentified as its metaphysical image, and the metaphysical image of the self that had always been mistaken as the real physical body. Does the light of the conscious intellect of the living soul within the mind go out, or is it instead transposed by the death of the body into another world?

One remaining problem to be resolved is the nature of the soul after it leaves the body. In both Chapters One and Four of this book, it is proposed that space is not empty, but is instead filled with a single universal substance, the stellar air or aether. Furthermore, this substance is far from being inert or homogenous, but is instead another highly complex form of various energy structures that are built upon and by other energy structures, both by and within itself. Accordingly, this complex of aethereal structures provides ample possibilities for the soul to have a real and meaningful spiritual existence outside of the physical body and within the aether. Each time scientists develop a new and better camera or explore our solar system with a new and better spacecraft, they discover new and unexpected things beyond anything they had previously imagined. Such is the case with the aether, as we have not even begun to understand the varieties and multiplicities of energy structures possible within the stellar air or the aether. As difficult as it is for us at times to believe in life after physical death, especially because of its seemingly one-way direction, it must be accepted as a definite and real possibility. Finally, when one remembers the stories, the faces, the dedication and the convictions of those special few who have experienced near-death experiences, life after death should be considered a near certainty.

Spiritual Life in the Heavenly World

The world that we perceive is actually an illusion created within the boundaries of our minds, and there instead exists another world beyond our human perceptions. It is accessible not only through the powers of our imagination, but also through physical death, near-death and/or out of body experiences. This then brings up the question of what would it be like when the soul of a person leaves the body within the physical world and then enters into spiritual life within the heavenly world? A compendium of answers can be found by defining those attributes that are a part of the soul living within the brain and those attributes that are merely a part of the brain or the nervous system alone. For example, our reflexes occur mostly within the spinal cord and not in the brain, so accordingly, reflexes would not go along with the soul. This makes a lot of sense, since you probably won't need reflexes in the spiritual world anyway. Likewise, further differentiation of the brain can also determine those attributes that are purely a part of the soul.

For example, the apparatus of the occipital lobes, which produce the images we see, and the temporal lobes which produce the sounds that we hear, are not a part of the soul; however, our perceptions of those images and our perceived sounds are a part of the soul. Therefore, when entering the heavenly world, the apparatus of producing images and sounds, will be replaced with the virtual images from the aura of holistic energy within the heavens. You will still be able to look back at the world and see the physical images of the world that you just left behind; however, the colors will probably be transparent instead of opaque as they are now, as if you were peering through a rainbow. You will also be able to hear the sounds of the physical world but they will be in a chorus of harmony. You will be able to see and to hear as the angels see and hear. Your words, your knowledge and your memory will go with you, so you will be able to recognize and to talk to your loved ones. Furthermore, attributes such as self-image, self-identity, and self-knowledge are all a part of the soul and will also make the transmigration along with the soul into the other world. In other words, when you get there, you will be in possession of who you are and what you know, and you will be able to see and to talk to others. You will also be able to visit with your lost loved ones or even your ancestors that you have never met, whom I am sure have all been eagerly waiting for your return so they can meet and share the memories of their bygone years with you.

Conclusion

Regardless of how difficult it is for us to believe, the simple truth is that our human perceived world exists solely within our minds, and that instead there actually exists another world beyond this physical world of our human perceptions. We get so entrenched in what we see that we do not realize that the things that we do not see also have their own existence, just as much as we do. Furthermore, there is a cause and effect relationship for everything within the Universe, including our own psychological constructs. Accordingly, there is no magic in the universe, but only our limited ability to perceive, to imagine and to understand the real truth behind reality. Until we accept these simple truths of our own limitations and the indisputable dichotomy between our uniquely human visual world and the real universal world, we will continue to have trouble uncovering the hidden truths of the universe – truths that will unlock both the secrets of world that is within us and the secrets of the world that surrounds us; but instead, remain hidden by the windows unto our minds.

Chapter Three

The Mind Game

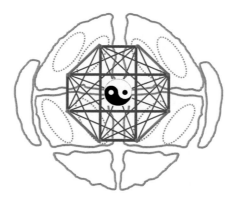

"By three methods we may learn wisdom:
first, by reflection, which is noblest;
second, by imitation, which is easiest; and
third by experience, which is the bitterest."
　　　　　　　　　- Confucius (551-479 BC)

Introduction

Confucius was a Chinese teacher, editor, politician and philosopher from the Lu State, Zhou Dynasty in China. The Zhou Dynasty was founded in the 11th century BC by King Wen of Zhou (1152-1056 BC). Although it was King Wen's second son King Wu of Zhou who conquered the nearby Shang Dynasty in 1046 BC after his father's death, King Wu only lived three more years, and it is his father King Wen who is therefore honored as the founder of the dynasty. King Wen is considered the first epic hero of China and is also credited with creating the 64 hexagrams of the Yi Jing from the eight trigrams. It is because of King Wen and the Yi Jing, that I am able to posit complex structures and corresponding tables for organizing those words that describe our collective human behavior into a single Organized Word Structure (OWS).

The OWS directly overlays the human brain, and thereby defines the mental processes functioning within the human brain. Moreover, the OWS can be expanded to include all of the words that describe each of the individual mental processes functioning within the human brain, including emotions, drives, conscience, will, mannerisms, gestures, behavior, etc. The OWS is then integrated and unified with the Yi Jing, the Kabbalah, and Lüscher's Color Test, which collectively posits volumes of detailed information about the human psyche and the human mind.

Decoding the Yi Jing (Yijing or I Ching)

A detailed physiological understanding of the various structures within the human brain is not necessary, since it is possible to reach end conclusions philosophically. The process begins by first realizing that human beings are organized beings. We see far too many recurring behavioral traits for this not to be true. Within our minds is the ability to interrelate and to interconnect muscular movements with visual perceptions and to form conceptual ideas from these perceptual events. They can even be remembered and reenacted at a later time through the mechanics of thought, as they are further assimilated into integrated concepts. Only a highly organized and structured mental apparatus can explain this recurring and unique ability within human beings. What must be accomplished is to find a corresponding organized mental structure, which allows for the diversity seen within human beings, while at the same time accounting for our shared similarities and oneness.

The second realization is that words by themselves mean nothing. They are just mere utterances of the mind. It is only when they are associated or connected with thoughts, knowledge, images, or sounds that they take on meaning. Words are more than just a method of communicating between ourselves; they are also a method of communicating within ourselves. This internal communication becomes an apparatus within the mind for our word structure to become and to grow. Words are not just verbal representations of our physical reality, but instead real entities, existing as three-dimensional energy arrays within the psyche of our human mind.

The third realization is by limiting the evaluation of our spoken language only to those words which are reflective of human nature, whether it be our own or someone else's, a word structure can be developed, which organizes our vocabulary of human nature into an integrated whole. For example, when we say we are considering our options, we know explicitly that we are considering and not meditating nor contemplating our options. Likewise, each of the words, which describe human nature, also describes a process within human nature; and, since the processes at work within human nature are organized, therefore it must also be possible to organize those words that describe that nature. This organization then represents a definition for the methods, and hence the apparatus at work within our minds.

One must then make a fourth realization in order to make this basic premise complete. That is, all knowledge and thoughts purported to be true by an individual must be considered mostly true, unless the individual is judged to be dishonest or not of sound mind, in which case it would then be discounted as useless. However, in each case, the final structure must account for both conditions. Therefore, the OWS must represent the collective knowledge of humanity and not simply one person's individual knowledge. Based upon reasoned faith, one must accept the collective knowledge of honorable and honest people as reasonably true. Accordingly, the OWS for human nature is proposed to be a four-dimensional bilateral/bipolar/bi-directional system, and corresponds to our psychological level of consciousness. It can be directly superimposed upon the parietal and frontal lobes of the human brain as shown in Figs. 3-1a, 3-1b and 3-2. This arrangement was chosen since incoming sensory perception or touch is connected to the parietal lobe, and since outgoing muscle control is connected to the frontal lobe. It is within this portion of the brain that the body of our soul exists.

Although sounds exist within the temporal lobes, our words are located within the parietal lobe and their integration into our soul also occurs within the parietal lobe, and it is there that our soul and its knowledge exist. Likewise, and although images are located within the occipital lobe, their integration into the soul also occurs within the parietal lobe, and it is also there that our perceptions exist. This same cause-and-effect relationship must exist for each of the organized, functioning processes existing within the brain, and accordingly a specific psychological trait must also occur. A similar relationship exists within both the conscious and the unconscious part of the brain, and thereby represents the complete structure of the conscious-unconscious mind. It is further proposed that each one of the six layers of brain cells within the cerebral cortex represents various overall mental processing functions, for example, being, knowing, thinking, or deciding. Accordingly, for this analysis to be complete, both the dynamic as well as the static conditions of the human psyche must be included. For example, in Fig. 3-1a, cognition is the combined process of learning, thinking, and understanding; and although they are dynamic processes, their end results are our static memories of experiences, knowledge, and thoughts, as illustrated in Fig. 3-1a. Cognition is then complemented by recognition, which is remembering, rethinking, and recollecting, and is a review of our static memories produced by cognition; and, although it is also a dynamic process, its end result is a further correction of our static memories.

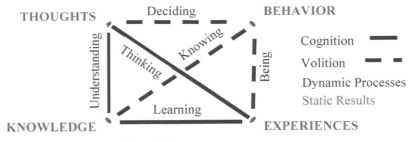

Fig. 3-1a – Four Point Diagram

Volition is the combined processes of being, knowing, and deciding and generates our will, and the act of exercising the will changes our will. These dynamic processes when attached to words represent our state of consciousness, and their static results represent our conscious and subconscious memories. These same dynamic processes, when not attached to words, represent the unconscious, and their static results are the memory traces of our preconscious and unconscious impressions.

The unconscious represents the overall integration of the content of the brain and always governs our behavior. Also, it should be noted that although words are rooted in the temporal lobe, knowledge and thoughts are distributed throughout the entire brain. For instance, whereas the base for understanding is in the left hemisphere, under-standing also extends into other areas of the brain in the form of intui-tion, imagination, and wisdom.

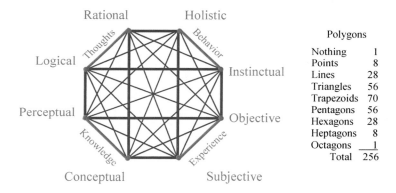

Polygons	
Nothing	1
Points	8
Lines	28
Triangles	56
Trapezoids	70
Pentagons	56
Hexagons	28
Heptagons	8
Octagons	1
Total	256

Fig. 3-1b – 8-Point Diagram with 28 dynamic lines
and associated list of Polygons

There are then two functions within each quadrant, collectively rep-resenting our static/dynamic and conscious/unconscious conditions. Accordingly, each quadrant in Fig. 3-1b is bipolar, as experiences are either subjective or objective, knowledge is either perceptual or concep-tual, thoughts are either logical or rational, and finally behavior is either instinctual or holistic. In the right brain the unconscious rules, and the conscious is projected onto it; and in the left-brain the conscious rules and the unconscious is projected through it. Our behavior is controlled solely by the right front brain, the seat of the unconscious, and is only influenced by the other three quadrants. We can think all we like, but our behavior is still an unconscious effect. Likewise, speech is a left-brain effect and is a window unto our soul.

I would like to briefly discuss free will before moving on. Basically, we have free will until we exercise it, and then it is gone. Free will is a dynamic process controlled by our past decisions and choices, which have formed the static memories of our personality. If we do not like what we have become, the only way to change is to rise to higher and higher levels of conscious awareness, re-choose our direction, and then endure until we have again reestablished our freedom to choose our own free and individual will.

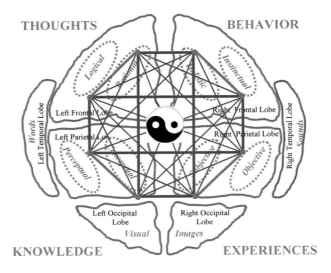

Fig. 3-2 – 8-Point Diagram superimposed on the parietal and frontal lobes of the cerebral cortex

The basic foundation for the total arrangement of our spoken words is then proposed as shown in Figs. 3-1a, 3-1b and 3-2. From this arrangement, and since instinctual spirit represents behavior, it is evident why lobotomies of the right front brain affected only our behavior and left the majority of our personality intact. Another significant characteristic noticed is its exact replication of the Chinese Yi Jing or the Book of Changes. For those unfamiliar with the Yi Jing, it is an ancient book of the intuitive understanding of the motivating forces of yin and yang within human nature. It is composed of eight fundamental trigrams, each represented by the unique and exclusive combinations of a three-line pictorial diagram ($\equiv\!\equiv$), which in this diagram can also be quantified as the three-digit binary number 010 or the single digit decimal number two.

According to Chinese tradition, these trigrams were invented by Fu Hsi (2953-2838 BC); however, this is difficult to prove, since his life predates the inception of written language within China. Actually, during his lifetime, China did not even exist as an integrated state, and he may simply have been a mythical character representing a collection of individuals and the evolution of these eight trigrams by those individuals. The next significant step in the evolution of the Yi Jing occurred almost two thousand years later during the reign of King Wen (1152-1056 BC) when the eight trigrams were coded into a dual matrix of sixty-four (64) unique and exclusive hexagrams (☰☰). The lower trigram in the matrix purportedly represents our earthly nature, and the upper trigram purportedly represents our heavenly or (divine) nature. I use the word divine here as an interpretation; since the Chinese people do not currently recognize divinity as a separate entity of nature. This phase of the Yi Jing's development ended shortly thereafter, when the Duke of Chou added commentaries to each of these sixty-four hexagrams, further reflecting upon the unique and exclusive vicissitudes of human nature. I propose that the eight-point arrangement for our spoken word structure is, in fact, the same arrangement that was perceived and identified by the originators of the Yi Jing almost 5000 years ago.

A second significant characteristic is the organizational progression of individually unique geometric arrangements, as listed in Fig. 3-1b. Whereas matter represents the four dimensions of space and time transcribed into three-dimensional space, man represents the three dimensions of the self, transcribed into the fourth dimension of being. Notice the fourth dimension of the space-time continuum is change or motion, and similarly the fourth dimension of man is motion or behavior. Also, each of the four dimensions is bilateral, bipolar, and bi-directional, just as the dimensions in the space-time continuum. Therefore, each human being is created by and of the universe and is carved from a common OWS fractal structure. Accordingly, human psychology is reduced to a branch of molecular physics, just as biology and chemistry and essentially all scientific disciplines must ultimately conform to the laws of physics.

Human beings have the potential to access all eight functions of the human mind; however, in most cases this never occurs. Most of us are born or grow at a reduced level of intellectual awareness and develop only a portion of these eight fundamental psychological traits. For instance, some people are logical, others rational, and some people do not think at all, but instead rely upon their intuitive assets. There are then 256 psychological combinations, as shown in the geometric progression in the right margin of Fig. 3-1b, which develop from just these eight points. This also helps to explain some of the diversities and the common traits of children from the same family. For instance, if the child's predisposition is aligned with his or her parents, he or she will develop knowledge and actions from them and hence adopt their personality traits. However, if the child is predisposed with a mental process different from the parents, that child will develop a personality based upon the knowledge and actions of his associates and peers. Granted, psychological types are mere generalizations for personalities and that the total number of personalities possible is unlimited on a practical basis. The unique combinations of the fundamental processes within the brain, the diverse potential for individual traits to develop within each of these processes and the subsequent changing of psychological types throughout our life causes the many variations within our personality. We may all be born with a blank slate, but not the same blank slate. Therefore we develop both radically different, as well as similar personalities, all molded from this same organized mental apparatus. Accordingly, we are each unique beings growing, sharing, and becoming within the common genetics of our human mind.

On the other hand, these same 256 psychological types can be rationalized into simpler groupings. For instance, the Yi Jing develops sixty-four types. Carl Jung developed only four types but his followers have extended this to sixteen types. Each of these generalizations reflects the psychological type of their developers; for instance in the latter case it is conceptual and intellectual, and based upon the four corner points. Other psychologists have developed six and even seven psychological types. These constructs tend to be more behaviorally oriented and can be explained by the rationalization shown in Figs. 3-1a and 3-1b. Note there are four points, but six interconnecting lines and that a seventh group can be included as an integration of the six lines into a single functioning whole. The flexibility of this organization can easily be illustrated by asking how many ways there are to cut an apple in half. The answer would be seemingly infinite, and likewise the human mind can be organized into many different schemes, dependent only upon the personality and psychological type of the person developing the schematic. Psychological types can also be applied collectively to entire cultures. Hence, our nations are dependent upon the values, principles, and ideals handed down by our forefathers. When departing from these prescribed values, unknown courses are charted in the human psyche, and both success and tragedy can develop.

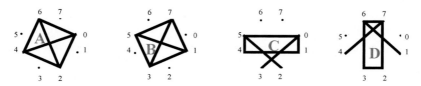

Fig. 3-3a – Four Six–Line Diagrams (**A, B, C, D**)

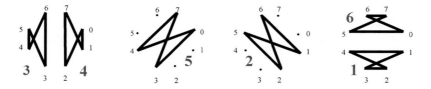

Fig. 3-3b – Six Four-Line Diagrams (**1 thru 6**)

QUADRANTS	GROUP #	1	2	3	4	5	6
12 Experiences	A	24	26	46	20	40	60
34 Knowledge	B	13	15	35	17	37	57
56 Thoughts	C	14	25	45	10	30	50
70 Behavior / Truth	D	23	16	36	27	47	67
21 Fantasies	A	42	62	64	02	04	06
43 Pretensions	B	31	51	53	71	73	75
65 Euphemisms	C	41	52	54	01	03	05
07 Lies	D	32	61	63	72	74	76

Fig. 3-3c – Combined Matrix of Six-Line and Four-Line Diagrams including both the Positive and Negative Attributes of Human Nature

Returning to the original eight-point arrangement, we notice that it can be disassembled into an arrangement of four groups of six lines or six groups of four lines as shown in Figs. 3-3a and 3-3b. With the inclusion of the four quadrants, these arrangements neatly combine, and thereby form a word matrix as shown in the chart shown in Fig. 3-3c. The upper half of the chart represents the proper or clockwise flow of energy within the brain, 1 through 7 to 0, and the bottom half represents the reverse or improper, or counter-clockwise flow or short-circuiting, of energy within the brain, 7 through 1 to 0. Another interesting similarity is now recalled; that is, there are six levels of brain cells in the cerebral cortex, or summarily four main lobes, which are interconnected by six levels of communication. Likewise, in the diagram there are four fundamental dimensions interconnected by six lines. Remember, if the original task is to be accomplished, the OWS must copy the physical structure of the brain. It is therefore proposed that there be six layers of diagrams, each representing a different aspect of human nature.

Another striking similarity is that when comparing the coding for the Yi Jing to the above diagram, each of the six lines in a hexagram can be set in correspondence with each of the six lines in the four-point diagram. It is from this perspective that many of its secrets and our mysteries begin to unravel. For instance, the Yi Jing diagram (45) is separated into heaven above (5) and the earth below (4). If these lines are pictorially coded by the rules shown in Figs. 3-4a and 3-4b, then corresponding images or pictures result as shown in Fig. 3-4c. This can then be expanded into the complete chart as shown in Fig. 3-5a. Reviewing the pictorial images, recurring identical images can be identified, but rotated 90 or 180 degrees. For example, hexagram (10) and hexagram (04) are the same but rotated 180 degrees. These relationships can then be divided into two distinct halves of red symmetry and blue symmetry, as illustrated in Fig. 3-5a, and as further illustrated in Figs. 3-7a and 3-7b.

An organizational definition for the four great attributes and their associated major and minor aspects of yin and yang are shown in the lower margin of Fig. 3-5b. I propose that the four great attributes are those energy lines as defined by the four comers of the pictorial coding sequence. In the case of human nature, they are our experiences (12), our knowledge (34), our thoughts (56), and the truth (70). Also note that in Fig. 3-5a these four lines are absent from the sixty-four pictorial hexagrams. However, note that when the six energy flow lines of our experiences, representative of the dashed lines of yin, are combined with the six energy flow lines of our knowledge, also representative of the dashed lines of yin; the same pictorial hexagram results as developed in the matrix code (00). This is the same code defined by the Chinese as yin. Similarly, when the energy flow lines of our thoughts and the truth are combined the pictorial hexagram for yang or hexagram (77) is developed.

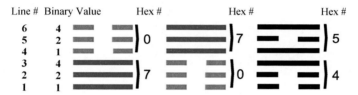

Fig. 3-4a – Binary Coding Method

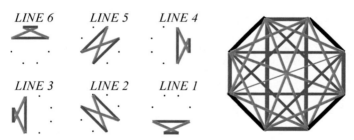

Fig. 3-4b – Line Identification for
Transposing Binary Codes

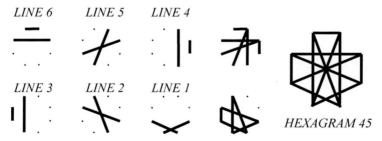

Fig. 3-4c – Sample Coding of Hexagram Binary Code #45

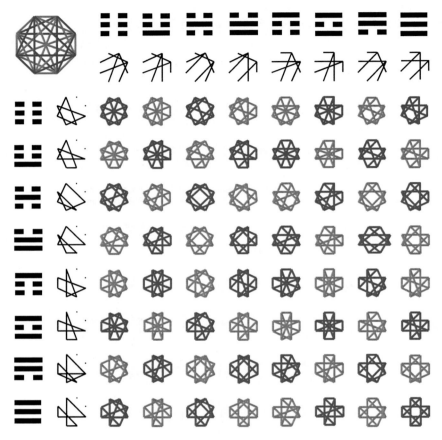

Fig. 3-5a - Coding of the 64 Hexagrams in the *Yi Jing (I Ching)*

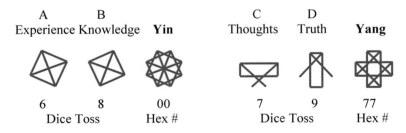

Fig. 3-5b - Pictorial Coding of the 64 Hexagrams in the Yi Jing (*I Ching*)

It is thereby evident that the definitions for yin and yang are very sophisticated and complex, utilizing the entirety of the brain, but each in its own way. For instance, objective logic becomes a part of yin, whereas subjective logic is a part of yang. Likewise, subjective rationale is a part of yin, whereas objective rationale is a part of yang. A similar duality of juxtapositions exists for each of the six dynamic energy flow-lines of yin and yang. Although each of the four aspects of the six energy flow-lines of yin and yang are identified in Fig. 3-5 by the divinations of the numbers 6, 7, 8, and 9 of the dice toss, this does not infer nor imply the legitimacy of that practice, as it can only be determined by a more complete analysis of the word structure. However, it is proposed that when that analysis is complete, it will probably be found to be mostly illegitimate and a part of the darker side of human nature. It is a little wonder that only the Chinese with their ancient visual vocabulary and verbal understandings of wisdom would be able to derive this pattern of human behavior. Recognition of the Yi Jing represents the predominant flow of energy lines within the academic minds of the Chinese people as established by their traditional cultural and value system. Moreover, it also illustrates the basic fundamental flow lines of energy within all human minds as represented by each of our own individual cultures. However, before an analysis can be completed, a more detailed understanding of the proposed word structure must be developed.

The completed word structure for understanding is then shown in Table 3-1 and represents 56 words of vocabulary. With the inclusion of learning and thinking, the combined process of cognition then represents 168 words of vocabulary. When other processes such as volition, will, and recognition are included, it then expands to almost 700 words. Also, it does not seem to be the end, as it appears there are processes for words like philosophizing, theosophizing, hypothesizing, and theorizing. Furthermore, only our internal mental processes have been discussed, and our goal, which was human behavior, has still not been reached. The combined word structure including verbs, adverbs, and adjectives then cascades into several thousand words and would more than allow for the myriad of words used to describe our human behavior by our various human languages.

In order to promulgate a precise and succinct understanding in lieu of complicated explanations, only the absolute simplest definitions were sought in this section. For example, apprehending can be thought of from a logical viewpoint as logical conceptions, or from a rational viewpoint as midway between grasping and understanding. An obvious conclusion from this format is that everything above the line in each group represents positive psychological traits, and everything below the line represents negative psychological traits,. Also, wisdom is a function of the unconscious spirit and not only of the conscious intellect. The only way to arrive at wisdom is through our logical instincts, with anything less being a concretization of already known facts. Therefore, there is certain shallowness within the conscious intellect in the form of false absolutes and the paradoxes of uncertainty.

Table 3-1 – OWS Word Matrix - Understanding

12 Experiences	24 Awareness	26 Associations	46 Prehensions	20 Tenets	40 Intuition	60 Prudence
34 Knowledge	13 Cognizance	15 Logic	35 Apprehensions	17 Opinions	37 Imagination	57 Intelligence
56 Thoughts	14 Views	25 Common Sense	45 Understanding	10 Beliefs	30 Insight	50 Judgment
70 Truths	23 Perspective	16 Rationale	36 Comprehensions	27 Convictions	47 Enlightenment	67 Wisdom
21 Fantasies	42 Ignorance	62 Misassociations	64 Mistakes	02 Myths	04 Illusions	06 Empiricism
43 Pretensions	31 Nonsense	51 Illogicality	53 Misapprehensions	71 Dogma	73 Dreams	75 Sciolism
65 Euphemisms	41 Omens	52 Mistruths	54 Misunderstandings	01 Superstitions	03 Hallucinations	05 Fanaticism
07 Lies	32 Occultation	61 Irrationality	63 Miscomprehensions	72 Idolatry	74 Delusions	76 Mysticism

Seq #	Hex #	Seq #	Hex #	Seq #	Hex #	Seq #	Hex #
1	77	17	13	33	47	49	53
2	00	18	64	34	71	50	63
3	12	19	30	35	05	51	11
4	24	20	06	36	50	52	44
5	72	21	15	37	56	53	46
6	27	22	54	38	35	54	31
7	20	23	04	39	42	55	51
8	02	24	10	40	21	56	45
9	76	25	17	41	34	57	66
10	37	26	74	42	16	58	33
11	70	27	14	43	73	59	26
12	07	28	63	44	67	60	32
13	57	29	22	45	03	61	36
14	75	30	55	46	60	62	41
15	40	31	43	47	23	63	52
16	01	32	61	48	62	64	25

Left Side represents the Sequential Listing of Right Side Pairs

Right Side Parings – Red Symmetry

Right side Parings – Correct Blue Symmetry

Right side Parings – Incorrect Blue Symmetry

Fig. 3-6a – King Wen Sequential Listing of the
64 Hexagrams in the Yi Jing (I Ching)

There are many ways to group the words listed in Table 3-1. For instance, there are groups of four words when reading vertically such as awareness, cognizance, views, and perspectives; or groups of three words when reading horizontally such as awareness, associations, and prehensions; or tenets, intuition, and prudence. The first group of three words is a part of our conscious intellect, and the second group of three words is a part of our unconscious intellect. The groups of four words, as in the initial example, represent individual mental processes, such as learning, for that example. Also, there are two groups of two words. For instance, awareness and tenets are conscious-unconscious complements or complimentary pairs, and awareness and ignorance are positive-negative complements or antithetical pairs. I also propose that for each word there will be two poles; for example, knowledge is either true or false.

Returning to the blue symmetry in Fig. 3-7a and the red symmetry in Fig. 3-7b, both are further enhanced by pairing identical images, which are 180 degrees out of phase with each other. The rotational axis of this phase relationship is illustrated by the symbol, Ø, shown on the solid and dotted lines connecting the complementary pairs. Basically these images represent the four dimensions of the human mind transposed onto a two-dimensional surface. All sixteen red symmetry pairs illustrated in Fig. 3-7b are the same as the red symmetry in the King Wen Sequence of the Yi Jing. In other words, they are same as the red arrows shown in Fig. 3-6a of the King Wen Sequential Listing for the Yi Jing. However, only six of the sixteen blue symmetry pairs in Fig. 3 -7a are the same as the blue symmetry arrows in Fig. 3-6a. To resolve this discrepancy, we must turn to Table 3-1a, which is a sequential listing of the paired groupings based on the premise that the proper flow of energy in the brain is from 1 through 7 and then to 0. The first column in Table 3-1a represents the perspective of Truth from the word grouping of Understanding in Table 3-1. It can also be transcribed into the other three perspectives of experiences, knowledge, and thoughts by utilizing the re-coding sequence as shown respectively in the last three columns in Table 3-1a. Accordingly, another level of symmetry is evident in that both the vertical and horizontal sequence of listed numbers follows a similar progression. The progression fails if the Chinese pairings are inserted; and therefore, it is further proof that the corrected blue symmetry is the proper one. Also, this clearly shows that the numbering sequence in Table 3-1 is both *a priori* and fundamental.

Table 3-1a - Four-Dimensional Transposition

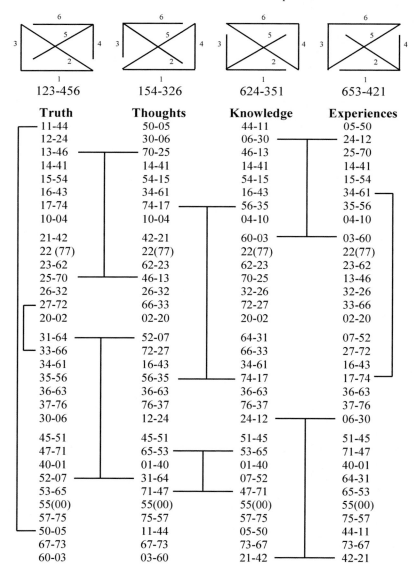

123-456   154-326   624-351   653-421

Truth	Thoughts	Knowledge	Experiences
11-44	50-05	44-11	05-50
12-24	30-06	06-30	24-12
13-46	70-25	46-13	25-70
14-41	14-41	14-41	14-41
15-54	54-15	54-15	15-54
16-43	34-61	16-43	34-61
17-74	74-17	56-35	35-56
10-04	10-04	04-10	04-10
21-42	42-21	60-03	03-60
22 (77)	22(77)	22(77)	22(77)
23-62	62-23	62-23	23-62
25-70	46-13	70-25	13-46
26-32	26-32	32-26	32-26
27-72	66-33	72-27	33-66
20-02	02-20	20-02	02-20
31-64	52-07	64-31	07-52
33-66	72-27	66-33	27-72
34-61	16-43	34-61	16-43
35-56	56-35	74-17	17-74
36-63	36-63	36-63	36-63
37-76	76-37	76-37	37-76
30-06	12-24	24-12	06-30
45-51	45-51	51-45	51-45
47-71	65-53	53-65	71-47
40-01	01-40	01-40	40-01
52-07	31-64	07-52	64-31
53-65	71-47	47-71	65-53
55(00)	55(00)	55(00)	55(00)
57-75	75-57	57-75	75-57
50-05	11-44	05-50	44-11
67-73	67-73	73-67	73-67
60-03	03-60	21-42	42-21

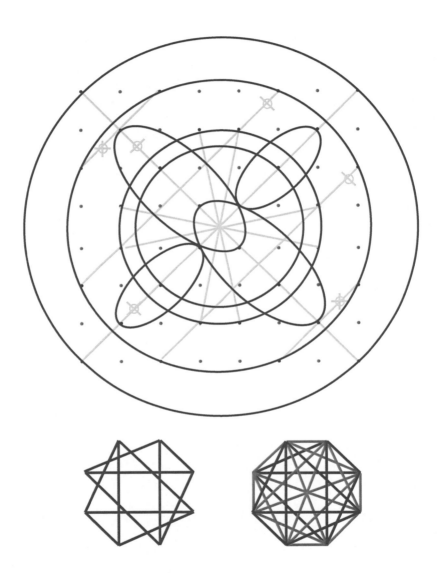

Fig. 3-6b – King Wen Blue Symmetry

Fig. 3-7a – OWS Corrected Blue Symmetry

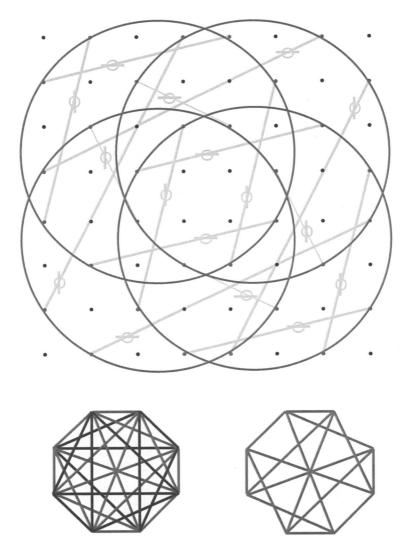

Fig. 3-7b – King Wen and OWS Red Symmetry

Accordingly, Table 3-2 broadly defines four individual stages or quadrants in the development of human nature, 11/44 objective /

perceptions, 22/77 subjective/holism, 33/66 conceptual rationalizations, and 55/00 logical instincts. The first stage of objective/perceptions begins at birth by developing our awareness and our prehensions. The first two pairings within the first stage, experience/awareness and cognizance/prehensions, represent the normal and natural way to develop our learned foundation for our behavioral traits. They are also the only two processes in the first stage, which yield solely positive psychological traits; that is, archetypes that are pairs of two positive complimentary opposites. In contrast, the rest of the pairings in the first stage develop negative psychological traits; that is an archetype that is paired with a negative complimentary opposite. These first two pairings within the first stage become the foundation for the further building of our soul within the next two stages. That is, the first pair of experiences/awareness in the first stage reappears as its antithetical opposite pair of fantasies/ignorance immediately before the beginning of the second stage. Similarly, the second pair of cognizance/prehensions in the first stage, reappears as its antithetical opposite pair of nonsense/mistakes immediately before the beginning of the third stage.

The second stage, subjective/holism, represents our subjective being and an opportunity to compensate for our lack of awareness, and the third stage, conceptual/rationalizations, is an opportunity to correct our mistaken prehensions. However, in both the second and third stages, there is again only one pair in each stage, common sense/truth and apprehensions/thoughts, which are both positive complimentary opposites and yield solely positive unconscious traits. These two stages then recombine immediately before the fourth stage, again as pairs of antithetical opposites, mistruths/lies and misapprehensions/euphemisms. Our last opportunity to correct our problems occurs in the fourth stage, logical/instincts, and the reward is wisdom and prudence. It should be noted the dual order of intelligence, judgment, wisdom, and prudence; that is, from the perspective of our conscious words, wisdom is supreme; but from the perspective of our unconscious behavior prudence is supreme. Moreover, when the relationship between a pair of hexagrams is either both positive complimentary or both negative complimentary, both hexagrams increase or decrease in value together, but when one hexagram is positive complimentary and the other hexagram is negative complimentary, as one goes up the other goes down. This same logic also applies equally to higher order symmetry pairings.

11-44	**OBJECTIVE**	-	**PERCEPTIONS**
12-24	Experiences	-	Awareness
13-46*	Cognizance	-	Prehensions
14-41*	View	-	Omens
15-54	Logic	-	Misunderstandings
16-43*	Rationale	-	Pretensions
17-74	Opinions	-	Delusions
10-04	Beliefs	-	Illusions
21-42	Fantasies	-	Ignorance
***22-77**	**SUBJECTIVE**	-	**HOLISM**
23-62	Perspectives	-	Misassociations
*25-70	Common Sense	-	Truths
26-32	Associations	-	Occultation
27-72	Convictions	-	Idolatry
20-02	Tenets	-	Myths
31-64*	Nonsense	-	Mistakes
33-66	**CONCEPTUAL**	-	**RATIONALIZATIONS**
34-61*	Knowledge	-	Irrationality
35-56	Apprehensions	-	Thoughts
36-63*	Comprehensions	-	Miscomprehensions
37-76	Imagination	-	Mysticism
30-06	Insight	-	Empiricism
45-51	Understandings	-	Illogicality
47-71	Enlightenment	-	Dogma
40-01	Intuition	-	Superstitions
*52-07	Mistruth	-	Lies
53-65	Misapprehensions	-	Euphemisms
***55-00**	**LOGICAL**	-	**INSTINCTS**
57-75	Intelligence	-	Sciolism
50-05	Judgment	-	Fanaticism
67-73	Wisdom	-	Dreams
60-03	Prudence	-	Hallucinations

Table 3-2 – OWS Sequential Order of the 64 Yi Jing (I Ching) Hexagrams

The entire sequence represents the natural flow of energy within the brain, with both positive and negative psychological traits. Positive psychological traits represent the proper clockwise flow of energy within the brain, and negative psychological traits represent the reverse flow of energy within the brain. I must discuss one additional item, pairings 22/77 and 55/00. In this case, the four-dimensional transposition did not dictate these pairings, as they can only be inferred from the overall blue symmetry. It could be an indicator of the relative interchangeability of these four attributes, since it is subjective logic, which yields the truth from our holistic instincts. Please remember that the entire preceding description for human behavior is a logical and rational procedure, with no hocus-pocus and with simple instructions that anyone can follow, and which thereby defines our four-dimensional human behavior.

It is, in fact, this sequential relationship between these four stages of human development in Table 3-2, which the Chinese intuitively recognized, but then incorrectly intermixed with the normal complementary and antithetical pairs, creating the ten mismatched pairs in the blue symmetry. For instance, the sequential relationship of hexagram pairs, 25/70 and 52/07 was recognized by the Chinese as a higher level of symmetry, but it was then mismatched as 70/07 and 52/25 in the lower level of symmetry. This error was then carried forward into hexagram pairs 22/77 and 55/00. Again, the sequential relationship of hexagram pairs, 13/46 and 31/64, incorrectly superseded the correct pairs as 31/46 and 13/64. Then, in order to maintain overall symmetry, pairs 14/41 and 36/63 were incorrectly changed to pairs 14/63 and 36/41, and likewise, pairs 16/43 and 34/61 were incorrectly changed to 34/16 and 43/61. Therefore, each of the ten mismatched pair errors can be explained by the primary and secondary effects of these two sequential relationships, thereby providing complete vindication of the proposed pictorial coding scheme.

Further evaluation of the King Wen sequential listings of the 32 pairs of hexagrams in Fig. 6a, shows that King Wen started by defining objective/perceptions as holistic instincts, and then followed a sequence utilizing convictions, tenets, imagination and mysticism to establish his own sequential version of seeking wisdom and truth. During the life of the Yi Jing, there have actually been several different sequential listings or progressions for the thirty-two pairs; and therefore there may not be only one order for the complete set of hexagram pairings, as can be inferred by the complex sequential interrelationship of the hexagrams in

Table 3-2. Even though various sequences may be possible, depending only upon the propensity of the psychological type of the person developing the sequence, I propose that the sequence in Table 3-2 is the basic fundamental sequence from which all others are derived.

Table 3-3 — Yi Jing (I Ching) and OWS Correlates

0 Receptive	1 Arousing	2 Water	3 Mist	4 Mountain	5 Fire	6 Wind	7 Heaven
Earth	Thunder	Abysmal	Joyous	Keeping Still	Sun	Gentle	Creative
Instinctual	Objective	Subjective	Conceptual	Perceptual	Logical	Rational	Holistic
Behavior	Experiences	Experiences	Knowledge	Knowledge	Thoughts	Thoughts	Behavior
Black	Orange	Red	Blue	Green	Yellow	White	Purple

Binary #	OWS Title	Hex # / Yi Jing Title	OWS Title	Hex # / Yi Jing Title
11-44	Objective	51 The Arousing/Thunder	-Perceptions	52 Keeping Still
12-24	Experiences	3 At the Beginning	-Awareness	4 Youthful Folly/Ignorance
13-46*	Cognizance	17 Following	-Prehensions	53 Development / Grad Progress
14-41*	View	27 Providing Nourishment	-Omens	62 Preponderance of the Small
15-54	Logic	21 Biting Through	-Misunderstandings	22 Grace/Beauty
16-43*	Rationale	42 Increase	-Pretensions	31 Tension/Influence
17-74	Opinions	25 The Simple/Innocence	-Delusions	26 Taming Power of the Great
10-04	Beliefs	24 Return/Turning Point	-Illusions	23 Splitting Apart/Collapse
21-42	Fantasies	40 Release	-Ignorance	39 Difficulty/Obstruction
22-77*	Subjective	29 The Deep/Abysmal	-Holism	1 Yang—The Creative
23-62	Perspectives	47 Oppression/Repression	-Misassociations	48 The Well
25-70*	Common Sense	64 Almost There	-Truths	11 Peace
26-32	Associations	59 Dispersion/Dissolution	-Occultation	60 Restraint/Limitation
27-72	Convictions	6 Conflict	-Idolatry	5 Waiting
20-02	Tenets	7 Soldiers/The Army	-Myths	8 Holding Together/Union
31-64*	Nonsense	54 The Marrying Maiden	-Mistakes	18 Fixing what has been spoiled
33-66	Conceptual	58 Joyous/Pleasure	-Rationalizations	57 Penetrating Wind/Gentle
34-61*	Knowledge	41 Decrease	-Irrationality	32 Continuity/Duration
35-56	Apprehensions	38 Neutrality/Opposition	-Thoughts	37 The Family
36-63*	Comprehensions	61 Understanding/InnerTruth	-Miscomprehensions	28 Preponderance of the Great
37-76	Imagination	10 Treading	-Mysticism	9 Taming Power of the Small
30-06	Insight	19 Approach/Conduct	-Empiricism	20 Contemplation/View
45-51	Understandings	56 The Wanderer/Stranger	-Illogicality	55 Abundance/Fullness
47-71	Enlightenment	33 Retreat	-Dogma	34 Power of Great Strength
40-01	Intuition	15 Modesty	-Superstitions	16 Enthusiasm
52-07*	Mistruth	63 After Completion	-Lies	12 Stagnation/Disjunction
53-65	Misapprehensions	49 Revolution/Molting	-Euphemisms	50 The Cauldron
55-00*	Logical	30 The Clinging/Fire	-Instincts	2 Yin—The Receptive
57-75	Intelligence	13 Fellowship/Society	-Sciolism	14 Possessions/Wealth
50-05	Judgment	36 Darkening of the Light	-Fanaticism	35 Advance/Progress
67-73	Wisdom	44 Temptation/Coupling	-Dreams	43 Resoluteness/Breakthrough
60-03	Prudence	46 Pushing Upward	-Hallucinations	45 Gathering Together/Accord

Table 3-3 is then a comparison of the word sequences just outlined in Table 3-2 with the actual abbreviated descriptions or titles given to each of the sixty-four hexagrams by Reifler in his book (1974) with commentary on the Yi Jing. Reifler's descriptive summaries are listed under the third and fifth columns labeled Hex # / Yi Jing Title, and the comparative OWS descriptions are listed under the second and fourth columns labeled OWS Title. This comparison yields a lot of insights and a few conundrums. For example, the hexagram with the binary code 64 in column one indicates 'mistakes' in column four as the word describing that particular process in the human mind. Similarly, in column five beside the Yi Jing hexagram number 18, Reifler in his 1974 book identifies this process as *'fixing'* - *(pg.86)* what has been spoiled, which is a perfect analogy for our mistakes which obviously need fixing. Likewise, our experiences and our awareness from the second line in Table 3-3 correlate to *'at the beginning'* or *'growing pains'* - *(pg.27)*, and *'youthful folly'* or *'youthful ignorance'* - *(pg.32)*, both respectively from Reifler's 1974 book.

Also, from Riefler's book, fantasies offer *'release'* - *(pg.178)*, opinions are *'the innocence'* or *'the simple'* - *(pg.114)*, and our comprehensions are our inner truth or our inner *'understanding'* - *(pg.264)*. Also, with common sense we are *'almost there' (pg.276)*, as it generates the real truth that grants us *'peace' (pg.58)*. However, some of the meanings behind some of the word pairings are more obscure. For example, rationale offers *'increase' (pg.186)*, while irrationality offers *'continuity' (pg.144)* and duration, compared to knowledge, which is a *'decrease' (pg.182)*. It seems that the descriptions for knowledge and irrationality should be reversed, and that if rationale is an increase, then irrationality should be a decrease. However, it may offer support to the old adage that the more you learn, the less you know for knowledge and truth are two entirely different processes and increasing our knowledge base, in some ways, just gets us further and further away from the real truth. It will take many years of hard work to expand the OWS, to correct any mistakes, to make the appropriate correlations to the Yi Jing and then to evaluate all of the information that will be generated.

One of the most remarkable things about the human psyche is that the various processes within the human psyche do not have to be consciously understood. The power of the unconscious far exceeds that of the conscious. Only the basic fundamentals need to be known, observed and remembered as we travel life's road. Sign language, gestures, mannerisms, and emotions are all forms of communication. Then intuition takes over and presents to our conscious many answers and solutions spontaneously as we require them. It is this basic understanding, which reflects the difference between our conscious and unconscious abilities. When we finally realize that we are not only our conscious thoughts and words, but also our unconscious intuition and imagination, collectively integrated into our memories, our perceptions, our images, and our feelings; can we hope to reach our full potential.

Truth can not be taught as illustrated in the charts in Tables 3-2 and 3-3, for truth taught by one is simply knowledge learned by another. Instead, truth is an integration of our own uniquely individual thoughts, knowledge, and experiences through the process of subjective logic or common sense. Knowing truth is a feeling of harmony created within the body, the heart and the mind, when proper conclusions have been reached from within. The greatest irony of knowing is to know that one knows and that the other person does not know; but instead, they think or pretend to know and that the knowers do not know. Such a paradox is then compounded by the many different ways of describing the truth, and by the knower who for the sake of quietude permits the pretention to prevail. At times, it seems almost impossible to intercommunicate with clear distinction because of these differences. However, during the entire process, two word groupings seemed to lead to thoughts which reflect the extremes of false thinking and, therefore, improper human behavior. These two are objective logic and subjective rationalizations.

They form the foundation for two widely diverging psychological types, and also closely resemble the common stereotype for the male and female psyche. Objective logic is simply pure logic and is paired with misunderstandings, whereas its counterpart, subjective logic, is common sense is paired with the truth. Objective logic becomes the Achilles Heel of science, in that it attempts to discover the ultimate truth by utilizing pure logic, which by definition from the Yi Jing always contains some level of misunderstanding. Our logical processes are then further complicated by our subjective rationalizations, or incorrect associations, which add even further confusion. When turned inward, subjective rationalizations distort our perspectives until the truth can no longer be seen. Concepts of ourselves and our surroundings must be rationalized with open eyes, open ears, and an open mind; and even then, we must realize that they will still contain mistakes, mistakes that can only be corrected by surrendering our egos and ourselves to the logic within our collective hearts. In doing so, we will finally achieve our goal of finding the single fundamental and ultimate truth of ourselves and of our universe.

It is from this perspective that we begin to account for some of the stereotyped differences between the sexes. It is not really a method for distinguishing the mental apparatus of the sexes, but instead, the tendencies for certain psychological types to develop within the sexes. The stereotype inaccurately persists that women know and men do not, and that men think and women cannot. An ancient Chinese proverb states that all words are part true and part false, and such is the case with the above stereotype. First of all, our lack of ability to think refers only to our visual projection of thoughts, and our lack of ability to know only refers to the intuitive truth. Secondly, this stereotype reflects only a percentage of the psychological types within each of the sexes. Furthermore, intuitive truth and visual thoughts are only as good as the discriminations and discernment upon which they are based. Often mystical insights or guesses are passed off as intuitive understandings.

Whereas men are categorized as logical and involved with the mechanical things of the world, women tend to be categorized as rational and more involved with people. It is this female interest in people that accounts for their intuitive understandings of human nature. The methods are diverse and inexact, but given enough bits and pieces, the mind arrives at startling truthful intuitions. You can observe almost everything human beings do, including their emotions; their actions; the style, color and condition of their clothes; their appearance, the jewelry they wear or do not wear; their mannerisms; or their gestures. Integrating such interesting complex variables into a composite picture is confusing and inexact. However, techniques exist for doing this, as many people know.

For instance, one of the easiest ways to better understand the feelings, thoughts, or intuitions of another person is to mimic his or her gestures, mannerisms, or posture. The feeling that arises within you will be an indication of what is going on within them. Other indicators are how they hold their head. For example, if they are looking down and to the left, they are searching their knowledge; down and to the right, their past experiences; up and to the left, their thoughts; and up and to the right, their intuition or imagination. I am therefore suggesting that the position of the head indicates and controls the mental process occurring within the mind; and furthermore, that the position of the eyes reveals the nature of the subject matter being reviewed by that process.

Our memory is therefore distributed throughout our mind and is organized first by process and then second by content. Congruency between the head and the eyes seems to indicate healthy perspectives while non-congruency indicates our more peculiar or eccentric ways. Each of our emotions, mannerisms, gestures, or postures represent specific processes or combinations of processes, which occur within our minds. Therefore, it should also be possible to organize our body language into an organized whole, just as we are able to organize our spoken language. Furthermore, there should then be a direct cause-and-effect relationship evident when comparing words to their equivalent behavior. It is because we are each born with this innate mechanism and its unconscious knowledge that we can possess intuitive insights into others intent and behavior. All we need to do is to learn a few fundamental behavioral truths. However, currently this remains an art and not a science, and instead takes many years of observation to develop.

Another visual aspect, which even more closely correlates with psychological types, is patterns. We wear vertical stripes, horizontal stripes, diagonal stripes, plaids, checks, prints, and even no patterns at all. Stripes can be broad or narrow, checks and plaids can be large or small, and prints can be paisley, flowery, or graphical. Vertical stripes represent logically thinking people and horizontal stripes represent rational people. Also, the width of the stripe represents the depth and/or breadth of the thoughts. Have you ever seen a professional golfer wear stripes, it is almost always horizontal stripes; whereas engineers tend to wear vertical stripe; and successful businessmen tend to wear dark striped suits? Plaids represent both logical and rational thoughts and the size of the plaid again represents both the depth and/or the breadth of the thoughts. By adding color intuition to these sizes and patterns, a further understanding of one's personality and psychological type can be determined. All of the variations in human preferences indicate a different aspect of our psychological type. Again, we do not have to even understand a relationship. All we need to do is to catalogue patterns with objective observations of behavior, and our intuition will do the rest. Granted pattern recognition is an art and not a science, and therefore requires a highly developed and integrated intuitive process, utilizing color, patterns, expressions, and gestures to be highly accurate.

Decoding the Kabbalah

The Kabbalah, which may also be written as Kabala, Qabala, Quaballa, Cabala, or QBLH, is the classical study of the meanings of the Hebrew alphabet and the implications of Hebrew text. Its history is somewhat uncertain, but it is proposed to have begun orally about the time of Adam or Moses, and then grew within the Hebrew culture for the next several thousand years. Earliest Kabbalah texts were recorded during the thirteen century AD by Rabbi Yitzhak Saggi Nehor (Isaac the Blind, 1160-1235 AD) in the Book of Bahir. The Kabbalah is comprised of ten vessels or ten spheres from the Tree of Life, plus the 27 letters of the Hebrew alphabet. It also has thirty-two paths of wisdom linked to the heart, which permeates the entire Torah. Each letter in the Hebrew alphabet has specific meanings born out of both reason and tradition, with each letter having an individual spelling and each having both an informal and a formal (sacred) meaning. The Hebrew alphabet, unlike English or Latin, is more like a set of mathematical symbols, and the words they form are more like equations. Therefore, the meanings of Hebrew words can be determined by the deeper meanings of the individual letters. Furthermore, there are no number symbols in ancient Hebrew, as numerical values are also represented by the alphabet.

Accordingly, the meaning of Hebrew letters represents simplified or distilled natural archetypes developed from older Hieroglyphic symbols. The meanings therefore, become more potent through the distillation process, and thereby represent various conscious/unconscious archetypes of the human mind. Therefore, just as the OWS is a method of communication both by and within the human mind, the evolutionary and historical development of the Hebrew language represents a uniquely traditional and cultural internal encoding method, which is historically purified and then distilled within the evolution of the language. Accordingly, the OWS, the Yi Jing and the Kabbalah must have common psychological roots. The following section is a proposed reconciliation for finding those common roots and for comparing the uniqueness of the Hebrew language to the integrated OWS / Yi Jing.

Table 3-4 – The Ten Vessels of The Tree of Life

1 Kether / Crown	70 Truth
2 Chochma / Wisdom	67 Wisdom
3 Binah / Understanding	36 Comprehension
Daarth / Knowledge	**34 Knowledge**
4 Chesed / Mercy	60 Prudence
5 Gevurah / Judgment	50 Judgment
6 Tiphareth / Beauty	57 Intelligence
7 Netzach / Victory	46 Prehensions
8 Hod / Glory	45 Understanding
9 Yesod / Foundation	35 Apprehensions
10 Malkkuth / Kingdom	12 Experiences

Rewriting these into the OWS matrix format would be as follows:

Red = little picture (impure) & Blue = big picture (pure)

12 Experiences 10-Malkkuth / Kingdom	24 Awareness	26 Associations	46 Prehensions 7-Netzach / Victory	20 Tenets	40 Intuition	60 Prudence 4-Chesed / Mercy
34 Knowledge / Daarth	13 Cognizance	15 Logic	35 Apprehensions 9-Yesod / Foundation	17 Opinions	37 Imagination	57 Intelligence 6-Tiphareth / Beauty
56 Thoughts	14 Views	25 Common Sense	45 Understanding 8-Hod / Glory	10 Beliefs	30 Insight	50 Judgment 5-Gevurah / Judgment
70 Truth 1-Kether / Crown	23 Perspective	16 Rationale	36 Comprehensions 3-Binah / Understanding	27 Convictions	47 Enlighten-ment	67 Wisdom 2-Chochma / Wisdom

Table 3-5 – The Hebrew Alphabet

א	ב	ג	ד	ה	ו	ז	ח	ט
Aleph	Bayt/Vayt	Ghimel	Dallet	Hay	Vay/Waw	Zayn	Hhyat	Tayt
1	2	3	4	5	6	7	8	9

י	כ	ל	מ	נ	ס	ע	פ	צ
Yod	Kaf/Khaf	Lammed	Mem	Nun/Noun	Sammekh	Ayn	Pay/Phay	Tsadde
10	20	30	40	50	60	70	80	90

ק	ר	ש	ת	ך	ם	ן	ף	ץ
Qof	Raysh	Seen/Shin	Tav	final Kaf	final Mem	final Nun	final Phay	final Tsadi
100	200	300	400	500	600	700	800	900

Please note that # 56 - Thoughts was included as the bars in the Tree of Life, but just was not recognized as such, making a total of twelve vessels including Daarth, instead of 10 vessels plus Daarth.

This causes one error (final Mem) in the Hebrew version of the alphabet which is corrected in the final version of the alphabet in the charts in Tables 3-6 and 3-7

The ten spheres or ten vessels of the Tree of Life along with the additional process of Daarth or Knowledge, are listed in the first column of Table 3-4. Their proposed equivalent matching words from the OWS are then listed in the second column of Table 3-4. In order to further clarify this comparison, it is then color coded into the 8-point OWS diagram in the upper right corner and then again into the OWS matrix in the middle of Table 3-4. This is a very easy and straight forward method for understanding the meanings behind the Tree of Life. It can be seen that these eleven words cover eleven of twelve key mental processes functioning within the human mind. The first three spheres Kether, Chochma, and Binah are shown in lavender and correspond to Truth, Comprehension (our inner Understanding), and Wisdom. The next three spheres, Chesed, Gevurah, and Tipareth are shown in blue, are commonly referred to as the big picture, and correspond to the three remaining key unconscious traits of Prudence, Intelligence, and Judgment. The last three spheres, Netzach, Yod, and Yesod are shown in red, are commonly referred to as the little picture, and correspond to the three remaining key conscious traits of Prehension, Apprehension, and Understanding. Finally, Daarth is the process for the accumulation of Knowledge. It is not my purpose to delve any deeper into this basic and fundamental analysis at this time, but only to show that the roots of both the OWS and the roots of the Hebrew Tree of Life are one and the same. One glaring exception is that thinking, or our thoughts, is the only process in this group of twelve key mental attributes of the human mind that is not included in this unique perspective of human nature.

The Hebrew alphabet itself is comprised of three sequences of nine letters each, for a total of twenty-seven letters, with the last five letters in the alphabet proposed to be final versions of five earlier letters as illustrated in Table 3-5. I propose that each one of the twenty-seven letters in the alphabet correlates to one each of the thirty-two matched pairs of yin-yang archetypes in the sequential listing for Being from the integrated OWS-Yi Jing as was shown in Tables 3-2 and 3-3. I further propose that these same thirty-two matched pairs in the OWS-Yi Jing are the same as the thirty-two paths to wisdom, which permeates the Torah. Accordingly, each matched pair from the Yi Jing correlates to a basic human behavioral archetype defined by the Kabbalah, with each of the three groups of nine pairs correlating to a basic overall function within the integrated OWS / Yi Jing, and therefore the human mind.

Table 3-6 – OWS Sequential Listing reconciled with the Kabbalah

(Binary#) OWS **Basic Archetypes - 1ˢᵗ Quad**	Kabala (#/Letter)	(Binary#) OWS **Existential Archetypes**

(Binary#) OWS **Basic Archetypes - 1st Quad**	Kabala (#/Letter)	(Binary#) OWS **Existential Archetypes**
11-44 Objective-Perceptions	1 Aleph	**33-66 Conceptual-Rationalizations**
12-24 Experience-Awareness	2 Bayt/Vayt	34-61 Knowledge-Irrationality
13-46 Cognizance-Prehensions	3 Ghimmel	35-56 Apprehensions-Thoughts
14-41 Views-Omens	4 Dallet	36-63 Comprehension-Miscomprehension
15-54 Logic-Misunderstandings	5 Hay	37-76 Imagination-Mysticism
16-43 Rationale-Pretensions	6 Vav/Waw	30-06 Insight-Empiricism
17-74 Opinions-Delusions	7 Zayn	45-51 Understandings-Illogicality
10-04 Beliefs-Hallucinations	8 Hhayt	47-71 Enlightenment-Dogma
21-42 Fantasies-Ignorance	9 Tayt	40-01 Intuition-Superstitions
		⎰ 52-07 Mistruth-Lies
Step 2 - transfer & eliminate 2 pairs →		⎱ 53-65 Misapprehensions-Euphemisms

11-44 Objective-Perceptions	1 Aleph	**33-66 Conceptual-Rationalizations**
12-24 Experience-Awareness	2 Bayt/Vayt	34-61 Knowledge-Irrationality
13-46 Cognizance-Prehensions	3 Ghimmel	35-56 Apprehensions-Thoughts
14-41 Views-Omens	4 Dallet	36-63 Comprehension-Miscomprehension
15-54 Logic-Misunderstandings	5 Hay	37-76 Imagination-Mysticism
16-43 Rationale-Pretensions	6 Vav/Waw	30-06 Insight-Empiricism
17-74 Opinions-Delusions	7 Zayn	45-51 Understandings-Illogicality
10-04 Beliefs-Hallucinations	8 Hhayt	47-71 Enlightenment-Dogma
21-42 Fantasies-Ignorance	9 Tayt	40-01 Intuition-Superstitions

11-44 Objective-Perceptions	1 Aleph	**33-66 Conceptual-Rationalizations**
12-24 Experience-Awareness	2 Bayt/Vayt	34-61 Knowledge-Irrationality
13-46 Cognizance-Prehensions	3 Ghimmel	35-56 Apprehensions-Thoughts
14-41 Views-Omens	4 Dallet	36-63 Comprehension-Miscomprehension
15-54 Logic-Misunderstandings	5 Hay	37-76 Imagination-Mysticism
16-43 Rationale-Pretensions	6 Vav/Waw	30-06 Insight-Empiricism
17-74 Opinions-Delusions	7 Zayn	50-05 Judgment-Fanaticism
10-04 Beliefs-Hallucinations	8 Hhayt	47-71 Enlightenment-Dogma
21-42 Fantasies-Ignorance	9 Tayt	40-01 Intuition-Superstitions

Reconciled and Corrected Hebrew Alphabet

11-44 Objective-Perceptions	1 Aleph	**33-66 Conceptual-Rationalizations**
12-24 Experience-Awareness	2 Bayt/Vayt	34-61 Knowledge-Irrationality
13-46 Cognizance-Prehensions	3 Ghimmel	35-56 Apprehensions-Thoughts
14-41 Views-Omens	4 Dallet	36-63 Comprehension-Miscomprehension
15-54 Logic-Misunderstandings	5 Hay	37-76 Imagination-Mysticism
16-43 Rationale-Pretensions	6 Vav/Waw	30-06 Insight-Empiricism
17-74 Opinions-Delusions	7 Zayn	45-51 Understandings-Illogicality
10-04 Beliefs-Hallucinations	8 Hhayt	47-71 Enlightenment-Dogma
21-42 Fantasies-Ignorance	9 Tayt	40-01 Intuition-Superstitions

Table 3-6 – OWS Sequential Listing reconciled with the Kabbalah (continued)

Kabala (#/Letter)	(Binary #) OWS	Kabala (#/Letter)

- 3rd Quad   Cosmic Archetypes - 2nd Quad

Kabala (#/Letter)	(Binary #) OWS	Kabala (#/Letter)
10 Yod	22-77 Subjective-Holism	100 Qof
20 Kaf/Khaf	23-62 Perspectives-Associations	200 Raysh
30 Lammed	25-70 Common Sense-Truths	300 Seen/Sheen
40 Mem	26-32 Dissociations-Occultation	400 Tav
50 Noun	27-72 Convictions-Idolatry	
60 Sammekh	20-02 Tenets-Myths	Step 1 - apply first 3
70 Ayn	31-64 Nonsense-Mistakes	Quads from the OWS
80 Pay / Phay		Sequential listing to
90 Tsadde		each of the three gen-
		erations of archetypes

Kabala (#/Letter)	(Binary #) OWS	Kabala (#/Letter)
10 Yod	22-77 Subjective-Holism	100 Qof
20 Kaf/Khaf	23-62 Perspectives-Associations	200 Raysh
30 Lammed	25-70 Common Sense-Truths	300 Seen/Sheen
40 Mem	26-32 Dissociations-Occultation	400 Tav
50 Noun	27-72 Convictions-Idolatry	
60 Sammekh	20-02 Tenets-Myths	Step 3 - replace 5
70 Ayn	31-64 Nonsense-Mistakes	pairs with 4th Quad
80 Pay / Phay	52-07 Mistruth-Lies	Logical Instincts
90 Tsadde	53-65 Misapprehensions-Euphemisms	as shown below

Kabala (#/Letter)	(Binary #) OWS	Kabala (#/Letter)
10 Yod	22-77 Subjective-Holism	100 Qof
20 Kaf/Khaf	23-62 Perspectives-Associations	200 Raysh
30 Lammed	25-70 Common Sense-Truths	300 Seen/Sheen
40 Mem	26-32 Dissociations-Occultation	400 Tav
50 Noun	55-00 Logical-Instincts (4th Quad)	500 final Kaf/Khaf
60 Sammekh	45-51 Understandings-Illogicality	600 final Mem
70 Ayn	57-75 Intelligence-Sciolism	700 final Noun
80 Pay/Phay	67-73 Wisdom-Dreams	800 final Pay/Phay
90 Tsadde	60-03 Prudence-Illusions	900 final Tsadde

Step 4 - Replace final Mem with final Sammekh

Kabala (#/Letter)	(Binary #) OWS	Kabala (#/Letter)
10 Yod	22-77 Subjective-Holism	100 Qof
20 Kaf/Khaf	23-62 Perspectives-Associations	200 Raysh
30 Lammed	25-70 Common Sense-Truths	300 Seen/Sheen
40 Mem	26-32 Dissociations-Occultation	400 Tav
50 Noun	55-00 Logical-Instincts (4th Pole)	500 final Kaf/Khaf
60 Sammekh	57-75 Intelligence-Sciolism	600 final Noun
70 Ayn	50-05 Judgment-Fanaticism	700 final Sammekh
80 Pay/Phay	67-73 Wisdom-Dreams	800 final Pay/Phay
90 Tsadde	60-03 Prudence-Illusions	900 final Tsadde

Accordingly, the first nine letters in the Hebrew alphabet, 1 thru 9, represent Basic Archetypes, the second group of nine letters, 10 thru 90, represent Existential Archetypes, and the third group of nine letters, 100 thru 900, represents Cosmic Archetypes. However, the OWS sequential listing of Being-Understanding is divided into four groups Objective/Perceptions, Subjective/Holism, Conceptual/Rationalizations and Logical/Instincts. It is the first three sections of this sequential listing for Being-Understanding that corresponds to the three sequences of letters in the Hebrew Alphabet; however, the second group and third group are interchanged. Therefore, the three correlated groups are Basic Archetypes (Objective/Perceptions), Existential Archetypes (Conceptual/Rationalizations) and Cosmic Archetypes (Subjective/Holism). The fourth group Logical/Instincts will be explained later. Each of the letters of the Hebrew alphabet can then be set in correspondence with each of the sequential pairings listed in Being-Understanding as illustrated in the top section of Table 3-6.

Accordingly, there are four repetitive sequences listed in the two-page Table 3-6, with each sequence illustrating the progressive correlation of the Hebrew alphabet to the sequential listing of Being-Understanding from the OWS/Yi Jing. In the top sequence in the chart, the three groups identified above are listed horizontally across the top of the two pages and in the same interchanged order (step 1) as they were defined above. That is, the first column represents the Basic Archetypes of our Objective/Perceptions, the second column represents the Existential Archetypes of our Conceptual/Rationalizations, and the third column represents the Cosmic Archetypes of Subjective/Holism. In the first column there are nine archetypal pairs, in the second column there are eleven archetypal pairs, and in the last column there are seven archetypal pairs for a total of twenty-seven pairs. In the next section of the page, the two last pairs from the middle column are transferred into the last column (step 2), creating three sequences of nine pairs, which is the same matrix as is purported by the Hebrew alphabet. Please note that the mental processes for each pair within each archetype that represent the darker side of our personality have been illustrated in black; while the mental processes that represent the good side of our personality have been illustrated in green. Also note that there are only two lines in the entire sequence that are totally good attributes, they are the title line and then the third line down. Finally, please note that most of the mental processes in the bottom half of the last column of cosmic archetypes represent many of our shortcomings and our fallibilities.

Table 3-7 - Final Archetype Relationships (4th Quad) within the OWS Word Matrix

12 Experiences	24 Awareness	26 Associations	46 Prehensions	20 Tenets	40 Intuition ←	60 Prudence
34 Knowledge ←————————	13 Cognizance	15 Logic	35 Apprehensions	17 Opinions	37 Imagination ←	57 Intelligence
56 Thoughts	14 Views	25 Common Sense	45 Understanding	10 Beliefs	30 Insight ←	50 Judgment
70 Truths	23 Perspective	16 Rationale	36 Comprehensions	27 Convictions	47 Enlightenment ←	67 Wisdom

The next step is to replace the last five pairs in the last column by the fourth quadrant from the OWS titled Logical/Instincts as alluded to earlier and as shown in the third section of Table 3-6 (step 3). These last five archetypes correspond to the last five hyper-archetypes as proposed by the Hebrew alphabet in Table 3-5 and as underlined in the second column of Table 3-6. Furthermore, Table 3-7 clearly shows the relationship between these final five archetypes and their base archetypes. First, Knowledge (final Khaf), the base root of Logic, was substituted for the OWS archetype Logical/Instincts. The only remaining discrepancy is that the Kabbalah indicates that hyper-Comprehension (final Mem) should be in the final four pairs of the Hebrew alphabet; whereas, the OWS indicates that it should be replaced by hyper-Insight, which is Judgment (final Sammekh). This change is illustrated by deleting hyper -Comprehension (final Mem) from the sequence and then by adding hyper-Insight or Judgment (final Sammekh) into the sequence as shown in the bottom section of Table 3-6 (step 4). Accordingly hyper-Imagination is Intelligence (final Noun), hyper-Insight is Judgment (final Sammekh), hyper-Enlightenment is Wisdom (final Phay), and hyper-Intuition is Prudence (final Tsadde). The correlation of this revised listing is validated both by the logic and the simplicity of the OWS Word Matrix as illustrated in Table 3-7. Furthermore, it clearly corroborates the revised sequence, as well as, adds an assured level of proof validating both the Kabbalah and the integrated OWS / Yi Jing.

Let us next return to the ten vessels of the Tree of Life. As I mentioned earlier, all of the major processes within the human mind were identified by the Tree of Life except for one, the conscious process of thinking or our thoughts. The process of thinking is in fact, unconsciously represented pictorially by the bars and the rods that are connecting the individual vessels of the Tree of Life together; however, it just has never been consciously recognized as a single process. Instead, each bar was included in the alphabet individually. Therefore, when the alphabet was put together, this failure impacted its construction. That is, the archetype 45/51 Understandings/Illogicality was incorrectly inserted into the sequence to take the place of archetype 50/05 Judgment/Fanaticism, which is the true final archetype for thinking but was instead deleted. This deletion caused 57/75 Intelligence/Sciolism to be moved down one letter to maintain sequential integrity in the alphabet.

These changes are triply evident when we look at the location of the primary or base word in each archetype in the OWS as listed in Tables 3-4 and 3-7. If you remember that our comprehensions are our inner understandings; then it is intuitively reasonable to link 36/63 Comprehension/Miscomprehension or Mem as the final version of 45/51 Understandings/Illogicality under the guise of final Mem. Second, our conscious Understandings are rooted in our Thoughts, which are then projected into the unconscious in the form of Judgment, and thereby Understandings occurs exactly in the middle of Thoughts and Judgment in the OWS. Please note that the base for the third horizontal line in the OWS in Fig 3-7 is Thoughts, that the highest form of the conscious intellect in that same horizontal line is the word Understanding, and that the highest form of the unconscious intellect in that same horizontal line is the word Judgment. Therefore, it was intuitively reasonable to switch 45/51 Understandings/Illogicality for 50/05 Judgment/Fanaticism. Thirdly, and in the end, this then becomes a method to compensate for the failure to recognize the process of Thinking as the mental process that had integrated the individual aspects of the Tree of Life together into a single and integrated whole.

Have you ever had someone say to you "Hold that thought?" How many thoughts can one hold at one time and where are they being held? There must be a method, a place or a vessel within the mind where these thoughts are saved for future reference. Finally, there are twelve tribes of Israel; and therefore, because of the mathematical nature of the

Hebrew alphabet, it seems only reasonable and appropriate that there would be twelve aspects to the Tree of Life, the ten mental processes recognized, plus the process for the accumulation of knowledge, plus the process for our ability to think.

Each of these three divisions of archetypes are then plotted in Fig. 3-7c in OWS eight-point diagram format to illustrate a composite picture of the actual energy flow lines within the brain for each group of archetypes. In the first group of Basic Archetypes in the top picture, all energy flow lines are based upon and around 11/44 Objective/Perceptions and represent our search for a better understanding of the visual world that surrounds us. Most of the energy in this group of archetypes flows back and forth between the Objective world, point 1, and our Visual Perceptions of that world, point 2. However, two energy flow lines culminate at point 3, our Conceptual world, and two more culminate at point 6, our Rationale of the world that surrounds us. Since no method exists for the release of the energy developed within this first group of archetypes, the trapped energy between points 3 and 6 then becomes the focus for the next group of archetypes. In other words, when we can't see how the visual world works, we then turn instead to devising a rational concept that best approximates or describes that world.

Accordingly, we continue or search in the second group of Existential Archetypes illustrated in the middle picture, by building a rational concept that better explains the world that surrounds us. Similarly, energy flows back and forth between point 3, Concepts, and point 6, our Rationale of those concepts,. However, in this case energy builds up again at point 1, the Objective world that surrounds us, and we are now back where we started. We are now faced with the decision to either learn additional information and to thereby expand our knowledge base, or to turn inward and to search for the answers from within. Accordingly, the Yi Jing and the Kabbalah both profess the same thing. That is, the real truth for both ourselves and the world that surrounds us can only be found from within our subjective being. Instead, science prefers to continue outward expanding both information and knowledge, believing that it is only one more fact away from discovering the real truth and putting the final piece of the puzzle together. Instead, science only strays further and further away from the real truth, as its entire pseudo religion is based upon the false assumptions of our visual world only, empty space and no higher power than the logic of itself.

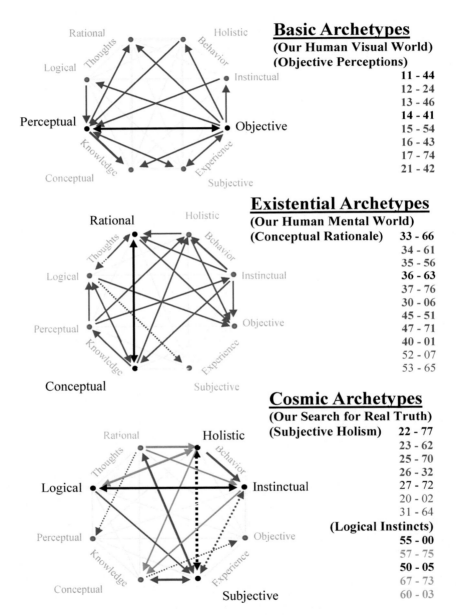

Basic Archetypes
(Our Human Visual World)
(Objective Perceptions)

11 - 44	
12 - 24	
13 - 46	
14 - 41	
15 - 54	
16 - 43	
17 - 74	
21 - 42	

Existential Archetypes
(Our Human Mental World)
(Conceptual Rationale)

33 - 66	
34 - 61	
35 - 56	
36 - 63	
37 - 76	
30 - 06	
45 - 51	
47 - 71	
40 - 01	
52 - 07	
53 - 65	

Cosmic Archetypes
(Our Search for Real Truth)
(Subjective Holism)

22 - 77	
23 - 62	
25 - 70	
26 - 32	
27 - 72	
20 - 02	
31 - 64	
(Logical Instincts)	
55 - 00	
57 - 75	
50 - 05	
67 - 73	
60 - 03	

Fig. 3-7c – Kabbalah Archetypes in OWS Format

Reconciled and Corrected Hebrew Alphabet

Basic Archetypes (1st Pole)		Existential Archetypes (3rd Pole)		Cosmic Archetypes (2nd Pole)	
OWS #/Name	Kabala #/Letter	OWS #/Name	Kabala #/Letter	OWS #/Name	Kabala #/Letter
11-44 Objective-Perceptions	1 Aleph	33-66 Conceptual-Rationalizations	10 Yod	22-77 Subjective-Holism	100 Qof
12-24 Experience-Awareness	2 Bayt/Vayt	34-61 Knowledge-Irrationality	20 Kaf/Khaf	23-62 Perspectives-Associations	200 Raysh
13-46 Cognizance-Prehensions	3 Ghimmel	35-56 Apprehensions-Thoughts	30 Lammed	25-70 Common Sense-Truths	300 Seen /Sheen
14-41 Views-Omens	4 Dallet	36-63 Comprehension-Miscomprehension	40 Mem	26-32 Dissociations-Occultation	400 Tav
15-54 Logic-Misunderstandings	5 Hay	37-76 Imagination-Mysticism	50 Noun	55-00 Logical-Instincts (4th Pole)	500 Kaf/Khaf
16-43 Rationale-Pretensions	6 Vav/Waw	30-06 Insight-Empiricism	60 Sammekh	57-75 Intelligence-Sciolism	600 Noun final
17-74 Opinions-Delusions	7 Zayn	45-51 Understandings-Illogicality	70 Ayn	50-05 Judgment-Fanaticism	700 Sammekh final
10-04 Beliefs-Hallucinations	8 Hhayt	47-71 Enlightenment-Dogma	80 Pay/Phay	67-73 Wisdom-Dreams	800 Pay/Phay final
21-42 Fantasies-Ignorance	9 Tayt	40-01 Intuition-Superstitions	90 Tsadde	60-03 Prudence-Illusions	900 Tsadde final

Table 3-8 – Reconciled and Corrected Hebrew Alphabet

Finally, in the third group of Fig. 3-7c in the bottom picture, through Cosmic Archetypes, our search finally reaches fruition, when the truth is finally realized through the subjective logic of common sense, when our attention is turned away from the visual world that surrounds us, and instead within our inner selves where the heart and the mind can become one. Please note that energy flow lines accumulate around our subjective feelings, point 2, and it is only through our sensitivity to those feelings that the truth can finally be realized by and within our mind. It is therefore necessary that we again return to the greater truths of a higher power as revealed by the integrated insights and prophesies of our many religions.

In conclusion, the most important single insight to be gleaned from this unique sequence of the OWS within the Kabbalah is the very aspect of God Himself as He relates to the Hebrew culture. That is, the third line mentioned previously and as shown in Table 3-8, (13/46 Cognizance/Prehensions - 3 Ghimel) (35/56 Apprehensions/Thoughts - 30 Lammed) (25/70 Common Sense/Truths - 300 Seen/Sheen) represents all positive psychological processes, and therefore all positive psychological traits within the human being. A descriptive narrative for this same sequence from the commentary of Carlos Suares on the Kabbalah is as follows: "Ghimel-Lammed-Sheen (3.30.300): these three letter-numbers express a movement in progressive enlargement, from the uncontrolled functional action of Ghimel (3), through the controlled connecting agent Lammed (30), going as far as the universal Sheen (300), mythically considered to be the *spirit*, of the *breath* of God." As mentioned earlier, the 3, 30, 300 line within the Hebrew Alphabet is the only line where all three pairings from the reconciled Yi Jing and OWS, are all positive psychological traits, thereby validating the progressive enlargement description by Carlos Suarez and also adding another level of proof for the reconciled Yi Jing, Kabbalah, and OWS. Moreover, it is this single archetypal pair of 300/Sheen or Common Sense/Truth that is the true *spirit* of the *breath* of the true living God.

Human cultures have been perplexed for two millennia by the meaning and the validity of the term 666 in the Book of Revelation in the Bible. From the above number sequence of 3, 30, 300, a similar description can be obtained for an alternative and reverse sequence of 600, 60, 6; instead of the number 666 as is commonly promoted. Accordingly, this sequence is 600 (Intelligence/Sciolism), 60 (Insight/

Empiricism), and 6 (Rationale/Pretensions) as shown in red in Table 3-8. Where better for this description to come from than the Hebrew Language itself where it was manifested and revealed? Accordingly, the force of 600, 60, 6 within human kind, begins with false intelligence that is based upon false insights from empirical evidence, and which is then pretended to be true.

When President Eisenhower left office in 1961, he warned us to beware of the military industrial complex. However today, a much more dangerous complex has emerged. That is, the governmental, pharmaceutical, academic, chemical, bureaucratic, health care complex. They first add poisons to our foods and then sell pills to fix our associated ailments. Our children are born with birth defects and develop life ending diseases at an early and tender age, all for the sake of regress and retrogress. Grants are issued in the name of research; however, universities and research centers get paid for looking for the truth instead of finding the truth. Are the established academic, governmental, and commercial institutions of contemporary science just asleep, or are they something far worse? Is there instead, an internal unconscious conspiracy within the dark side of science, purely for the advancement of science itself? The dark side of science wants to be god, and the dark side of our government wants to be the lord of our lives, and they both use the spirit of logic to complete this unholy trinity. The battle between science and religion has been waged within the minds of human kind for millennia. Instead, science is merely one more tool in the toolbox of God. I will discuss this premise in more detail in Chapter Five.

Accordingly, and from the Kabbalah, there is only one way to become conscious of God and His Real Truth, and that is to first surrender ourselves to His greater spirit of that same greater truth, that is within each of us. In other words, stop lying, for that perpetuates evil both within our souls and within our cultures. When we avoid lying, we have the freedom to begin our collective journey through the mental process of learning through awareness and cognizance. Accordingly, we must listen with respect to the sincere and honest proposals of others, and at least try to grasp the context of their point of view. We must then integrate these new personal and uniquely individual prehensions into our own personal conscious apprehension of reality. The thoughts that are generated by such a process must then be seared by our own good sense and by the common good sense of all good people.

Good sense is the coming together of the logic of our mind with the feelings of our heart, and then sensing the feeling of inner harmony and inner peace. Common sense is then the collective good sense of all human kind, by combining the feelings within our collective hearts with the logic of our collective minds. Logic and feelings cannot be separated but instead must be integrated into a single whole, if our desire is to find the real truth. The real truth is a great puzzle and each of us has our own unique perspective on our part of that puzzle; and it is only by integrating and assimilating all of our individual pieces of that puzzle, that we will be able to find that one and only, real absolute truth. This long and arduous process then represents the only pathway for human beings to achieve the real truth, and that final truth will then reside both within our minds and within our hearts; and it will be without a doubt the true and single *spirit* of the real *breath* of the true living God.

The Physics of Human Psychology

Dr. Max Lüscher spent his entire lifetime analyzing and correlating personality to the colors we prefer. He was born in Basel, Switzerland in 1923 and is a Swiss psychotherapist. He invented the Lüscher Color Test, which is a tool for measuring one's psychological state and associated physical condition based upon the colors we prefer. He actually developed a long system with over fifty colors, and an abbreviated system as used in this analysis with eight colors. Please recall from Chapter Two that the images we see and that are perceived within our human mind are also coded and stored psychically within our minds in a derivative of color. This interaction of the laws of molecular physics with the rest of our mind causes preferences for certain colors, depending upon our psychological makeup. Accordingly, Color Psychosomatics is illustrated in the left image in Fig. 3-8a as was defined by the colors associated with the Yi Jing in Table 3-3 earlier in this chapter, and in the right image as defined by the eight-color abbreviated Lüscher Color Test, Even though these two systems were generated from two totally different perspectives and over many millenniums apart from each other, they exhibit a very close equivalency to each other.

Whereas the Yi Jing only defines light or bright colors, the eight-color Lüscher system utilizes both light and dark colors. Such recognitions are significant, since the two systems are nearly identical and since Dr. Lüscher's dark colors are merely different versions of the Yi Jing's light colors. Therefore, both systems can be compared by simply correlating the light and dark colors, for example, by assigning brown to dark red (orange) and gray to dark white. Moreover, the colors that we prefer do not represent a single psychological type, but instead the diversities of our personality. It therefore represents our mood at the particular time we choose the color. The colors of our clothes, our cars, and our houses each reflect different aspects of our personality, depending upon the various values and priorities we have assigned to each of those decisions throughout our lifetime.

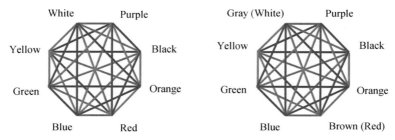

Fig. 3-8a – Yi Jing (left) & Lüscher Color Psychosomatics (right)

An interesting variance between the order the colors as listed in Fig. 3-8a for the Lüscher Color Test and the RGB-CMYK color wheel is further illustrated in Fig. 3-8b. The ability to perceive orange and to therefore add orange to the color wheel, is explained by the overlapping bandwidth of the red and green color cones in the human eye. Selecting the six most visually recognizable colors can also be verified by simply looking at the International Commission on Illumination color chart, CEI 1931. Only six colors can be chosen, for when an additional color distinction is added, one must also be dropped, cyan in this case, for their can only be a total of six spatial directions in the universe and therefore the human mind. The dropping of cyan can also be explained by the overlapping of the bandwidths of the red and blue cones making purple more pronounced than cyan.

Finally, I do not know why the six colors of the psychosomatic color wheel influence the mind in the order as shown; however, the three polar color axes and the one additional black and white axis may shed some light on this conundrum for future investigators. The interaction of color preference and psychological mood is very, very complex. It took Lüscher a lifetime of analytical study to develop a detailed conscious understanding of color preference. However, until this process is more completely understood, it remains an unconscious process for each individual. That is, if we are to develop this ability without developing associated prejudices, we must simply observe colors and associated moods and behavior and then, as our objective color experiences increase, so will the accuracy of our color intuition.

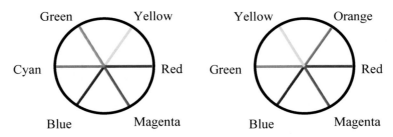

Fig. 3-8b – RGB-CMYK Color Wheel (left) &
Lüscher Color Psychosomatics (right)

An integrated comparison of the OWS as discussed earlier, with the Chinese Yi Jing and with Dr. Lüscher's Color Test is listed in the two page format in Tables 3-9a & 3-9b. The format used is the same as the original OWS matrix word format with fifty-six squares as presented earlier in Table 3-1. Accordingly, the first line in each square is the corresponding OWS coding sequence number and its respective word description. The second line is then the hexagram number and the word description from the Yi Jing, and the third line is the color number and its associated word descriptions as presented in the Lüscher Color Test. Many of these three line combinations read like a sentence in a book. For example, the very first square represents our experiences occurring at the beginning of life through sensual gratification. The second square represents our awareness, our youthful ignorance and our insistence on comfort. And in the last row and the fourth square down wisdom uses cautious sensitivity to resist temptation. And finally, in the third square over and the third square down we are almost there, when we use our common sense and achieve total security. Also from both Tables 3-3 and 3-9a, common sense is subjective logic, which yields both truth and its reward of peace. However, please note in the third row over and the seventh row down in Table 3-9b that after completion we still have only a close approximation of the truth or still a mistruth, and therefore an assumed resistance. The real truth exists above and beyond any concept of itself, and which therefore has its own existence beyond any concept or any scope of that concept.

I can remember as a boy in elementary school being taught to draw the picture of a tree. It was a very simple tree with a big brown trunk and lots of green leaves. I went through much of my childhood thinking that was a tree, not realizing that instead it was a picture of a tree. Instead, a real tree has crooked trunks, bark that scratches your arms and legs, limbs that are broken, a shape that is as irregular, leaves that have holes in them, and bugs that crawl all over you, the bark, the leaves and the tree. Still, a tree is more than that or any concept that we may develop, for trees have an existence of their own, and that is the true beauty of life. My analysis will not go any further other than to say that whole chapters or books could be written about each of the fifty-six squares, and it is therefore beyond the scope of this dissertation, which is instead intended to merely unite philosophy with psychology and metaphysics. More importantly, it is the essence of truth that is being conveyed anyway, instead of any individual abstraction of that truth.

Cataloging some of the basic propositions advanced by the science of psychology will then conclude this chapter. For instance, Sigmund Freud developed many concepts such as the ego, superego, libido, and id. The conscious self and the unconscious spirit must also be included along with the libido, ego, super ego, and id to complete this analysis as shown in Fig. 3-9. Remember, as indicated earlier, that just as there are many ways to quarter an apple, so are there many ways to rationalize the human psyche. These four do not represent just a portion of the human psyche, but its entirety quartered in its own unique way. The libido is proposed to be the instinctual aspect of our being, based upon our subjective and objective experiences and our limited conceptual knowledge. It is the result of the repressed self, living within the unconscious. It can best be observed as the spontaneity of our activities, as it seeks its release. The ego is proposed to be the measure of our conscious awareness or the lack of conscious awareness of our self. When the conscious and the unconscious become one, the ego and the libido unite into a single whole. The libido is then freed to move upon

Table 3-9a - Positive Attributes of OWS, Yi Jing, Lüscher Color Test Correlates

12 Experiences 03 At the Beginning 36 Sensual Gratification	24 Awareness 04 Youthful Ignorance 62 Insistence on Comfort	26 Associations 59 Dispersion Dissolution 60 Exhaustion Depletion	46 Prehensions 53 Development Gradual Progress 20 Defensive Superiority	20 Tenets 07 Soldiers The Army 67 Self Disparagement	40 Intuition 15 Modesty 27 Obstinate Exclusion	60 Prudence 46 Pushing Upward 07 Total Non Involvement
34 Knowledge 41 Decrease 12 Self Contained Orderliness	13 Cognizance 17 Following 31 Cooperative Enterprise	15 Logic 21 Biting Through 34 Expansive activity	35 Apprehensions 38 Neutrality 14 Emotional Dependency	17 Opinions 25 The Simple 35 Susceptible to Stimulus	37 Imagination 10 Treading 15 Erotic Sensitivity	57 Intelligence 13 Society 45 Lure of Fantasy
56 Thoughts 37 The Family 40 Indecision Lack of Resolution	14 Views 27 Nourishment 32 Purposeful activity	25 Common Sense 64 Almost there 64 Total Security	45 Understanding 56 The Wanderer The Stranger 24 Ambition	10 Beliefs 24 Returning 37 Exaggerated Desire	30 Insight 19 Conduct 17 Absolute Peace	50 Judgment 36 Darkening of the light 47 Sudden Crisis
70 Truths 11 Peace 57 Compulsive Blending	23 Perspectives 47 Repression 16 Sensual Ease	16 Rationale 42 Increase 30 Impulsiveness	36 Comprehensions 61 Understanding Inner Truth 10 Tranquility Recuperation	27 Convictions 06 Conflict 65 Sensuousness	47 Enlightenment 33 Retreat 25 Irresponsible Charm	67 Wisdom 44 Temptation Coupling 05 Cautious Sensitivity

Table 3-9b - Negative Attributes of OWS, Yi Jing, Lüscher Color Test Correlates

21 Fantasies / 40 Release / 63 Insecurity from lack of allies	42 Ignorance / 39 Difficulty / 26 Demand Esteem	62 Misassociations / 48 The Well / 06 Demand Esteem as Exceptional	64 Mistakes / 18 Fixing what has been spoiled / 02 Unresolved Pressure	02 Myths / 08 Seeking Union / 76 Demand for Perfection	04 Illusions / 23 Collapse / 72 Unacceptable Restrictions	06 Empiricism / 20 Contemplation / 70 Intense Involvement
43 Pretensions / 31 Tension Influence / 21 Pressure from stress & discord	31 Nonsense / 54 Marrying maiden / 13 Helpless Disharmony	51 Illogicality / 55 Abundance Fullness / 43 Unrealistic Self-Justification	53 Misapprehensions / 49 Revolution / 41 Emotional Disappointment	71 Dogma / 34 Great Strength / 53 Empathic Frustration	73 Dreams / 43 Break through / 51 Emotional Dissatisfaction	75 Sciolism / 14 Wealth / 54 Watchful mistrust
65 Euphemisms / 50 The Cauldron / 04 Apprehensive insecurity	41 Omens / 62 Smallness in excess / 23 Helpless rebellion	52 Mistruths / 63 After Completion / 46 Assumed Indifference	54 Misunderstandings / 22 Grace / Beauty / 42 Frustrated Vacillation	01 Superstitions / 16 Enthusiasms / 73 Frustrated Independence	03 Hallucinations / 45 Accord / 71 Restless Instability	05 Fanaticism / 35 Advance Progress / 7 Watchful Self Protection
07 Lies / 12 Disjunction / 75 Demands Straight Dealing	32 Occultation / 60 Restraint / 61 Undue Self Restraint	61 Irrationality / 32 Continuity & Duration / 03 Helpless irritability	63 Miscomprehension / 28 Greatness in excess / 01 Restless Dissatisfaction	72 Idolatry / 05 Waiting / 56 Esthetic Discrimination	74 Delusions / 26 Major Restraint / 52 Humiliated Belittlement	76 Mysticism / 09 Minor Restraint / 50 Controlled Response

and through the conscious ego. The ego can best be observed in our attitudes, our gestures, and our posture in the form of self-defense. The superego is the complex of our logical and rational thoughts integrated into our limited perceptual understanding of our selves and the world that surrounds us. We can best observe this by listening to the forceful-ness by which we try to convince ourselves and others of the validity of our thoughts. Finally, the id is the combined integration of the libido, ego, and superego into our own unconscious individual behavior.

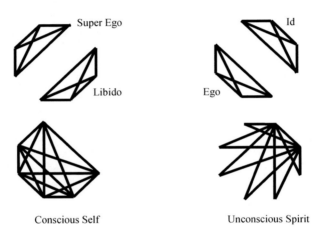

Fig. 3-9 - Composite Psychological Types in OWS Format

Recalling the flow of energy within the mind, the libido represents the premature flow of energy caused by the domination of the ego com-plex, and the ego represents the premature flow of energy caused by the superego complex. In this case, the ego and superego represent our false self-identity and our false self-image; only when they are surren-dered to, or transformed into, a healthy self-identity or a positive self-image, can good feelings of self-esteem develop. If the process of sur-render does not occur and the super-ego battles the libido, a psychosis exists; likewise if the ego battles the id, a neurosis exists. In the case of the ego, it is our false self-identity struggling against the truth; and in the case of the superego, it is our illogical and irrational thoughts strug-gling against the realities of our everyday world. Each of these four quadrants could be individually dominated by either good or bad traits.

Therefore, when the ego or the id struggles against either the superego or the libido, character disorders develop. Furthermore, complete integration of all four quadrants produces either a completely good or a completely evil mind, and at that point it is probably no longer reversible.

Carl Jung used terms like anima, animus, and shadow, which all arise from the resulting confusions acted out within the id by our limited knowledge of our own self-nature. The animus represents someone else's thoughts tied to our own feelings; the anima represents someone else's feelings rationalized into our own thoughts, and the shadow represents the reflection of our own collective conscious into our own unconscious id. The collective conscious and the collective unconscious are the same aspects but from different points of view.

Instinctual behavior is then our intuitively innate human spirit, and holistic behavior is the Holy Spirit within us. It is proposed that the potential for the Holy Spirit to arise within us is firmly established at birth, as the truth was genetically coded within each of our minds. Therefore, each of us was born with this intuitive understanding of the truth, but can only achieve its potential when we surrender ourselves to its greater spirit within us. We must constantly remind ourselves that the perception of the self is only the conscious part of the psyche, and that the spirit is the unconscious part. Therefore, we can never feel, know, or be the spirit but can only allow it to move within and through us. This refutes another unconscious myth of today, that by defining our psychological makeup, we can control the destiny of our own lives. Regardless of how high our intellect ascends, it always remains an approximation of the truth, and can only become the absolute truth when it instead transcends through the power of the Holy Spirit. Only when we combine the study of psychology with our religious beliefs, can we begin to sort out our problems and attain true freedom and happiness.

As we grow, we are taught both truths and mistruths, both by actions and by words. This menagerie of facts along with our past behavior is integrated into an organized whole by the apparatus of the brain. Accordingly, good behavior results from good teachings, and improper behavior results from false teachings. Somewhere at the beginning of this process, self-awareness and later, self-identity develop. It is at this point that this integrated structure of good and bad traits sets upon its own course toward maturity.

The holistic approach is to consciously sort out the good from the bad, and if completed, will result in good character, but if incomplete, will result in confusion and insanity. The instinctual approach is to act out both the good and the bad aspects of our combined learned and innate nature in a more natural and normal way, and then, heuristically discover what is good or bad. As the developing self interacts with the id, the spirit develops, and when based upon truth and honesty, it will be the Holy Spirit. However, when it is based upon lies, it becomes the spirit of evil. Our instinctual behavior by itself is not evil, but can become evil when based upon mistruth, lies, and bad habits. The spirit of evil thinks, but is illogical and irrational. It senses, but has no feelings. It possesses knowledge, but is composed of prejudices, misperceptions, and misconceptions. It randomly strikes out in uncontrollable rages against reality. It is organized chaos, has no self-identity, has no value, and is based upon a lie. In contrast, the Holy Spirit is the spirit of truth; and when the self surrenders, the Holy Spirit enters and takes possession of our soul, and then transforms us into what we were intended to be from the beginning. If the self does not surrender, our only recourse is to ascend to higher and higher levels of conscious awareness, until we have each recognized the folly of our self-actions; and then through the spirit of truth, to individually repossess our freedoms to choose our direction and our destiny.

Christ said that no servant can serve two masters; for either he will hate the one, and love the other, or else will hold to the one and despise the other. Again in the Book of Mathew, Jesus reminded his followers that there are only two choices within this world, either good or evil. It would seem to be a self-evident truth that we would choose those things, which are ultimately good for each of us; however, history has proven this wrong. It is not easy to choose right over wrong, to choose good over bad, or to choose honesty over lies, while many of those around us are doing wrong, being bad, and constantly lying. Accordingly, we each become a slave to those choices that we make throughout our lives. Our journey is further complicated by those among us who have chosen the dark side of life as their master, and who deviously spread their evil lies throughout our lives and who poison our cultures. We now seem to be at a point in our civilization where we have but one last chance to resolve our problems. It is this choice that each of us must make as we travel life's road and which will ultimately determine our final end. However, we must remember that each time we exercise our freedom of will; our choice is fixed within our soul and affects all of the succeeding decisions of our soul.

Conclusions

There are several reasons why I believe that the foundation for the OWS cannot possibly be wrong. The first reason is the many coincidental characteristics of four independently derived, complex and very sophisticated approaches to defining and describing human nature. The OWS defines the learning processes of cognition and volition, the Yi Jing describes the behavioral sequences within human nature, the Kabbalah defines the constructs of our spoken language, and Lüscher's color test describes the influence of color upon our human choices and our human condition. Each of these approaches was derived independently and over several thousands of years.

The second reason is the unique numbering sequence of archetypes in the sequential listing of the pairs of Yi Jing hexagrams, which repeats itself from all transpositions. A third reason is the near perfect match of the Hebrew Tree of Life with both the sequential and the OWS matrix format. Also, the numerical match of the Hebrew thirty-two steps to wisdom with the same thirty-two paired sequences of both the Yi Jing and the OWS culminating with prudence and wisdom. Another reason is the many squares in the combined word matrixes that read like sentences in a book. The OWS is the noun, the Yi Jing is the verb, and Lüscher's Color Test is the direct or indirect object for the combined and integrated newly formed sentences. The structure of language is a fractal, and the words that we speak, write and obey are the tunes that we play upon our instrument of mind.

Another reason is the final five letters in the Hebrew Alphabet duplicating the final five sequences in the sequential listing of the OWS. Finally, the unique sequence of the third line in the integrated Hebrew Alphabet and OWS relating to a progressive enlargement that ends with the very aspect of God Himself, which the OWS confirms as the *Truth,* and which is mythically considered, and beyond any doubt, the true *spirit,* of the *breath* of true living *God.*

Chapter Four

Eye Spy

*"Nor do I seek to understand that I may believe,
but I believe that I may understand. For this I
too believe, that unless I first believe, I shall not
understand."* - St. Anselm (1033-1109 AD)

Introduction

St. Anselm was born circa 1033 A.D in the provincial city of Aosta
in the Aosta Valley, which is near the Italian and French border and
surrounded by the Italian Alps. He was descended from noble families
and his parents owned considerable property. His father would not let
him enter the monastery at the young age of 15, so he instead lived a
carefree life until 1060 AD when he finally fulfilled his earlier desire
and entered the Abbey at the age of twenty-seven. He later became
Archbishop of Canterbury in 1093 AD and became one of the Church's
greatest theologians and leaders. He received the title "Father of Scho-

lasticism" for his attempt to analyze and illumine the truths of faith through the aid of reason.

Similarly in this chapter, I will attempt to illumine the truths of science and understanding through the aid of common sense and reason. I will present an integrated summary of my various papers about the physics of the world beyond, including explanations and descriptions for aether, the electromagnetic wave spectrum, fractals, the structure of sub-nuclear particles, atomic structure, a new model for the universe, and a new paradigm for physics. These concepts were developed over my lifetime and have been presented to the Natural Philosophy Alliance (NPA) during the last ten years and to the Chappell Natural Philosophy Society (CNPS) during the last few years. It was my intention not to publish this second edition of my book until all fundamental aspects of the universe were clearly defined, integrated and unconditionally proven. Instead, for the sake of posterity, I am publishing this second edition including the best of my past and current insights leaving further advances to others.

Much work is still required to verify my assumptions, to corroborate my decisions, and then to validate my conclusions. Therefore, unlike the last chapter which has been posited as the foundation of an absolute truth, this chapter is presented as a theory; and so it shall remain until all missing pieces are realized, all errors are corrected, and all conundrums are solved. My purpose has always been to provide for a comprehensive foundation, from which to build a more thorough and complete understanding of the physical phenomena of the universe and their associated mechanical and spatial attributes within the universe. It includes the use of those visualizing techniques presented earlier in the first chapter of this book, the fundamental characteristics of fractal based structures, and the unconditional acceptance of the mathematical predictions of contemporary physics. As we have learned from the OWS, things in the real world come in groups of four as was shown while decoding the Yi Jing - experiences, knowledge, thoughts and truth. Accordingly, the basic four word structure for physics is proposed to be substance, structure, mechanism and process.

In addition, there are four basic assumptions upon which my proposals were derived. First, there is an energy-laden aether that pervades all of the spaces within the universe and throughout the cosmos, and through which electromagnetic waves travel and from which all things are made; just as sound waves travel through the air that we breathe and just as snowflakes form from the water vapor that is in the air. When the energy of the aether is free to roam throughout the heavens, it is in the non-material world of x-rays, gamma rays, sunlight, the sun's heat, and radio, television and other communication signals; and when it is captured in self sustaining loops of the energy of liquid light, it is in the material world of particles, atoms, matter and mass. One of the goals of this book is to make the former non-material invisible world just as visible and just as real to each of us as the latter material world that we see, for only then will we finally realize that there is indeed another world that is even more real than world that we perceive.

The second assumption is that the aether has a fine structure within which there is a limit to the smallest electromagnetic wave that can be manifested and where beyond this point, waves, particles and matter cannot form and do not exist. Accordingly, the universe is not infinite but is instead limited in both the scale of size and the fineness of resolution. The third assumption is that all particles and mass are fractal based structures made from the aether. Specifically, I propose that aetherons are created within the aether from high energy electromagnetic waves in the middle of the electromagnetic wave spectrum, and then combine together to form the particles, matter and mass of our material world. Since the fineness of the aether is so incredibly small, it is only through the repetitive structures of fractals that we have any chance of projecting our understanding into the smallness of this process. And finally, the fourth assumption is that this composite aether/aetheron soup is a hyper-dynamic, non-homogeneous, elastic substance that includes a plethora of various field structures that exist as holistic arrays of constantly changing motions and structures within a finite and non-infinite athereal fractal plenum, which by definition is the sum total of all energy and all forces within a finite sized universe.

Unfortunately, most of these definitions and descriptions are not currently accepted or understood by the scientific community as viable explanations, and are therefore discounted as useless and ineffective. Instead, they propose the nonsense of the vacuum of space and the magic of creating things out of nothing, which anyone should absolutely know beyond any doubt cannot be true. Accordingly, reconciling these disciplines into a simple common sense integrated theory has been an arduous task, as can be seen by the multitudes of scientists and physicists who are actively involved in this endeavor and to the level of mystery and confusion that still exists. The problem with contemporary physics is not their findings, nor their mathematics, but instead the lack of a proper foundation from which to apply their findings and their mathematics. Contemporary science preaches objective logic; that is, to take our heart out of the analysis. However, the OWS has shown that analysis of the object is an endless, fruitless and hopeless task; and that although it increases our knowledge base with each step forward, it actually takes us further and further away from the real truth. Instead, the OWS indicates that the ultimate truth can only be found from within, through our inner God-given mental process of subjective logic or common sense. Accordingly, we must leave the confines of this earthly world, and instead through the powers of our imagination and our common sense, transpose our point of view into the other world that is beyond our earthly senses. Hopefully, we can get just a momentary glimpse of the true world within which we actually live. Finally, it is of upmost importance, that all things become known so that errant, perverted and unscrupulous philosophies have no where left to hide. We simply must understand how both the macroscopic universal world that surrounds us and the microscopic mini-world that is within us are put together. Please join me on this journey within our minds, as we explore these worlds together.

The Philosophy of Aether

The idea of aether has been around since ancient times. In Greek mythology aether was the bright, glowing upper air, and was the personification of the elemental God of the upper sky, of space and of heaven. It was the pure upper air that the gods breathe, as opposed to the normal air that we mortals breathe. Aristotle included aether as the "fifth element" (the *quintessence*) of his system of the classical elements of Ionian Philosophy. In the 19th century, luminiferous aether was proposed as a light-bearing substance that described a medium for the propagation of electromagnetic waves. Isaac Newton, Bernhard Riemann, and Lord Kelvin, among others, have all proposed models of the universe that included an aether based medium for the propagation of electromagnetic wave energy. However, the theory of aether has always been confronted with its inability to explain even some of the most basic physical observations without paradox and conflict.

Accordingly, mainstream physics has been unwilling to accept the existence of aether in the universe, but instead professes a vacuum of empty space in which unreal or make-believe energy travels in some miraculous and unexplainable fashion. This make-believe world of contemporary physics includes the magic of gravity with no conceivable mechanism or explanation necessary; and light waves that can be a wave or a particle, but with no clear explanation for how waves can even wave since there is no substance for them to wave in. Mainstream physics conveniently looks past the mechanics of these omissions, and instead concentrates on gaining more knowledge about the universe in the hope that they will finally find the solutions to their answers. However, again the OWS says that increased knowledge is not an increase in understanding, but instead a decrease. Likewise, the Kabbalah mapped on an OWS format indicates that it is this insistence on obtaining additional knowledge based on the objective world that is the problem.

Accordingly, all of our conflicting descriptions and mathematical derivations are not a limitation to a universal theory of aether, but instead a limitation of our ability to imagine the true hyper-dynamic qualities of the aether, the one that really exists within the universe. It is absolutely preposterous to believe that this make-believe world of mainstream physics can possibly be correct; although granted, much of what they profess mathematically is true, but only based upon the wrong foundation. In contrast, the following theory argues that there is a single universal substance that fills the entire universe, through which all energy travels and from which all matter is made. Moreover, there are hundreds of thousands of differing structures that naturally occur within the aether, of which only a special few fractal-based structures have the ability to form matter as we know it. Finally, the aether and its aether based fractals form the basis of an aethereal fractal plenum that pervades a finite sized universe. These electromagnetic aethereal light waves that fills this universe, are then condensed into the various visible forms of liquid light that constitute the atoms and the matter of our physical world.

A Modern Day Theory for Aether

Accordingly, I, like many others, believe that there is a single fundamental substance that pervades the entire universe, which is the substance from which all matter and energy are made and which thereby provides the mechanism for both wave and particle energy. However, I also accept the contemporary standards of modern-day physics including Planck's Length as the fundamental fine structure for aether. I further believe that there are multiple states of the aether. First, the aether can exist as complex superimposed wave structures within the aether; or second, as aetheron energy cells, which combine and fuse together to form other more complex energy cells such as strings, rings, loops and bubbles, and which can thereby create particles, atoms, matter and mass. One of the problems that aetherists have encountered is trying to equate force fields in the aether directly to mass equations and particle structures. However, this new theory is at minimum, a two step process with the force fields within the aether aligning the force fields within the aetherons, so that the aetherons can combine and fuse together by themselves to form particle and mass structures. Accordingly, the so called empty space of the universe is instead filled with a multiplicity of energetic structures constantly changing their form and shape. It is these independent energy cells that allow for the transmission of electromagnetic waves, for the creation of mass, and for the mechanics of gravity, as strings and charged rings are pulled into the bodies of galaxies, stars and planets to create the matter that fuels the continuous and ever expanding growth within the galaxies, the stars and the planets.

A reasonable analogy of this process would be a microscopic version of spinning yarn, where fibers of cotton are spun or twisted into strings of yarn; or the process for making nylon, where two liquid chemicals are placed in a jar, and from their common incidence, strings of nylon can be pulled from the mixture within the jar. Accordingly, as the energy cells are either tensed and/or compressed, their spin axes align; and the energy cells can thereby fuse into various patterns of fibers, strings, loops, rings and particles. These patterns may also disband just as quickly as they were formed when no particles are created and the tensed or compressed conditions have passed. The energy cells of the aether are constantly forming and reforming a net holistic array of energy patterns within the universe, which are reflective of the complex distribution of matter and energy within the universe. Both matter and energy interact with each other and both mutually affect each other. It is like a kaleidoscope of patterns of lights that are reflections from the various patterns of matter, while at the same time the cause for the distribution of matter throughout the universe. I will discuss this process in more detail in the fractal section of this chapter.

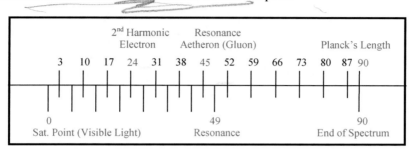

Fig. 4-1 – Particle Distribution in the Electromagnetic Wave Spectrum

I further propose that the energy within the aether was atomized or aetherized possibly by an event such as the Big Bang, precisely midway between Planck's Frequency and the frequency of visible light or the photon, as illustrated in Fig. 4-1. This event caused the breakup of saturated high energy waves on both three and four dimensional axes, into individual fragmented octal polar energy cells. I prefer to use Steven Rado's term of aetheron; however, the term gluon may also apply, although gluon more than likely refers to the aethereal field instead of the aetheron itself. Steven Rado (1920-2012) was born in Budapest, Hungary, as a Jewish descendent living in a Nazi world. He was a musician, artist, journalist and scientist who wrote two books on physics, Aethro-kinematics in 1994 and later in his life Aethro-dynamics, which are both based upon concepts of 17th century philosopher and mathematician, Rene Descartes. The term aetheron is taken from his teachings presented on his website at *www.aethro-kinematics.com*. Accordingly, there are now three variables proposed within the aether; first electromagnetic waves, second aetherons, which are complex energy cells constructed from the aether, and third, field structures, which are polar distribution patterns of the aetherons within the aether.

Since aetherons can only orient their axes in one direction at a time, they can only fuse or combine into uniquely congruent patterns when their axes are properly aligned, otherwise they repel each other. There are no average trends at this level, and therefore there is an implied limit to the number of patterns that can form due to their orientations. It may seem that infinity exists due to the large mathematical distance between our world and the astronomical size of the universe or the fine resolution of the aether; however, infinity does not exist except within the minds of men. Granted, aether does have some very interesting properties at the aetheron level. That is, axes of individual aetherons can be aligned and their energy traveling in one direction while an adjacent cell is nonaligned and its energy traveling in an entirely different direction. Also, they can both attract or repel each other depending on their velocities and the orientation of their axes.

Electromagnetic Waves

Electromagnetic waves are the mechanism by which we transmit and receive radio and television signals. It is also how we see light, feel the suns heat, perform x-rays and MRI scans. They each must undoubtedly have a real absolute existence of their own just as we do, and the lack of our imagination is no excuse for denying that existence. Table 4-1 is a tabulated list of various oscillating systems. In each case, energy oscillates back and forth from the static or potential energy state to dynamic or kinetic energy and vice versa. For example, in the case of a pendulum, the energy is transferred into kinetic energy while the pendulum is swinging to the left or to the right, however in between reversals of the pendulum the energy is stored as static or potential energy as the height of the mass of pendulum swings upward to its rest position. This process is the same for all oscillating systems.

	Static energy (potential energy)	Dynamic Energy (kinetic energy)
Pendulum	Left Side - Height of Pendulum Right Side - Height of Pendulum	Forward Velocity – No Static Energy Reverse Velocity – No Static Energy
Water Wave	Positive Height of Water Negative Height of Water	Forward Motion of Water Reverse Motion of Water
Clock Timing Spring	Tension of Spring – No Velocity Compression of Spring – No Velocity	Forward Velocity of Rotational Mass Reverse Velocity of Rotational Mass
Electromag- netic Wave	(Electrostatic Energy – Charge) Tension of Aether – No Velocity) Compression of Aether – No Velocity	(Electromagnetic Energy – Motion) Forward Rotation of Aethereal Mass Reverse Rotation of Aethereal Mass

Table 4-1 - Various Oscillating Systems

It is preposterous to believe that electromagnetic waves are any different from any other waves, and that instead they are only make-believe and that they travel through a non-functional vacuum of space. We know that air oscillates to cause sound waves and that water waves travel through the water. Likewise, electromagnetic waves must travel through some medium that is made of something or we would not call them waves. Historically, most ancient philosophers and scientists have called this medium aether. Our only limitation is imagining what these invisible waves traveling through an invisible aether looks like. The importance of knowing the inner composite structure of an electromagnetic wave is of prime importance and cannot be overestimated in understanding the big picture within physics.

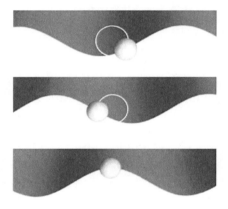

Fig. 4-2 - Motions of surface molecules
within a wave of water.

A three pictorial sequence of the motion of a molecule of water at the surface of the water, as a wave of water passes by that point is illustrated in Fig. 4-2. Note that there is a circular motion of the molecules at the surface of the water that traces out the pattern of a circle as a wave of water passes through the water. If a molecule of water is chosen below the surface, then the circle only gets smaller. Also, the wave causes a static pressure to develop within the water by the height of the wave. It should be noted that without the force of gravity and the subsequent pooling and/or ponding of water, there could be no water waves for there would be no bodies of collected water, but only droplets and splashes of molecules of water traveling chaotically throughout the cosmos. Likewise, this same logic applies to sound waves, as without gravity there would be no bodies of air for the sound waves to travel through. Similarly, the aether must be held together by something, either an internal force of attraction between aetherons or a similar universal force of gravity.

Likewise, something very similar to the preceding process must also occur within the aether. I therefore propose that there is a circular motion of the aether that is caused by the aetheron particles within the aether; however in this case, the circular motion would be tangential to the direction the wave is traveling. It would also have a forward or longitudinal component depending only upon how far the point chosen inside the wave is located from the center of the wave, similar to the smaller circles mentioned above as a molecule of water is chosen below the surface of the water. Accordingly, there would be an electrostatic component developed within the wave and a dynamic or electromagnetic component of aetheron particles circling the center of the wave, similar to patterns within the water wave illustrated in Fig. 4-2.

Moreover, I propose that electromagnetic waves oscillate like the timing spring in a mechanical watch as they propagate through the aethereal fractal plenum. The timing spring is different from the main spring, which stores energy that powers the mechanism; instead the timing spring just rotates back and forth on a center shaft thereby controlling the timing or the speed of the mechanism. Similarly, electromagnetic waves oscillate back and forth from a condensed or compressed inner position to a stretched or tensed outer position around a central axis, as they propagate forward through the aether. Accordingly, a first order or first generation electromagnetic wave is proposed to be as illustrated in Fig. 4-3. The circular arrows represent the electromagnetic component, the size of the wave represents the electrostatic component and the length of the wave represents the frequency of the wave. I further propose that when the frequency of the wave is high enough to saturate the aether, that a second generation wave is developed as illustrated in Fig. 4-4. Again, these illustrations are proposed to be actual renditions as much as possible, of the various electromagnetic television, radio, heat, light and particle waves that promulgate throughout

the cosmos. Accordingly, they have both a real existence and a structure of their own, that is just as real as our own existence.

Fig. 4-3 - A First Generation Electromagnetic Wave

Fig. 4-4 - A Second Generation Electromagnetic Wave

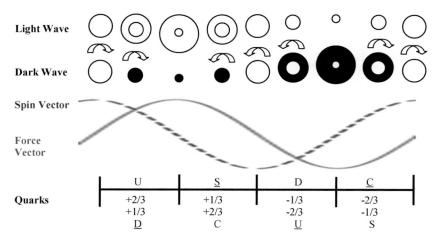

Fig. 4-5 - One Cycle of an Electromagnetic Wave

A single 360 degree cycle of an electromagnetic wave is graphed in
Fig. 4-5 along with proposed cross sections of the wave. The spin or
electromagnetic vector of the wave is illustrated in blue and the force or

electrostatic vector is illustrated in red. The black and white circles
above the wave illustrate the various charge segments that grow, develop and then dissolve back into the aether as the wave propagates
through the aether. The chart at the bottom of Fig. 4-5 locates and identifies each of the associated quarks within the wave. I further propose
that quarks are simply charge segments of an electromagnetic wave
with both a charge and a magnetic vector, as the wave both oscillates
and propagates through a hyper-dynamic, elastic and fluidic aethereal
fractal plenum. Please note the order of the eight quark charge segments in the bottom of Fig 4-5. Quarks of the first generation are
charge segments of a saturated light wave, and quarks of the second
generation are charge segments of a saturated dark wave. Furthermore,
the three colors of a quark are simply quarks that are oriented in each of
the three x,y,z polar dimensions of space. The w+ and w- bosons are
wave segments or couplets, and are unique and special since these two
segments of the electromagnetic wave have the ability to regenerate
themselves as they are the only portions of the wave that are stable.
Therefore, a U quark can regenerate a D quark and a U quark can regenerate a D quark. This is because of the momentum of the previous
C or C quark respectively, and the up direction of the spin, and resulting
in a slightly lower frequency of the wave.

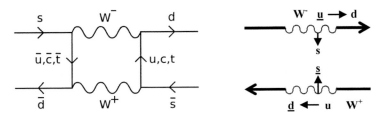

Fig. 4-6a - Standard Feynman   **Fig. 4-6b** – Simplified Feynman

    A standard and a simplified Feynman Diagram for Kaon Meson in-
teraction is shown in Figs. 4-6a and 4-6b. Please note that in Fig. 4-5
both the S and S quarks are on the outside of the wave, therefore they
could be stripped off of the wave and annihilate each other as the two
gamma rays pass by. Then according to the previous conclusion, the U
quark in the one gamma ray then regenerates the D quark, while simultaneously the U quark in the other gamma ray regenerates the D quark.

The reverse of this same process would also occur as a C quark could regenerate an S̲ quark and a C̲ quark could regenerate a S quark.

Quarks and the Formation of Particles

Once you have a visual idea of what an electromagnetic wave looks like, then a quark is simply a segmented portion of that wave. Three of any of the eight first and second generations of quarks can be charted into their respective particles on a 3D polar axis as illustrated by the red lines on the picture of a Dodecahedron Quark Ball (DQB) as shown in Fig. 4-7. To create this image, draw three red perpendicular lines on a spherical ball, representing the three phases or colors of energy in each of two polarized directions, forward & reverse spin. Then, draw a point at the center of each of the eight red triangles, representing four of the basic fundamental particles of Up, Down, Charm & Strange quarks, and with the remaining four points representing their four corresponding anti-quark particles. Then identify each of the eight points within this picture, according to the following procedure. Locate UUU and DDD in any of the top two opposing quadrants, locate C̲C̲C̲ and S̲S̲S̲ in the remaining top two opposing quadrants, and locate U̲U̲U̲, D̲D̲D̲, CCC, and SSS in the appropriate opposing bottom four quadrants.

Fig. 4-7 - Dodecahedron Quark Ball (DQB)

These eight points represent the spin axes for eight different sub-atomic structures, and their layout on the DQB exactly matches the lay-out for the equivalent eight quarks in an electromagnetic wave. It is simply 360 degrees of the electromagnetic wave from Fig. 4-5 wrapped around 360 degrees of the ball. Next, draw four pairs of concentric circles with each circle intersecting three of the eight single points. The intersect points of the red lines on the polar axes and the additional concentric colored lines then illustrate the locations of forty mixed triple-quark combinations. Furthermore, these same intersect points of the red lines on the yellow triangle exactly replicates the Baryon family of particles. The rest of the family is represented by the rest of the intersect points within the yellow triangle.

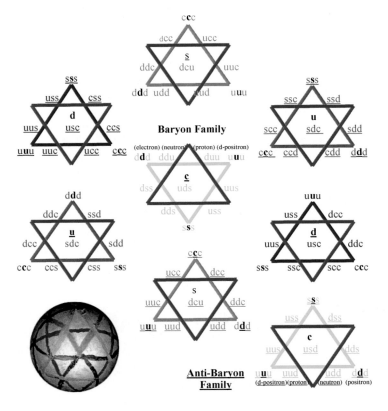

Fig. 4-8 - Unfolded Surface of the Dodecahedron Quark Ball (DQB)

Furthermore, each of these particles is formed with its own inner construct, since each of its three constituent quarks has its own individual and unique combination of shape, spin and size. Accordingly, each of those eight points on the DQB represent the spin axis of a new and different particle, which has just been created by superimposing three force fields from three quarks in the same space and at the same time; thereby coalescing the aetherons within that space into a single and unique structure. The aetherons cannot escape as they do in a single electromagnetic photon wave, since their spin axes are all lined up and magnetically coupled to each other. If the axis of spin for the overall structure is in the direction of any one of the individual aetherons it is a ½ spin particle and if it is in the composite direction of the combined three quark segments it is a $^3/_2$ spin particle. The new particle is then locked into place and takes on its own characteristics and identity, including mass. The synthesizing of aetherons from quarks into particles can then be charted as illustrated on the DQB as shown in Fig.4-8.

The DQB was derived from the same logic and rationale used in the development of the previous electromagnetic wave structure and then similarly applied to each of the three polar axes of the proposed DQB ball. It thereby represents not only a method for organizing particles, but also a method for defining the process, as well as the structure by which particles are formed. This structural process proposes that there are four energy packets in each of the two concentric waves, which together with their anti-energy packets form eight basic quarks: up, down, charm, strange and their four anti-quarks. Furthermore, it requires three identically sized waves coincident at the same point and time to possess enough energy to form the new particles, since the energy required to build a particle comes from only a quarter of a wavelength of each of the three individual electromagnetic waves. Finally, quarks are not particles, but only charge segments of an electromagnetic wave and thereby cannot exist individually by themselves, but only within the constructs of an electromagnetic wave. There are then eight sets of triangles, which develop from the previous charting method, of which each unfolds into a repetitive diagram as illustrated in Fig. 4-8.

Fractal Structures

Fractals are geometric patterns that repeat themselves both structurally and mathematically at a constant scaling ratio for each successive and repetitive scale of size. Accordingly, this scaling ratio is very important in determining a fractals overall size and structure. The internal structure of a snowflake is an example of a fractal as shown in the selection of photographs taken by Wilson Bentley (1861-1931) in Fig. 4-

9.   Other examples are crystals, river networks, fault lines, mountain ranges, stress cracks, cauliflower, broccoli, trees, blood vessels, animal coloration patterns, and yet to be proven, the internal structure of sub-atomic particles. Not only am I suggesting that subatomic particles are fractals, but also I believe that atoms, molecules, matter, mass, our minds, our bodies and DNA are all examples of fractals. It is only be-cause our DNA and our minds are fractals, that there is a common or-ganizational structure underlying the mechanics of our minds as was found and delineated in the Organized Word Structure (OWS) pre-sented in the last chapter. Digressing for a moment, I therefore suggest that the OWS is a fractal, and accordingly when expanded, will com-pletely define all of the mental processes, both good and bad within the human mind. Likewise, I suggest that the behavior of societies and cul-tures are also fractals, and therefore an equivalent Social and Cultural OWS will totally define and delineate both good and bad behavioral traits within our various civilizations and cultures. For example, not only do we consider our options, but we should also maximize incen-tives, encourage good behavior and promote the general welfare. These are all examples of phrases of good behavior that will develop within a cultural OWS, and therefore should be models of good behavior for the citizens and the governments of our societies.

Fig. 4-9 - Various Fractal Patterns of Snowflakes
by Wilson Bentley (1861-1931), via Wikimedia Commons

In the case of subatomic particles, fractals are our only method to determine their internal structure, since it is impossible to measure these ultra microscopic dimensions. For example, the fine resolution of an aetheron is as much smaller than an electron as an electron is to us. Therefore, the only way to determine their internal structure is through fractals and arithmetic theory. If particles are a fractal, then through theory we can figure it out, but if they are not a fractal, then we will never know. Don Briddell (1945-) who is an artist, scientist and a fellow member of the Chappell Natural Philosophy Alliance, has spent many years studying and is an expert on field structures, which are the fundamental distribution patterns of the various forces within the aether fractal plenum. Briddell proposes that even numbered looped structures are always energy loops, since they prematurely return to their point of origin on their first trip around the loop. Therefore, even numbered looped structures disallow the large scale accumulation of enough aetherons to form a particle. In contrast, odd numbered looped structures can accumulate large scale quantities of aetherons, since they go around the loop many times before returning to their point of origin. This structural concept will be discussed in more detail later in this section, including other looped fractal structures that can theoretically accumulate large scale quantities of aetherons, and thereby form the much heavier and more massive particles.

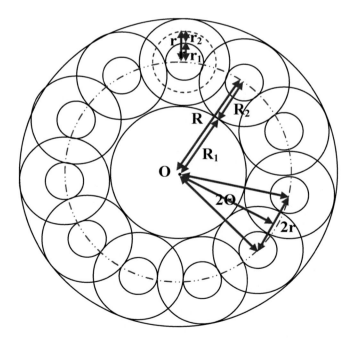

Fig. 4-10 – 1st Generation 11 twist-loop fractal

Fig. 4-10 is an illustration of the first generation of an odd-numbered eleven twist-loop fractal structure. By definition, each inner circle is an exact replica of the larger outer circle but at a reduced scaling ratio. The following equations can then be written as dimensioned in Fig. 4-10, where R_1 is the inner radius of the single large loop, and $R = R_1 + R_2$ is the centerline radius for the same large loop, and O is the center point for the same large loop. Likewise, r_1 is the inner radius of each of the eleven smaller twist-loops, and $r = r_1 + r_2$ is the corresponding centerline radius for the same smaller twist-loops, and o is the center point for each of the same smaller twist-loops. S is then defined as the ratio or the scaling factor scalar ratio of r to R, r_1 to R_1 and r_2 to R_2. Also $C = 2\pi R$ is the circumference of the centerline or midline of the outer loop, 2Θ is the angle between adjacent smaller twist-loops and N is the number of twist-loops within the fractal, which in this case is the number eleven. Therefore the eleven smaller twist-loops are proposed to be exact but smaller replicas of the larger loop that they are within. From Fig. 4-10, N isosceles triangles oOo', with o and o' adjacent small circle centers, each containing angle 2Θ, fill the entire circle around O with 2π radians.

Basic equations are: $\qquad r = r_1 + r_2 \qquad R = R_1 + R_2 \qquad$ (1)

$$S = r / R = r_1 / R_1 = r_2 / R_2 = \sin \Theta \qquad (2)$$

Each angle is: $\qquad 2\Theta = 2\pi / N \quad => \quad S = \sin \pi / N \qquad$ (3)

Also from Fig. 4-10, we find that R_2 is the sum of r and r_2:

$$R_2 = r_2 / S = r + r_2 \quad => \quad r / r_2 = (1 / S) - 1 = (1 - S) / S \quad (4)$$

From this we also obtain relations between all the r's and R's:

$$r_1 / r_2 = R_1 / R_2 = (r / r_2) - 1 = (1 / S) - 2 = (1 - 2S) / S \quad (5)$$

$$r_2 / r = R_2 / R = S / (1 - S) \qquad (6)$$

$$r_1 / r = R_1 / R = 1 - (r_2 / r) = (1 - 2S) / (1 - S) \qquad (7)$$

Table 4-2 is then a summary of 6 thru 12 twist-loop fractal structures, of which only 6 loops and larger are possible within this construct.

N	$S = \pi/N$	$S = \sin \pi/N$	r^1/r^2	r^1/r	r^2/r
12	.26179939	.258819045	1.86370331	.349198186	.650801814
11	.28559933	.281732557	1.55946553	.392239074	.607760926
10	.31415927	.309016994	1.23606799	.447213595	.552786405
9	.34906585	.342020143	.92380440	.519803365	.480196635
8	.39269908	.382683432	.61312593	.619914404	.380085596
7	.44879895	.433883739	.30476487	.766421615	.233578385
6	.52359878	.500000000	0	1	0

Table 4-2 - Summary of Various Twist-Loop Fractals

Figs. 4-11a, 4-11b & 4-11c – 1st & 2nd Generation 11 twist-loop fractal

A second illustration of this same eleven twist-loop fractal is shown in Fig. 4-11a but this time showing two generations of the fractal. In both cases, the fundamental outer loop and all secondary and tertiary loops are exact replicas of each other, except at varying scalar levels. Also, each of the smaller twist-loops are colored in red and blue to illustrate that there are two outer, larger trip-loops that each represent one trip around the outer loop, with the first loop colored in red and then a second trip around the outer loop colored in blue. Please note that the end of the red loop is connected to the beginning of the blue loop and that the end of the blue loop is connected to the beginning of the red loop, illustrating that it is one continuous string of energy of two trip-loops. Fig. 4-11b is then a further illustration of Fig. 4-11a by adding an imaginary black cylinder inside the larger loop, upon which the trip-loops are wound.

Figs. 4-10 and 4-11a are two-dimensional planar views of a three dimensional object; whereas Fig. 4-11b is a three-dimensional view of the same structure helically wound around an imaginary cylinder like the strands of a loosely wound rope. Both cases are actually the same with just two different ways of looking at them. It is like trying to see two images in a picture at the same time, like one of the old woman and the young woman, or like the face and a vase in the same picture. Both of the above illustrations are just two different ways of looking at the same thing. Both illustrate eleven twist-loop fractals within its single parent loop, and which is one continuous non-ending strand of energy of multiple trip-loops around an outer parent loop. Within this fractal arrangement, trip-loops would double with each succeeding generation, whereas twist-loops would increase by a multiple of eleven with each succeeding generation.

Fig. 4-11c is then a similar illustration except showing four trip-loops around a second generation eleven twist-loop fractal. Please note that the green trip-loop connects to an orange trip-loop, which connects to a blue trip-loop, which connects to a yellow trip-loop, which then connects back to the original green trip-loop. In all cases of odd num-bered trip loops, the number of trip-loops within the fractal structure is the power of two to the number of generations. Also, not only would there be an imaginary cylinder inside the first generation of twist-loops, but there would also be other imaginary cylinders inside each of the second generation green, orange, blue, and yellow trip-loops loops. As it is obvious by now, there are actually two different kinds of loops in-volved in this fractal arrangement, including both twist-loops and trip-loops. Therefore, a two generation, eleven twist-loop fractal would contain 4 trip-loops and 121 twist-loops as illustrated in Fig 4-11c; and eleven generations of an eleven twist-loop fractal would contain 2048 trip-loops and over 285 billion twist-loops. Although the size of sub-atomic particles is incredibly small, the fine resolution of the aether is astronomically small.

Various generations of a 7 twist-loop fractal are illustrated in Fig. 4-12 for the purpose of comparison. However, in this fractal the energy pathways and the imaginary cylinders are much more difficult to visual-ize. This level of complexity continues with multiple combinations of any odd number of twist-loops, thereby creating myriads of various field structures. The number of generations is only theoretically limited by the fine structure of the aether or by the size of the universe, and then yet comes more complexity. That is, not only can multiple generations of odd numbered fractals form, but also, multiple generations of fractional numbered trip-loops can form. Fig. 4-13 is an illustration of a 9 1/2 twist-loop fractal; however in this case, it now requires four trip-loops per generation to complete the entire cycle. Moreover, this is still not the end of the complexity, for third, fourth, fifth … etc. fractional numbers of twist-loops can also be created as illustrated in Fig. 4-14.

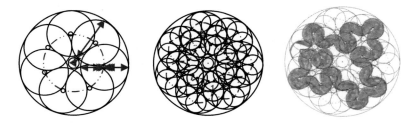

Fig. 4-12 - 1ˢᵗ & 2ⁿᵈ Generations of a 7 Twist-Loop Fractal

Fig. 4-13 - 9 1/2 twist-loop fractal

Although at first it may seem complex, an understanding of the variety, versatility and simplicity of fractal structures is of upmost importance in understanding the basic foundation of sub-nuclear particle formation and how the basic elements of the periodic table are formed, since we could then engineer those elements just as nature does. This understanding would also elucidate another level of proof that there is indeed another world beyond our perceived world that exists solely within our minds. We simply must understand the true reality of both the micro-miniature world within us and macro-universal world that surrounds us, if we are ever to truly understand and appreciate our own unique human relationship both within and to those worlds. In other words, to answer those questions about who we are, and how and from where did we come?

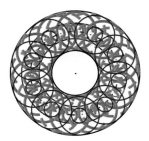 

Fig. 4-14 - 1st Generation 9 2/3 twist-loop fractal

Fractionally based fractal structures would be very similar to helically wound structures, such as winding coils or ropes except that in this case, the structure would be composed of one continuous unending single fiber of energy. For example, within 16 generations of the 9 1/2 twist-loop fractal, there would be $(4)^{16}$ or 4,194,304 trip-loops that are comprised of $(19)^{16}$ or 2.88 E+20 twist-loops. Obviously, both a visual drawing of the structure and the structural mathematics is exceedingly complex and can only be done by a computer. Physicists Bohr and Olsen at the Department at the Technical University of Denmark discussed similar mathematical limitations for the limits to the art of winding ropes in 2010 in their paper titled "The ancient art of laying rope."

However, in the case of looped structures, the imaginary cylinders that the fibers are wound around, are a torus instead of a linear cylinder, and therefore, the structural mathematics offers a unique possibility. That is, a more simplified technique in my paper titled *Aether Fractal Structures for the Electron and the Proton* listed on the World Science Database website at *www.worldsci.org* for determining exactly wound torus structures for almost any particle mass ratio as shown in Tables 4-3. This is accomplished by using rates of precession with multiple and overlapping loops, such that at the end of the final precession the final loop returns back to its exact point of origin, thereby creating a continuous thread of multiple loops of energy exactly matching the particle mass ratio. It is accomplished by first, determining the numbers of loops and the number of generations in the fractal. Then take the generational root of the mass ratio and divide it by the number of loops in one trip around the torus, and then the remainder becomes the rate of precession. However, some twist-loop fractal structures cannot be built, since their remainders cause them to prematurely terminate similar to even number fractals. If you divide the trips per cell by the rate of precession, and if this new remainder is the number one then the structure can be built, and if it is the number two then only odd numbered gradients per sequence can be built. Otherwise, when this new remainder is equal to zero or to any prime number of the divisor except one, then the structure cannot be built, since it will terminate early by returning to its point of origin before the entire structure is completed.

1.5189905381 E+63 Total Energy Cells in Particle
857 Energy Cells (Twist-Loops) / Trip
1,061,540,183 Energy Cells (Loops) / Generation
1,061,540,183 / 857 = 1,238,669.991832 Trips / Generation
1,238,670 Trips (Gradients) / Cell
(1 - 0.991832) 857 = Remainder of 7 (Rate of Precession)
7 Gradients / Trip (Total # of Sequences)
1,238,670 / 7 = 176,952.857 Gradients / Sequence
176,953 Gradients (Loops) / 1st Sequence
176,953 Gradients (Loops) / 2nd Sequence
176,953 Gradients (Loops) / 3rd Sequence
176,953 Gradients (Loops) / 4th Sequence
176,953 Gradients (Loops) / 5th Sequence
176,953 Gradients (Loops) / 6th Sequence
176,952 Gradients (Loops) / 7th Sequence
1 Advance / Sequence
7 Total Advance
1,238,670 Total Trips / All 7 Sequences
(1,238,670 x 857) - 7 = 1,061,540,183 Total Cells / Each Generation
$(1,061,540,183)^7$ = 1.5189905381 E+63 Total Energy Cells in Particle

Table 4-3 – Determining Torus Structures for Twist-Loop Fractals

The Hexagonal Fractal

The hexagonal fractal, which is composed of six repetitive loops in inside each greater loop, has several unique properties in that it has no empty space in its middle, forms another exact replica of itself at its middle, and has a scaling ratio of exactly 2 or its inverse of ½ as was listed in red in Table 4-2. In the following section, the hexagonal fractal structure will be shown to replicate the fundamentals of Sierpinski's Triangle, which is a fractal pattern that was named after Warclaw Sierpinski (1882-1969), and who was a polish mathematician that wrote extensively on set theory and number theory. The triangle was named after him in recognition of his works, although it first appeared as a decorative pattern many centuries earlier. An overall view of Sierpinski's Triangle is illustrated in Fig. 4-15, and then the top triangle from that image is enlarged and expanded in Fig. 4-16, along with the arithmetic numbers of Pascal's Triangle superimposed on the top of it. Blaise Pascal (1663-1662) was a French mathematician, physicist, inventor and Christian philosopher, who among many other things wrote a treatise on a similar arithmetic triangle. The number zero is then added between each of the numbers in Sierpinski's triangle to indentify the empty spaces. Then by highlighting only the odd numbers, a pattern develops that merges the two concepts into one.

Fig. 4-15 - Sierpinski's Triangle

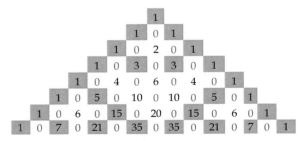

Fig. 4-16 - Pascal's Triangle

The basic structure of Pascal's Triangle is normally associated with a triangular three loop fractal arrangement. For example, if you mark any three points on a blank sheet of paper creating an outline of an imaginary triangle, and then select any point within the triangle, and then progressively jump half the distance to any of the three first selected points, the above image of Sierpinski's or Pascal's Fractal will develop. Similarly, this one half of the distance is the same scaling factor for a six-loop hexagonal fractal as highlighted in red in Table 4-2 earlier in this chapter, or as its inverse scaling ratio of two. Therefore, this same fractal arrangement should also apply to the six-loop hexagonal fractal as illustrated in Fig. 4-17. The left picture in Fig. 4-17 is a single loop containing six half-sized additional loops. The middle picture is then the same as the left picture except that each of the smaller six loops now contains an additional six half-sized loops. The right two figures are then a continuation of this same process, such that the number of loops within any successive generation of the fractal is a multiple of six. However, six is not the same as three as in Sierpinski's and Pascal's Triangle, so at this point the two concepts do not appear to correlate.

Fig. 4-17 – Second, Third, Fourth & Fifth Generations of the Hexagonal Fractal

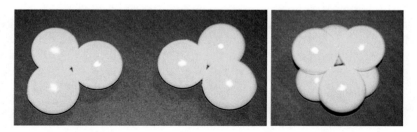

Fig. 4-18 - Six Energy Cells in the Hexagonal Fractal

Fig. 4-19 - Thirty-Six Energy Cells in the Hexagonal Fractal

Fig. 4-20 - 216 Energy Cells (left) & 36 Quark Balls (right)

As mentioned earlier, the hexagonal fractal is unique in that it has no vacant space at the center of the fractal. Moreover, an interesting structural component develops in that even though there are only six loops within each greater outer loop, there is an additional six-loop arrangement that concentrically emerges in the center of the greater loop, which is illustrated in the fourth and fifth generation pictures in Fig. 4-17 by the progressively smaller concentric circles in the center of each image. The next challenge is to create a real three-dimensional structure that is based upon and corresponds to the hexagonal fractal. In the left image of Fig. 4-18, three energy cells are connected together along with three more energy cells in the middle image, and then the first three energy cells are placed on top of the second three energy cells to create a grouping of six energy cells in the right image of Fig.4-18. I propose that this structure is the real 3D version of the hexagonal fractal illustrated in Fig. 4-17, since it replicates the same structural mathematical progression. Moreover, it is isometric on each of its three x, y

& z coordinates of a 3D polar coordinate system. The process is repeated with six energy cells in each subgroup to form a thirty-six energy cell group as illustrated in the middle image of Fig. 4-19. Please note the six different colored clusters of six cells each in this thirty-six cell grouping. This same process is then repeated in the left image in Fig. 4-20 by creating the next generation of six subgroups of 36 energy cells each for a total of 216 energy cells in a single octahedral structure.

There are many unique characteristics of this fractal structure. First, the overall octahedral structure is easy to recognize in all of the images, but especially in the larger versions like the 216 energy cell version in the left image in Fig. 4-20. Also, as shown in yellow in the right image of Fig. 4-19, another six energy cell structure forms in the center of each overall structure that is identical to the hexagonal fractal as was illustrated in Fig 4-17. Furthermore, when each of the energy cells is replaced with a DQB ball, as shown in the right of Fig. 4-20, all DQB lines of force that were drawn on the quark ball can be made to line up perfectly. That is, all of the red 3D polar coordinate axes line up, and each of the pairs of 4D yellow, blue, green and black concentric lines line up with each other. The three x, y & z red polar axes are evident by drawing three axis lines between each two of the six opposing corners forming the octahedron. Accordingly, both the octahedron and the DQB ball have similar 3D and 4D characteristics.

Therefore, I propose that aetheral energy is strung together in four dimensions when forming mass, but is charged in three dimensions. Also, you can visually see in the left image of Fig 4-20, a perfect replication of Sierpinski's Triangle on each of the eight faces of the hexagonal octahedron; and therefore, preliminary correlation emerges. That is, it is not the volume of the octahedron, but instead the surface area of the octahedron that correlates to Sierpinski's Triangle. In addition, the entire structure is a modified octahedral version of Sierpinski's Pyramid as shown in Fig. 4-21 along with its inverted image, such that the base of the red pyramid sits atop the base of the inverted or upside down blue pyramid. Accordingly, the surface of the hexagonal fractal structure does correlate with the combined Pascal & Sierpinski Triangle and is therefore proposed to be the basic structure for much of the distribution of particle energy within the aether. I have now defined two different fractal arrangements that can exist within the aether, the first is the twist-loop fractals illustrated earlier, and now the six-loop hexagonal fractal arrangement.

Fig. 4-21 - Sierpinski's Pyramid
Licensed under CC BY-SA 3.0 via Wikimedia Commons - http://commons.wikimedia.org/wiki/
File:Sierpinski_pyramid.png#/media/File:Sierpinski_pyramid.png

The next step in this process is to develop a periodic table for the six -loop hexagonal fractal as shown in Table 4-5. First, the scaling factor of two was multiplied by itself 22 times as listed in the 22 rows of the second column. Next, a correction factor of one half of the quantum limit of the fine structure of the aether is subtracted from each of the 22 rows in the third column, since a fractal must have a seed to form around or from, just as a pearl forms from an irritant in a mollusk. That is, when a fractal forms there must be a center circle representing the quantum limit to the fractals own individual and unique micro world. Accordingly, if there is no limit to the infinitely small, then fractals cannot form and we are not here; but since we are here, there is a quantum finite limit. Then in the next column of the chart, new ratios are calculated based upon this previous subtracted correction factor of one half of the quantum limit. Then in each of the successive columns of these new scaling factors are multiplied together for the various layers of a fractal arrangement, and is then repetitively recalculated for the various levels that each fractal could occupy.

In the first red column to the left in Table 4-5, eleven scalar numbers are multiplied together for each of the eleven different layers that an eleven layered fractal could exist. In the bottom row of the eleven layer fractal is the number 2049, which is the last eleven scalar numbers mul-

Table 4-5 - Periodic Table for a Six-Loop Hexagonal Fractal

Level	Scalar	Correction	Ratio	(1)	(2)	(3)	(4)	(5)	(6)	(7)	(8)	(9)	(10)	(11)
1	2	0.5	3.000000	3.000										
2	4	1.5	2.333333	2.333	7.000									
3	8	3.5	2.142857	2.143	5.000	15.000								
4	16	7.5	2.066667	2.067	4.429	10.333	31.000							
5	32	15.5	2.032258	2.032	4.200	9.000	21.000	63.000						
6	64	31.5	2.015873	2.016	4.097	8.467	18.143	42.333	127.000					
7	128	63.5	2.007874	2.008	4.048	8.226	17.000	36.429	85.000	255.000				
8	256	127.5	2.003922	2.004	4.024	8.111	16.484	34.067	73.000	170.333	511.000			
9	512	255.5	2.001957	2.002	4.012	8.055	16.238	33.000	68.200	146.143	341.000	1023.000		
10	1024	511.5	2.000978	2.001	4.006	8.027	16.118	32.492	66.032	136.467	292.429	682.333	2047.000	
11	2048	1023.5	2.000489	2.000	4.003	8.014	16.059	32.244	65.000	132.097	273.000	585.000	1365.000	4095.000
12	4096	2047.5	2.000244	2.000	4.003	8.007	16.029	32.122	64.496	130.016	264.226	546.067	1170.143	2730.333
13	8192	4095.5	2.000122	2.000	4.001	8.003	16.015	32.061	64.247	129.000	260.048	528.484	1092.200	2340.429
14	16384	8191.5	2.000061	2.000	4.001	8.002	16.007	32.030	64.123	128.498	258.008	520.111	1057.000	2184.467
15	32768	16383.5	2.000031	2.000	4.000	8.001	16.004	32.015	64.062	128.249	257.000	516.024	1040.238	2114.032
16	65536	32767.5	2.000015	2.000	4.000	8.001	16.002	32.008	64.031	128.124	256.499	514.004	1032.055	2080.492
17	131072	65535.5	2.000008	2.000	4.000	8.000	16.001	32.004	64.015	128.062	256.249	513.000	1028.012	2064.118
18	262144	131071.5	2.000004	2.000	4.000	8.000	16.001	32.002	64.008	128.031	256.125	512.500	1026.002	2056.027
19	524288	262143.5	2.000002	2.000	4.000	8.000	16.000	32.001	64.004	128.016	256.062	512.250	1025.000	2052.006
20	1048576	524287.5	2.000001	2.000	4.000	8.000	16.000	32.001	64.002	128.008	256.031	512.125	1024.500	2050.001
21	2097152	1048575.5	2.000001	2.000	4.000	8.000	16.000	32.000	64.001	128.004	256.016	512.062	1024.250	2049.000
22	4194304	2097151.5	2.000000	2.000	4.000	8.000	16.000	32.000	64.001	128.004	256.016	512.062	1024.250	2048.500

tiplied together. Then the number located right above the number 2049 was calculated by shifting up one row and then multiplying the next eleven scalar numbers. This process was then continued for each of the eleven various fractals that could exist within the eleven fractal arrangement. Accordingly, this process was then continued for all possible fractals from one layer through eleven layers. Of particular interest is the 7-layer fractal with a scaling ratio of 136.466667 in the center of the column. Accordingly, I am proposing that fractals are a key component in sub-nuclear particle formation; and hence, the formation of all matter including ourselves is created from pre-existing energy patterns found within the aethereal heavens. There is no magic in the world of things, instead aether is real, aetherons are real, particles are real, atoms are real, and matter is real, and just as we are real, all are formed from and out of the aetheron energy within the heavens.

Vector Particle Physics

This next section is a comparison of the preceding DQB fractal theory with Lockyer's Vector Particle Physics (VPP) for the purpose of developing mathematical support for the DQB theory. Tom Lockyer (1926-2012) was an electrical engineer and a past member of the Natural Philosophy Alliance dedicated to the understanding of particle physics and nuclear structure. Lockyer's theory precisely calculates a host of standard subatomic CODATA (Committee for Data on Science and Technology) values which adds credibility to his methods; and therefore becomes a great roadmap for understanding subatomic structure. However, first a correlation must be made between our two theories. Both of our theories are based upon a sin-cosine relationship between the electric and magnetic fields within an electromagnetic wave, with the DQB theory further proposing that an electromagnetic wave is in reality and in fact, an aethereal based mechanical rotary oscillating system. The first step is to compare the fundamental wave forms as presented by each author for their respective theories as shown for VPP in Fig. 4-22 and DQB in Fig. 4-23. Please note that the effective RMS value for the propagation speed of an electromagnetic wave in Fig. 4-22 is $\sqrt{2}/2$ or .707 times the radius (R). This is confirmed in the graph in Fig. 4-23 as both the spin vector and the force vector cross at the same .707 rms value; therefore both theories are in agreement.

Secondly, as proposed by DQB and as illustrated in Fig. 4-23, particles can only form at the 45, 135, 225 and 315 degree positions in an electromagnetic wave where the sine and cosine waves cross. Also please note that the sine-sine paradox is solved by defining two sine-cosine wave functions for each of the two dual concentric waves. This was one of my mistakes in that I recognized that there are two dual concentric waves, but then failed to draw both waves in my summary. Essentially, there is an electric and a magnetic transverse component vector in each of the dual concentric waves plus a longitudinal velocity vector for direction of travel. Measuring the inner E field and the outer H field is simply measuring the same thing twice, from two different points of view, and that is the essence of the sine-sine paradox. Below the saturation point of the wave, the two waves remain intact; however above the saturation point the two waves separate and particles can form. At each of the four intersect points of the sine-cosine functions, eight unique complex vectors are formed representing each one of the eight basic Up, Down, Strange, and Charm quarks and their four anti-quarks. Quarks are simply forward and reverse wound charge segments or vector force fields within the aether, and therefore are not particles.

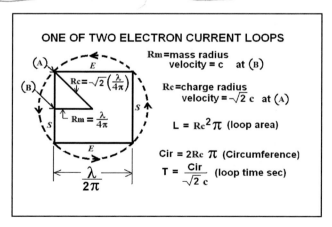

Fig. 4-22 - Lockyer's Vector Particle Physics (VPP)

The two transverse vector components of magnetic spin and electric force, and the one longitudinal component of the direction of travel are added to each of these eight quark field vectors are illustrated on the

x,y,z Cartesian coordinates in the lower chart of Fig. 4-23. I suggest
that electromagnetic waves are caused by spinning particles, which not
only wind up and distort the aether transversely due to their coupling
coefficient with the individual aetherons, but also draws energy into this
ball of energy longitudinally. When the coupling coefficient is ex-
ceeded, the ball of energy is released, and thereby launched on its forward trajectory, just as an arrow is launched from a drawn bow. Accordingly, a first generation unsaturated wave oscillates back and forth
as a rotary oscillating system as it propagates forward. Likewise, a second generation saturated wave oscillates back and forth as a dual rotary
oscillating system, except in a ratcheting or leap frog forward motion.

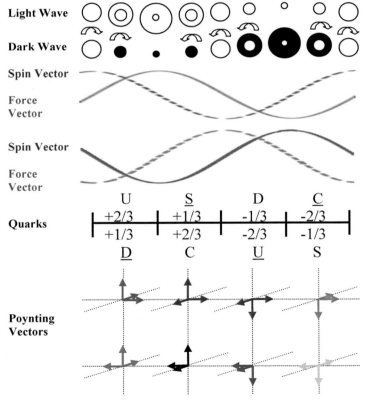

Fig. 4-23 - Various Illustrations of 360° of an Electromagnetic Wave (DQB)

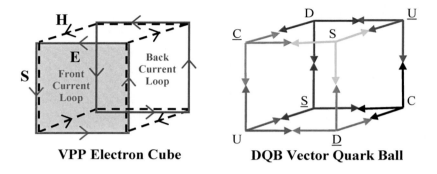

VPP Electron Cube   **DQB Vector Quark Ball**

Fig. 4-24 - DQB Quark Ball & Lockyer's VPP Electron Cube

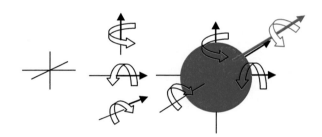

Fig. 4-25 - Spin Coordinates Used in Creating the Quark Ball

These eight possible x,y,z quark-vector Cartesian coordinates from the lower chart in Fig. 4-23 can then be combined into a single cube as shown in the right of Fig. 4-24; and likewise, it along with the VPP electron cube fits precisely inside the DQB ball. Furthermore, these are the same eight possibilities and are exactly the same cube that the both Lockyer and I discovered many years ago. The only difference being that DQB professes to represent one cycle of an electromagnetic wave where VPP professes to be the actual structure of an electron. Both theories have merit as the DQB was generated from three quarks from three individual waves on x,y,z Cartesian coordinates as shown in Fig. 4-25. The Baryon Octet and Decuplet Family charts can then be directly derived as shown in Figs. 4-26 and 4-27 from the unfolded Baryon Family chart shown earlier in Fig. 4-8, and the Meson Family cube can be derived from the DQB ball. While VPP generates and predicts exactly a host of mathematical characteristics of the electron as shown in Figs. 4-28 & 4-29. The blue circle has been added in Fig 4-28 for the purpose of clarification. The volume and surface area circled in red are of prime importance, since any polyhedral structure must match these numbers in order to arrive at the correct electron charge. The challenge is to find a structure that satisfies both theories, with two structures being considered, the cube as proposed by VPP and an octahedron as proposed by the hexagonal fractal.

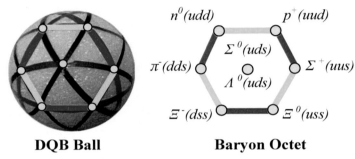

DQB Ball   **Baryon Octet**

Fig. 4-26 - DQB & The Baryon Octet

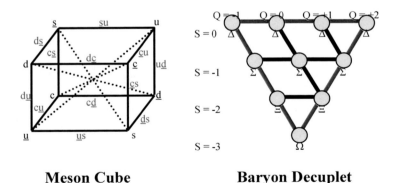

Meson Cube   **Baryon Decuplet**

Fig. 4-27 - DQB , The Meson Family Cube & The Baryon Decuplet

The cube and the octahedron are complimentary dual polyhedral structures as illustrated in the left half of Fig. 4-30. Also, both the VPP Electron Cube and the Octahedral Hexagonal Fractal (OHF) share three squares within their structure as illustrated by the red, green and blue squares in the right side of Fig. 4-30 supporting both the VPP theory that electron circuits form squares and the DQB theory that all particles are formed from three quarks on x,y,z Cartesian coordinates. Furthermore, I suggest that the two VPP arrangements for the Poynting Vectors as shown in Fig. 4-31 represent the flow of energy in the 2nd generation electromagnetic wave as previously proposed by the DQB dual sine-cosine waves.

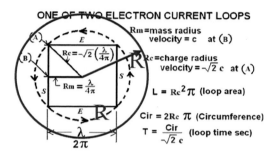

ONE OF TWO ELECTRON CURRENT LOOPS

Rm = mass radius
velocity = c at (B)

Rc = charge radius
velocity = $-\sqrt{2}\,c$ at (A)

$Rc = -\sqrt{2}\left(\frac{\lambda}{4\pi}\right)$

$Rm = \frac{\lambda}{4\pi}$

$L = Rc^2\,\pi$ (loop area)

$Cir = 2Rc\,\pi$ (Circumference)

$T = \dfrac{Cir}{\sqrt{2}\,c}$ (loop time sec)

$\frac{\lambda}{2\pi}$

Fig. 4-28 - Lockyer's VPP Electron Current Loops

Electrical potential energy (electron)

$Js := \dfrac{(h \cdot c \cdot \alpha)}{\lambda}$ $Js = 5.97441869080294 \times 10^{-16}\,kg\,m^2\,s^{-2}$

Volume of the QVPP electron model

$Vol = \dfrac{\lambda^3}{16\pi^2}$ $Vol = 9.04522247606751 \times 10^{-38}\,m^3$

Power density, QVP electron model

$Pe := \dfrac{(2 \cdot Js \cdot c)}{Vol}$ $Pe = 3.9602910136836 \times 10^{30}\,kg\,s^{-3}$

QVP electric field strength

$E := \sqrt{Pe \cdot Zo}$ $E = 3.86259197299146 \times 10^{16}\,kg\,m\,s^{-3}\,A^{-1}$

Charge density of QVP electron model

$D := \varepsilon_0 \cdot E$ $D = 3.4200114789303 \times 10^{5}\,s\,A\,m^{-2}$

QVP two current loop areas

$L2 = \dfrac{\lambda^2}{4\pi}$ $L2 = 4.68471084627891 \times 10^{-25}\,m^2$

$em := D \cdot L2$ $em = 1.60217648697431 \times 10^{-19}\,s\,A$

NIST published value $e = 1.602176487 \times 10^{-19}\,s\,A$ Check

Fig. 4-29 - Lockyer's VPP Electron Mathematical Calculations

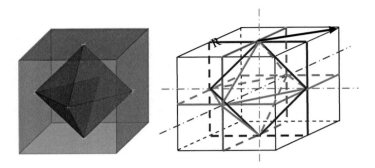

Fig. 4-30 - Dual Polyhedra – The Cube and the Octahedron

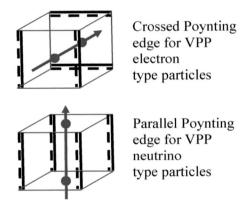

Crossed Poynting
edge for VPP
electron
type particles

Parallel Poynting
edge for VPP
neutrino
type particles

Fig. 4-31 - Lockyer VPP Poynting Vectors

Moreover, the time axis coordinates for the VPP electron cube are
defined by the blue arrows as shown in Fig. 4-31; and accordingly, in
the bottom example of Fig. 4-31, the Poynting vector travels between
the two faces or therefore between the two concentric waves, whereas
in the top example the Poynting vector travels solely within each of the
two faces, or therefore within each of the two concentric waves. This
latter case exists when the two dual concentric waves have become
saturated and therefore separated from each other. Both waves contain
an internal sin-cosine wave function as defined by the DQB, except that
their functions are 180 degrees out of phase with each other and reversed, which is the basic structural construct for the $\sin^2 EH + \cos^2 HE$

= 1 function. Accordingly, the two faces at R radian spacing in the VPP Electron Cube are determined by the internal structure of the two waves proposed by the DQB quark ball.

Accordingly, the front and back faces of the Electron Cube are formed from the inner light wave and the outer dark wave of a 2nd generation electromagnetic wave just as the DQB waveforms were derived as shown previously in Fig. 4-25. Incorporating Lockyer's VPP Theory descriptions into my own DQB Theory, the internal wave would function as a capacitor while the external wave would function as an inductor, thereby creating a normal LC circuit. VPP Theory proposes that this LC circuit resonates at the Compton Frequency for an Electron. The relative values of the capacitor and the inductor would create a significant difference between the magnitudes of the associated E and H vectors in each wave, such that the E vector resides mostly in the inner wave and the H vector resides mostly in the outer wave depending upon the dielectric values of the materials through which they are oscillating. Since the these two vectors are in phase, the apparent measured waveform only appears to be a sine-sine relationship, since the associated cosine E & H vectors were not defined nor included in any previous measurement techniques or theories. Although, it may be that they have already been defined but by other names, such as the curl of the electron current, and simply have not been included properly in an overall theory. Mechanically, each of these two dual concentric waves is an individual rotary oscillating system with the spin vector from the inner wave in phase with the force vector of the outer wave.

It is easy to understand why two of the three spatial dimensions of the VPP Electron Cube would have a value of R, because it is a square of size R that fits perfectly inside the .707 rms circle as was shown in Fig. 4-28. However, why does the length of the cube also have the same value of R, instead of $2\pi R/4$ or a quarter of a wavelength? VPP theory proposes that this third dimension, length or the time coordinate of the electron cube is related to the ratcheting motion of the electromagnetic wave as it propagates forward. However, as will be shown later, combining three electromagnetic waves on x,y,z Cartesian coordinates, describes a more reasonable explanation, since in this case an equilateral regular octahedron develops for the internal structure of an electron solely within a quarter of a wave-length and directly relative to the value R.

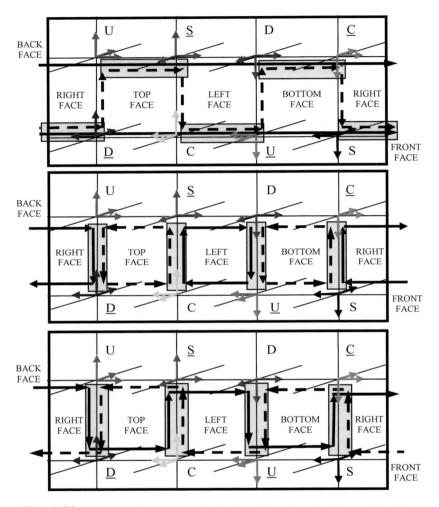

Fig. 4-32 - VPP Poynting Vectors for Lockyer's Electron (top), Muon Neutrino
(middle) & Neutrino (bottom) shown in 360° graphical form

Finally, just as there was a correlation between the DQB waveform
and the DBQ ball by wrapping the waveform around the ball; the VPP
vectors defined by the VPP Electron Cube can also be unwrapped into
analogous waveform graphs as shown in Fig. 4-32. This technique aids
considerably in understanding the concepts developed by Lockyer and

as presented in his Electron Cube. Note in top graph the Poynting vectors travel solely within each of the two proposed dual concentric electromagnetic waves, but in the bottom two graphs the Poynting vectors travel between the two proposed dual concentric electromagnetic waves. The difference is that the first case the wave is saturated and in the latter two cases the waves are unsaturated. The first characteristic can be seen in a pendulum or a tether ball that are driven beyond their limited motion and the energy is transferred into a distorted pendulum or a compressed ball, which violently oscillates between the two limits of their free oscillations.

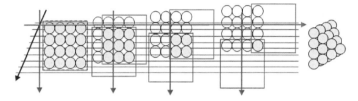

Fig. 4-33 - Stacked Construction Technique for an Octahedron

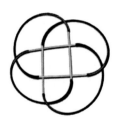

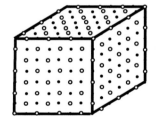

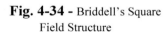

Fig. 4-34 - Briddell's Square   **Fig. 4-35** - Virtual Electron
Field Structure   Positron Field Array

At this point the two theories diverge significantly, since VPP was derived from a single wave, while DQB proposes three separate waves coincident on x,y,z Cartesian coordinates. Accordingly, construction for a DQB octahedral hexagonal fractal can be delineated and illustrated as shown in Fig. 4-33. That is, as each of the three electromagnetic waves travel forward on each of their paths, illustrated as red, green and blue below, the respective squares would decrease their overlap area. This would in effect create a sequence of smaller and smaller squares stacked on top of one another both up to and following the center larger square, as illustrated in the right half of Fig. 4-33. This concept is also supported by Briddell's Field Structure Model for squares as shown in Fig. 4-34. It is from this pattern that half of an octahedral hexagonal fractal would develop, as was shown previously in Figs. 4-18 thru 4-20.

In contrast, the VPP model would require successive cube faces to develop within a single cycle or from several cycles of an electromagnetic wave. This again is in conflict with the DQB model which instead generates a virtual Simhony's electron-positron field where three waves are congruent on x,y,z Cartesian coordinates, as illustrated in Fig. 4-35. This is purely a virtual lattice field in that only the potential exists to create electrons and positrons. Likewise, other potential lattice fields could also exist simultaneously at the same place and same time. Accordingly, if the octahedral hexagonal fractal is the correct structure, then a structural mathematical correlation must be made with the VPP Electron Cube, since previous mathematical characteristics were derived from it exactly.

Electron Charge

In this section, concepts for determining electron charge will be developed utilizing Lockyer's mathematical equations in Fig 4-29, but instead based upon my own DQB octahedral fractal structure. I suggest that exact correlations are possible, since the volume of objects varies by the cube of the scaling ratio while the surface area varies by the square of the scaling ratio. Therefore, at some scale of size, all structures will possess the correct volume to surface area ratio. Summarizing Lockyer's proposals, the equations for Radius (R), the Mass Radius (R_m), and the Charge Radius (R_c) from Fig. 4-28 are listed in Eqs. 8 thru 10; and corresponding volume and surface areas from Fig. 4-29 are as defined in Eqs. 11 thru 14 and as further illustrated in Fig. 4-36:

$$R = \lambda/2\pi \text{ (Radians)} \qquad [8]$$
$$R_m = \lambda/4\pi = .5\ R \text{ (Mass Radius)} \qquad [9]$$
$$R_c = \sqrt{2}\ (\lambda/4\pi) = 1.414\ R_m = .707R \text{ (Charge Radius)} \qquad [10]$$
$$\text{Volume (VPP electron cube)} = \mathbf{R}^3 \qquad [11]$$

Surface Area (VPP electron cube) = $6R^2$ [12]
Volume (Rotating VPP electron cube) = $(\pi/2)R^3$ [13]
Surface Area 2 Ends (Rotating VPP electron cube) = πR^2 [14]

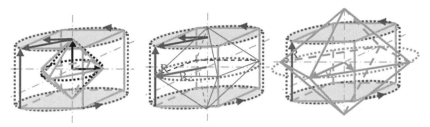

Fig. 4-36 - Octahedral Hexagonal Fractal vs. VPP Spinning Electron Cube

Corresponding structural relationships between Lockyer's rotating electron cube illustrated in red, and my own octahedral hexagonal fractal (OHF) successively illustrated in blue, green and brown, are shown in Fig 4-36. Volumes of the three fixed or stationary Octahedrons and three rotating Octahedrons relative to the VPP electron cube are as follows:

Fixed: $R^3/6$ $2\sqrt{2}\ R^3/6 = \sqrt{2}R^3/3$ $(2\sqrt{2})\ \sqrt{2}R^3/3 = 4/3R^3$
Rotating: $(\pi/2)\ R3/6$ $(\pi/2)\ \sqrt{2}R3/3$ $(\pi/2)\ 4/3R^3$

Corresponding surface areas for each of the three fixed or stationary Octahedrons and the three rotating Octahedrons relative to the VPP electron cube are as follows:

Fixed: $\sqrt{3}\ R^2$ $2\sqrt{3}R^2$ $4\sqrt{3}R^2$
Rotating: $(\sqrt{2}/2)\ \pi R^2$ $\sqrt{2}\ \pi R$ $(\sqrt{2}/2)\ \pi R^2$

An interesting matrix develops, which includes a scaling ratio for volumes of fixed octahedrons of $2\sqrt{2}$ or $\sqrt{2}^3$, and a scaling ratio for surface areas of fixed octahedrons of 2 or $\sqrt{2}^2$ both when going from left to right.   Also, there is a multiplication scaling ratio of $\pi/2$ for volumes and $\sqrt{2}/(2\sqrt{3})$ for surface areas both when going from fixed to rotating octahedrons. When considering mass structures $\sqrt{2}$ or (1.414) and its reciprocal (.707) are important numbers, for not only are they reciprocals of each other but the latter is exactly half of the former, which is the same multiplication scaling factor of the hexagonal fractal. However, at this point, none of these alternates directly match the numbers that Lockyer used in his derivations.

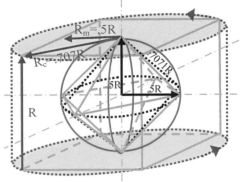

Fig. 4-37 - An Octahedron (blue) and a Sphere (green) nested within
Lockyer's VPP Spinning Electron Cube (red)

But as mentioned earlier, an interesting possibility does exist since volume varies by the cube and surface area varies by the square; therefore, there must be a point somewhere on the electromagnetic spectrum where the scaling factors are such that Lockyer's numbers are an exact match. Accordingly, all polyhedral structures are candidates for electron charge providing they meet the correct volume to surface area ratio. Furthermore, when evaluating any polyhedron, such as the three incremental sizes of octahedrons as shown in Fig. 4-36, it does not matter which size is used in the derivation, since the results are merely different scaling ratios of each other. That is, as long as reciprocal of the change in the reciprocal of the square root of the volume is equal to the surface area, then the two changes cancel each other out and the derivation for electron charge remains intact. Accordingly, this single point on the electromagnetic spectrum can be derived from any given initial size of the polyhedron. This expression can also be written that "the change in the reciprocal of the square root of the volume must equal the reciprocal of the surface area" or "the change in the square root of the volume must equal the change in the surface area" or "the change in the volume must equal the square of the change in the surface area." Accordingly, solving for the value of R of both the octahedron and the sphere nested inside the VPP electron cube as shown in Fig. 4-37, solves for R = 1/3. Accordingly, results for the R = 1/3 scaling factor for the VPP electron cube, the Octahedron, and the Sphere are as follows:

Scaling Factors:	VPP Cube	Octahedron	Sphere
$1/\sqrt{}$Volume:	1	12.72792206135	9.0
Surface Area:	1	.07856742013	0.11111111

As noted, this philosophy works, that is, using the total volume and only two ends of the VPP electron cube yields a result at the desired Compton's Wavelength as derived by Lockyer. Also, please note that 12.7279 is the reciprocal of .07586 for the octahedron and that 9 is the reciprocal of .1111 for the sphere. Accordingly, both the octahedron and the sphere work, but at 1/3 of the size of Compton's Wavelength or at a frequency of three times the Compton Frequency. Moreover, and most importantly, no polyhedron of any type or size will ever meet the requirements except in the case of the cube, and then only when the two ends of the cube are used for the surface area instead of the entire cube, which is a very unlikely and untenable scenario. However, there is another option, that is if electrons are formed from three electromagnetic waves on x,y,z Cartesian coordinates, then the same volume would be charged three times, each time from each of the three coincident electromagnetic waves. However, the end result would still be only one unit of surface area, since only one electron is created as the final result. Accordingly, there would be three units of volume but only one unit of surface area, and the scaling ratios then solves for R = 1 for both the octahedron and the sphere and R = 1/3 for the VPP electron cube. Entering these values into the preceding formulas generates the following results.

Scaling Factors:	VPP Cube	Octahedron	Sphere
Volume:	.1111	.5	1.0
1/Volume:	9	2	1.0
$1/\sqrt{}$Volume:	3.000	1.414213562373	1.0
Surface Area:	0.333	.7071067811865	1.0

Again, this process works in each case with each generating reciprocals for the scaling factor for the corresponding volumes and surface areas.

However, both the octahedron and the sphere occur at the Compton Wavelength for the electron, while the VPP Cube now occurs at 1/3 the Compton Wavelength. This is exactly why Lockyer had to choose to use only 1/3 of the cubes total surface area, to make the numbers work out. By coincidence, the final derivation results for the sphere would be identical to Lockyer's original numbers as was shown previously in Fig. 4-29.

Accordingly, I propose that quarks are not particles, but instead are charge segments or charge vectors of an electromagnetic wave, and that when three waves or vectors coincide at the proper phase relationship, an octahedral electron is formed on the surface of an octahedral hexagonal fractal with one unit of electron charge. I further propose that only the outer shell of the octahedron forms the electron, since it was the surface cells of the octahedron that matched Sierpinski's Triangle as presented earlier; and furthermore, that is the only way that heavier particles such as the proton or neutron can form at the proper size. Entering the above data into Lockyer's derivation method and formulas generates the following results with the correct electron charge value for the octahedron as shown in Eq. 23. Accordingly, an exact and precise structure has now been determined for the electron along with an exact calculation for electron charge.

Electrical Potential Energy of an Electron
$$Js = 5.97441869080294 \times 10^{-16} \ kgm^2s^{-2} \qquad [15]$$

Volume of Triple Octahedron = [.5] Lockyer Volume $\qquad$ [16]

$$Vol_{TrOcta} = 4.522611238033755 \times 10^{-38} \ m^3 \qquad [17]$$

Power Density – Triple Octahedron
$$Pe = 7.9205820273672 \times 10^{-30} \ kgs^{-3} \qquad [18]$$

Triple Octahedron Field Strength
$$E = 5.46252995411794 \times 10^{16} \ kgms^{-3}A^{-1} \qquad [19]$$

Triple Octahedron Charge Density
$$D = 4.836626616974897 \times 10^5 \ sAm^{-2} \qquad [20]$$

Octahedron SA = [.7071067811865] Lockyer SA $\qquad$ [21]
$$SA = 3.31259080730198 \times 10^{-25} \ m^2 \qquad [22]$$

Octahedral Electron Charge
$$e = 1.60217648697431 \times 10^{-19} \text{ sA} \qquad [23]$$
$$\text{NIST Published Value} = 1.602176487 \times 10^{-19} \text{ sA}$$

Electron & Positron Structure

Although the previous mathematics has been quite extensive and maybe to some quite boring, it is necessary in order to prove my stated goal of determining a viable explanation for how matter and mass are formed out of the aether. Accordingly, this next section of this chapter is the final step in that initial process of defining the internal structure of an electron, thereby validating that there is indeed another world beyond our human perceptions, where fractal structures of matter and mass are made from the aethereal energy of the heavens. The next and last step in this process is to add Briddell's Field Structure Lines (FST) to the Octahedral Hexagonal Fractal (OHF) structure as shown in Figs. 4-38 and 4-39. However, first in Fig. 4-38, lines of force have been added to Lockyer's free forming squares or electron cube. Please note the red square in the middle of the picture represents one of three squares on the three coordinates contained within the 3D octahedral structure. It is proposed that these squares of aetheron energy form within a vortex of aethereal energy of an electromagnetic wave just as Lockyer had proposed, and which is why he was able to derive exact mathematical calculations for electron charge. However, in the new combined VPP-OHF model three individual and discontinuous square structures would be required, with each containing four continuous loops of energy as was also shown previously in Fig. 4-34, for a total of 12 loops of energy. Please note that each of these loops is connected to opposite and non adjacent energy cells in a single plane.

Accordingly, there are only two more ways that these energy cells can be interconnected as shown in the two diagrams in Fig. 4-39. And then, instead of three structures of four loops, you now have four discontinuous and interlocked structures of three continuous loops, again for a total of 12 loops just as Briddell had proposed. The mechanism for this process is the relative rotational direction of the aethereal lines of force, and due to their geometry it is self sustaining. When the three electromagnetic waves are rotating clockwise the lines are skewed and reconnected in the forward direction forming the electron, and when the electromagnetic wave is rotating in the counter clockwise direction (180 degrees out of phase as shown previously in the graph in Fig. 4-23), the lines of force are skewed and reconnected in the opposite or reverse direction forming the positron. So the only difference between an electron and a positron is their rotational axis relative to their direction of travel. As Feynman had suggested, a positron truly is just an electron traveling backwards. This opens up many other possibilities which will be discussed later in this chapter.

Fig. 4-38 - Briddell's Field Structure Lines illustrated in Lockyer's VPP Squares

Fig. 4-39 - Positron (Left) & Electron (Right) Charged Field Structure Lines

This noted difference is clearly seen as illustrated by the white and black arrows in Fig. 4-39. No matter how you hold these two models, the relative slope of the aethereal field structure lines of force remains the same and are counter to each other. These two models are clearly identical in every way except in the way that their field lines are interconnected and sloped; which therefore, most certainly represents the structures of the electron and positron and their corresponding mechanism for charge. Also from this model, remnants of the original three quarks can be clearly seen, including viable explanations for the causes of the strong and the weak nuclear forces. The weak force is caused by Briddell's skewed, twisted or charged lines of force that bring the aetherons together, the strong force is the interactions of the spinning vortexes in the octa-pole or quadra-dipole aetherons, and the normal electromagnetic forces are caused by the collective sum of all field lines of force from the entire structure and are only dependent upon the type and the size of the field structure that is created.

Proton & Neutron Mass

The entire purpose of this chapter has been to make real to each of us the invisible world that we cannot see, by developing actual structures for atomic and subatomic particles that correlate directly with known mathematical values. Those structures are then integrated into a viable theory for the creation of the visible mass and matter that we do see, thereby eliminating the mystery and confusion that currently exists within the existing theories of mainstream science. Moreover, it is only the electron and the proton that are naturally stable, while the neutron is only stable when captured by the proton within the nucleon or nucleus of an atom. Normally, half of the non-captured or free neutrons dissolve or decay every fifteen minutes, while other particles have even shorter half lives of normally less than microseconds. Therefore only the electron, proton and neutron are important in this evaluation of how matter and mass are formed.

I have already proposed a simple bubble octahedral structure for the electron. Likewise, there are many clues for determining the internal structure of both the proton and the neutron. For instance, both proton and neutron to electron mass ratios can be calculated by counting the number of cells on the surface of the proposed octahedral fractal structures within higher order hexagonal fractals, and then utilizing formulas proposed by Briddell. A top, frontal and/or side view of the surface area of the proposed octahedral fractal structure that develops from the hexagonal octahedral fractal is shown in Fig. 4-40. It is based upon

aetheron energy cells connected together on the surface of an octahedron with each face being identical to Sierpinski's and Pascal's Triangle. Accordingly, fractals can be built down where each larger cell on
the surface contains three smaller cells, or they can be built up where
three smaller cells on the surface combine together to form one larger
cell. This also implies that another particle must exist at each end of the
fractal spectrum; for instance, if the overall structure represents an electron then each dot would represent a much smaller particle such as the
aetheron, from which the electron is made. Cells can be counted by
three different methods - counting the face, edge or quadrant cells. In
the following charts, I counted the number of cells in each method by
looking down into the fractal and then calculating the number of
smaller cells in each larger overall unit, however this method would
apply equally in both directions.

Fig. 4-40 - Top, Frontal and/or Side View of the Octahedral Electron

The first counting method is to count the face cells and then to sub-
tract from that total the total number of duplicate cells along the edges
as shown in Table 4-6. The second method is to count the edge cells
and then to add to that total the total number of cells between the edges
as shown in Table 4-7. The third method is to count the cells by quad-

rant and then to add the four quadrants together as shown in Table 4-8. Please note that in the bottom line number 31 in all three methods and under the column labeled Total Surface Cells is the circled number 4.9414E+15 (4.941361400467810E+15) verifying that each of the formulas and that all of the cell count numbers are correct.

Level	Total Cells per all levels	Scalar Ratio	Cells per face	Total of 8 face cells	Duplicate cells	Total Surface Cells Quantity	Ratio	%
0	1.000E+00	2.000E+00	1.00E+00	8.000E+00	7.000E+00	1		
1	6.000E+00	2.000E+00	3.00E+00	2.400E+01	1.800E+01	6	6.000	1.00E+00
2	3.600E+01	4.000E+00	9.00E+00	7.200E+01	4.200E+01	30	5.000	8.33E-01
3	2.160E+02	8.000E+00	2.70E+01	2.160E+02	9.000E+01	126	4.200	5.83E-01
4	1.296E+03	1.600E+01	8.10E+01	6.480E+02	1.860E+02	462	3.667	3.56E-01
5	7.776E+03	3.200E+01	2.43E+02	1.944E+03	3.780E+02	1,566	3.390	2.01E-01
6	4.666E+04	6.400E+01	7.29E+02	5.832E+03	7.620E+02	5,070	3.238	1.09E-01
7	2.799E+05	1.280E+02	2.19E+03	1.750E+04	1.530E+03	15,966	3.149	5.70E-02
8	1.680E+06	2.560E+02	6.56E+03	5.249E+04	3.066E+03	49,422	3.095	2.94E-02
9	1.008E+07	5.120E+02	1.97E+04	1.575E+05	6.138E+03	151,326	3.062	1.50E-02
10	6.047E+07	1.024E+03	5.90E+04	4.724E+05	1.228E+04	460,110	3.041	7.61E-03
11	3.628E+08	2.048E+03	1.77E+05	1.417E+06	2.457E+04	1.3926E+06	3.027	3.84E-03
12	2.177E+09	4.096E+03	5.31E+05	4.252E+06	4.915E+04	4.2024E+06	3.018	1.93E-03
13	1.306E+10	8.192E+03	1.59E+06	1.275E+07	9.830E+04	1.2656E+07	3.012	9.69E-04
14	7.836E+10	1.638E+04	4.78E+06	3.826E+07	1.966E+05	3.8067E+07	3.008	4.86E-04
15	4.702E+11	3.277E+04	1.43E+07	1.148E+08	3.932E+05	1.1440E+08	3.005	2.43E-04
16	2.821E+12	6.554E+04	4.30E+07	3.444E+08	7.864E+05	3.4359E+08	3.003	1.22E-04
17	1.693E+13	1.311E+05	1.29E+08	1.033E+09	1.573E+06	1.0315E+09	3.002	6.09E-05
18	1.016E+14	2.621E+05	3.87E+08	3.099E+09	3.146E+06	3.0962E+09	3.002	3.05E-05
19	6.094E+14	5.243E+05	1.16E+09	9.298E+09	6.291E+06	9.2918E+09	3.001	1.52E-05
20	3.656E+15	1.049E+06	3.49E+09	2.789E+10	1.258E+07	2.7882E+10	3.001	7.63E-06
21	2.194E+16	2.097E+06	1.05E+10	8.368E+10	2.517E+07	8.3658E+10	3.000	3.81E-06
22	1.316E+17	4.194E+06	3.14E+10	2.510E+11	5.033E+07	2.5100E+11	3.000	1.91E-06
23	7.897E+17	8.389E+06	9.41E+10	7.531E+11	1.007E+08	7.5304E+11	3.000	9.54E-07
24	4.738E+18	1.678E+07	2.82E+11	2.259E+12	2.013E+08	2.2592E+12	3.000	4.77E-07
25	2.843E+19	3.355E+07	8.47E+11	6.778E+12	4.027E+08	6.7779E+12	3.000	2.38E-07
26	1.706E+20	6.711E+07	2.54E+12	2.033E+13	8.053E+08	2.0334E+13	3.000	1.19E-07
27	1.023E+21	1.342E+08	7.63E+12	6.100E+13	1.611E+09	6.1003E+13	3.000	5.96E-08
28	6.141E+21	2.684E+08	2.29E+13	1.830E+14	3.221E+09	1.8301E+14	3.000	2.98E-08
29	3.685E+22	5.369E+08	6.86E+13	5.490E+14	6.442E+09	5.4904E+14	3.000	1.49E-08
30	2.211E+23	1.074E+09	2.06E+14	1.647E+15	1.288E+10	1.6471E+15	3.000	7.45E-09
31	1.326E+24	2.147E+09	6.18E+14	4.941E+15	2.577E+01	**4.9414E+15**	3.000	3.73E-09

Table 4-6 - Octahedral Surface Cell Count by Face

Level	Total Cells (all levels)	Scalar Ratios			Edges (12)	Faces (8)	Total Surface Cells	
							Total	%
0	1.0000E+00	2	0.5	1			1	100.00%
1	6.0000E+00	2	3	3.00E+00	6	0	6	100.00%
2	3.6000E+01	4	2.333	7.00E+00	30	0	30	83.33%
3	2.1600E+02	8	2.143	1.50E+01	78	48	126	58.33%
4	1.2960E+03	16	2.067	3.10E+01	174	288	462	35.65%
5	7.7760E+03	32	2.032	6.30E+01	366	1200	1,566	20.14%
6	4.6656E+04	64	2.016	1.27E+02	750	4320	5,070	10.87%
7	2.7994E+05	128	2.008	2.55E+02	1518	14448	15,966	5.70%
8	1.6796E+06	256	2.004	5.11E+02	3054	46368	49,422	2.94%
9	1.0078E+07	512	2.002	1.02E+03	6126	145200	151,326	1.50%
10	6.0466E+07	1024	2.001	2.05E+03	12270	447840	460,110	0.76%
11	3.6280E+08	2048	2.067	4.23E+03	24558	1368048	1,392,606	0.38%
12	2.1768E+09	4096	2.032	8.60E+03	49134	4153248	4,202,382	0.19%
13	1.3061E+10	8192	2.016	1.73E+04	98286	12558000	12,656,286	0.10%
14	7.8364E+10	16384	2.008	3.48E+04	196590	37870560	38,067,150	0.05%
15	4.7018E+11	32768	2.004	6.97E+04	393198	1.14E+08	1.1440E+08	0.02%
16	2.8211E+12	65536	2.002	1.40E+05	786414	3.43E+08	3.4359E+08	0.01%
17	1.6927E+13	1.31E+05	2.001	2.79E+05	1.57E+06	1.030E+09	1.0315E+09	0.01%
18	1.0156E+14	2.62E+05	2.067	5.77E+05	3.15E+06	3.093E+09	3.0962E+09	0.00%
19	6.0936E+14	5.24E+05	2.032	1.17E+06	6.29E+06	9.286E+09	9.2918E+09	0.00%
20	3.6562E+15	1.05E+06	2.016	2.37E+06	1.26E+07	2.787E+10	2.7882E+10	0.00%
21	2.1937E+16	2.10E+06	2.008	4.75E+06	2.52E+07	8.363E+10	8.3658E+10	0.00%
22	1.3162E+17	4.19E+06	2.004	9.52E+06	5.03E+07	2.509E+11	2.5100E+11	0.00%
23	7.8973E+17	8.39E+06	2.002	1.91E+07	1.01E+08	7.529E+11	7.5304E+11	0.00%
24	4.7384E+18	1.68E+07	2.001	3.81E+07	2.01E+08	2.259E+12	2.2592E+12	0.00%
25	2.8430E+19	3.36E+07	2.067	7.88E+07	4.03E+08	6.778E+12	6.7779E+12	0.00%
26	1.7058E+20	6.71E+07	2.032	1.60E+08	8.05E+08	2.033E+13	2.0334E+13	0.00%
27	1.0235E+21	1.34E+08	2.016	3.23E+08	1.61E+09	6.100E+13	6.1003E+13	0.00%
28	6.1409E+21	2.68E+08	2.008	6.48E+08	3.22E+09	1.830E+14	1.8301E+14	0.00%
29	3.6846E+22	5.37E+08	2.004	1.30E+09	6.44E+09	5.490E+14	5.4904E+14	0.00%
30	2.2107E+23	1.07E+09	2.002	2.60E+09	1.29E+10	1.647E+15	1.6471E+15	0.00%
31	1.3264E+24	2.15E+09	2.001	5.20E+09	2.58E+10	4.941E+15	4.9414E+15	0.00%

Table 4-7 - Octahedral Surface Cell Count by Edges

Next, in Table 4-9, ratios are developed between all levels of the fractal, comparing 1st, 2nd, 3rd, and 4th thru 7th levels of the fractal. Please note that all surface count numbers are near multiples of three even though the basic fractal was developed by scaling six octahedrons together to form the new octahedron structure double its original size. All of these ratios would be exact multiples of three if it wasn't for the duplicated cells on the edges of the surface of this three dimensional fabric of energy, which is exactly why Sierpinski's triangle is only a close approximation to mass ratios, but not an exact replication. Then, I used Briddell's proposed formula for calculating the proton mass ratio by subtracting out three separate levels that could each form individually, to project very close correlations with the current accepted proton and neutron to electron mass ratios. Note that on the 31st level of Table 4-9, the proton to electron mass ratio is determined within about 4 parts per million of the current accepted CODATA value. Furthermore, note that on the 24th level of the same chart the neutron to electron mass ratio is determined within about 5 parts per million of the current accepted CODATA value.

Lvl	Scaling #	Quad 1	Quad 2	Quad 3	Quad 4	Quad Tot	Grand Tot	Total Cells
1		1.00E+00	0.00E+00	0.00E+00	0.00E+00	1.00E+00	1.00E+00	6.0000E+00
2		3.00E+00	1.00E+00	1.00E+00	0.00E+00	5.00E+00	5.00E+00	3.0000E+01
3	1.00E+00	9.00E+00	8.00E+00	2.00E+00	2.00E+00	2.10E+01	2.10E+01	1.2600E+02
4	2.00E+00	1.80E+01	1.80E+01	1.00E+01	1.00E+01	5.60E+01	7.70E+01	4.6200E+02
5	4.00E+00	5.40E+01	5.40E+01	3.80E+01	3.80E+01	1.84E+02	2.61E+02	1.5660E+03
6	8.00E+00	1.62E+02	1.62E+02	1.30E+02	1.30E+02	5.84E+02	8.45E+02	5.0700E+03
7	1.60E+01	4.86E+02	4.86E+02	4.22E+02	4.22E+02	1.82E+03	2.66E+03	1.5966E+04
8	3.20E+01	1.46E+03	1.46E+03	1.33E+03	1.33E+03	5.58E+03	8.24E+03	4.9422E+04
9	6.40E+01	4.37E+03	4.37E+03	4.12E+03	4.12E+03	1.70E+04	2.52E+04	1.5133E+05
10	1.28E+02	1.31E+04	1.31E+04	1.26E+04	1.26E+04	5.15E+04	7.67E+04	4.6011E+05
11	2.56E+02	3.94E+04	3.94E+04	3.83E+04	3.83E+04	1.55E+05	2.32E+05	1.3926E+06
12	5.12E+02	1.18E+05	1.18E+05	1.16E+05	1.16E+05	4.68E+05	7.00E+05	4.2024E+06
13	1.02E+03	3.54E+05	3.54E+05	3.50E+05	3.50E+05	1.41E+06	2.11E+06	1.2656E+07
14	2.05E+03	1.06E+06	1.06E+06	1.05E+06	1.05E+06	4.24E+06	6.34E+06	3.8067E+07
15	4.10E+03	3.19E+06	3.19E+06	3.17E+06	3.17E+06	1.27E+07	1.91E+07	1.1440E+08
16	8.19E+03	9.57E+06	9.57E+06	9.53E+06	9.53E+06	3.82E+07	5.73E+07	3.4359E+08
17	1.64E+04	2.87E+07	2.87E+07	2.86E+07	2.86E+07	1.15E+08	1.72E+08	1.0315E+09
18	3.28E+04	8.61E+07	8.61E+07	8.60E+07	8.60E+07	3.44E+08	5.16E+08	3.0962E+09
19	6.55E+04	2.58E+08	2.58E+08	2.58E+08	2.58E+08	1.03E+09	1.55E+09	9.2918E+09
20	1.31E+05	7.75E+08	7.75E+08	7.74E+08	7.74E+08	3.10E+09	4.65E+09	2.7882E+10
21	2.62E+05	2.32E+09	2.32E+09	2.32E+09	2.32E+09	9.30E+09	1.39E+10	8.3658E+10
22	5.24E+05	6.97E+09	6.97E+09	6.97E+09	6.97E+09	2.79E+10	4.18E+10	2.5100E+11
23	1.05E+06	2.09E+10	2.09E+10	2.09E+10	2.09E+10	8.37E+10	1.26E+11	7.5304E+11
24	2.10E+06	6.28E+10	6.28E+10	6.28E+10	6.28E+10	2.51E+11	3.77E+11	2.2592E+12
25	4.19E+06	1.88E+11	1.88E+11	1.88E+11	1.88E+11	7.53E+11	1.13E+12	6.7779E+12
26	8.39E+06	5.65E+11	5.65E+11	5.65E+11	5.65E+11	2.26E+12	3.39E+12	2.0334E+13
27	1.68E+07	1.69E+12	1.69E+12	1.69E+12	1.69E+12	6.78E+12	1.02E+13	6.1003E+13
28	3.36E+07	5.08E+12	5.08E+12	5.08E+12	5.08E+12	2.03E+13	3.05E+13	1.8301E+14
29	6.71E+07	1.53E+13	1.53E+13	1.53E+13	1.53E+13	6.10E+13	9.15E+13	5.4904E+14
30	1.34E+08	4.58E+13	4.58E+13	4.58E+13	4.58E+13	1.83E+14	2.75E+14	1.6471E+15
31	2.68E+08	1.37E+14	1.37E+14	1.37E+14	1.37E+14	5.49E+14	8.24E+14	4.9414E+15

Table 4-8 - Octahedral Surface Cell Count by Quadrant

172 Divine Revelations

Lv	Total Surface Cells Qty	Ratio	7	6	5	4	3	2	1	Std. Codata Values
	Cell Count by Face		Multiplication Ratios for Octahedral Fractal Structures — Number of Layers							
0	1.00.E+00									Neutron 1836.6837
1	6.00.E+00	6.000							6.00	
2	3.00.E+01	5.000						30.00	5.00	
3	1.26.E+02	4.200					126.00	21.00	4.20	Proton 1836.1527
4	4.62.E+02	3.667				462.00	77.00	15.40	3.67	
5	1.57.E+03	3.390			1566.00	261.00	52.20	12.43	3.39	Calculated
6	5.07.E+03	3.238		5070.00	845.00	169.00	40.24	10.97	3.24	Values
7	1.60.E+04	3.149	15966.00	2661.00	532.20	126.71	34.56	10.20	3.15	13812.0000
8	4.94.E+04	3.095	8237.00	1647.40	392.24	106.97	31.56	9.75	3.10	7054.0000
9	1.51.E+05	3.062	5044.20	1201.00	327.55	96.63	29.85	9.48	3.06	4290.8000
10	4.60E+05	3.041	3651.67	995.91	293.81	90.75	28.82	9.31	3.04	3092.4762
11	1.39E+06	3.027	3014.30	889.28	274.68	87.22	28.18	9.20	3.03	2545.2208
12	4.20E+06	3.018	2683.51	828.87	263.21	85.03	27.77	9.13	3.02	2261.5096
13	1.27E+07	3.012	2496.31	792.70	256.09	83.64	27.51	9.09	3.01	2101.0343
14	3.81E+07	3.008	2384.26	770.25	251.56	82.73	27.34	9.06	3.01	2005.0139
15	1.14E+08	3.005	2314.72	755.97	248.63	82.15	27.22	9.04	3.01	1945.4245
16	3.44E+08	3.003	2270.51	746.75	246.72	81.76	27.15	9.03	3.00	1907.5474
17	1.03E+09	3.002	2241.96	740.73	245.47	81.50	27.10	9.02	3.00	1883.0866
18	3.10E+09	3.002	2223.33	736.78	244.64	81.34	27.07	9.01	3.00	1867.1223
19	9.29E+09	3.001	2211.08	734.16	244.09	81.22	27.04	9.01	3.00	1856.6295
20	2.79E+10	3.001	2202.99	732.43	243.73	81.15	27.03	9.01	3.00	1849.7005
21	8.37E+10	3.000	2197.63	731.29	243.48	81.10	27.02	9.00	3.00	1845.1104
22	2.51E+11	3.000	2194.08	730.52	243.32	81.07	27.01	9.00	3.00	1842.0632
23	7.53E+11	3.000	2191.71	730.01	243.21	81.04	27.01	9.00	3.00	1840.0376
24	2.26E+12	3.000	2190.14	729.68	243.14	81.03	27.01	9.00	3.00	1838.6897
25	6.78E+12	3.000	2189.09	729.45	243.10	81.02	27.00	9.00	3.00	1837.7922
26	2.03E+13	3.000	2188.39	729.30	243.06	81.01	27.00	9.00	3.00	1837.1944
27	6.10E+13	3.000	2187.93	729.20	243.04	81.01	27.00	9.00	3.00	1836.7961
28	1.83E+14	3.000	2187.62	729.13	243.03	81.01	27.00	9.00	3.00	1836.5306
29	5.49E+14	3.000	2187.41	729.09	243.02	81.00	27.00	9.00	3.00	1836.3537
30	1.65E+15	3.000	2187.28	729.06	243.01	81.00	27.00	9.00	3.00	1836.2258
31	4.94E+15	3.0000	2187.18	729.04	243.01	81.00	27.00	9.00	3.00	1836.1572

Table 4-9 - Extended Octahedral Surface Cell Count by Face

Accordingly, the proton and neutron mass ratios can be calculated from this chart as circled in red, but still not their actual structure, since when removing part of the overall octahedral structure the remaining structure would more than likely collapse into a different smaller structure. Also, please note that Table 4-9 also mirrors and duplicates the Hexagonal Periodic Table proposed earlier in Table 4-5 of this chapter that was calculated by scaling ratios instead of energy cell count ratios. Very unusual that these two charts should be so much alike unless they are revealing something very basic and fundamental. Note the 'seven' level column of ratios in the Table 4-5 Scaling Chart (1st, 4th, 11th) have three initial levels followed by seven ratio levels exactly the same as the Surface Mass Ratio Chart (0, 3rd, 10th, 17th, 24th, 31st) in Table 4-9. The only difference was that I started the first number for the Scaling Chart with the number 'One', while I started the first number for the Surface Mass Ratio Chart with the number 'Zero'. This change was made for ease in developing the math energy cell counting formulas. Also, it is very interesting that all contributing charts repeat at the seventh level of the fractal, which is very unique and therefore definitely warrants further investigation. Finally, each value listed in Table 4-9 represents an exact number of energy cells on the surface of a precisely sized octahedral structure from a specific layer of the hexagonal fractal proposed earlier. Therefore it is possible to draw the equivalent of any of these numbers or any combination of these numbers into its equivalent 3D octahedral structure.

Scaling	Red Light	Visible		Bohr $(\alpha)^1$	Compton $(\alpha)^2$	Classic $(\alpha)^3$
Level	420-680 nm	1	3	10	17	24
Ratio	440 - 710 Ghz	1	15	137.036	137.036	137.036
Freq.	4.409E+14	4.386E+14	6.580E+15	9.017E+17	1.236E+20	1.693E+22
Wvlnth	6.80E-07	6.835E-07	4.556E-08	3.325E-10	2.426E-12	1.771E-14
Radians	1.082E-07	1.088E-07	7.252E-09	5.292E-11	3.862E-13	2.818E-15
Ang. Freq.	2.770E+15	2.756E+15	4.134E+16	5.665E+18	7.763E+20	1.064E+23
Energy	2.921E-19	2.906E-19	4.360E-18	5.974E-16	8.187E-14	1.122E-11
Time	2.268E-15	2.280E-15	1.520E-16	1.109E-18	8.093E-21	5.906E-23

Table 4-10 - Zero Reference Cell Count Spectrum for Mass Ratio Charts

Accordingly, exact octahedral sizes can simply be determined by defining the one or zero reference level, which calculates extremely close to the point on the electromagnetic spectrum between infrared and visible red light where the photon occurs, as shown in Table 4-10. Electromagnetic waves exist below the frequency of visible light, while particles are created above the frequencies of visible light, and at the frequencies of visible light saturation occurs and photons are created. These conclusions can be directly correlated to Lockyer's five basic VPP Electron Cubes as illustrated previously in Fig. 4-32, with the bottom picture illustrating electromagnetic waves instead of Lockyer's neutrino, the middle picture illustrating visible light waves instead of Lockyer's muon neutrino, and the top picture illustrating wave to particle formation. There are many more inferences from this chart including the radius of the neutron, which should be alpha times larger than the proton; however the exact shape of both the neutron and the proton still requires more study.

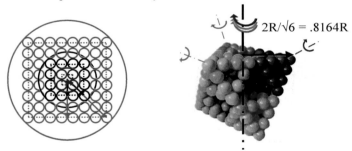

2R/√6 = .8164R

Fig. 4-41 - Octahedral Diagonal & Lateral Scaling
Factor for $^1/_2$ Spin Particles

Next, look at the number 136.466666... in Table 4-5 of the periodic table for the hexagonal fractal, which was calculated by taking the number 1023.5 (2^{10} – ½) divided by 7.5 (2^3 – ½). Note that this number can also be structurally derived directly from both the lateral and the diagonal positions of the energy cells within the base squares on any one of the three x,y or y,z or x,z planes in the octahedron as illustrated in Fig. 4-41. Furthermore, this ratio is structurally stable, that is, if you change the positions of the cells uniformly by expanding or contracting the overall structure, or if you change the size of the cells, this ratio still remains the same. Three different scaling ratio examples are shown in the Octahedral Scaling Constant Calculator in Table 4-11. I have labeled this number the Octahedral Scaling Constant and not the Fine

Structure Constant since they disagree with each other by about ½ percent, although I believe them to be derived from the same thing. There are probably one or two more small considerations that have been missed by one or the other of the two concepts.

Level	Octahedron Scaling Factor Calculator					Octahedron Ratios		
	2	0.5	0.414	0.20711	0.7071			
1	2	1.5	0.414	0.20711	0.621	2.121	3.000	0.879
2	4	3.5	1.243	0.20711	1.450	4.950	2.333	2.333
3	8	7.5	2.899	0.20711	3.107	10.607	2.143	2.143
4	16	15.5	6.213	0.20711	6.420	21.920	2.067	2.067
5	32	31.5	12.841	0.20711	13.048	44.548	2.032	2.032
6	64	63.5	26.095	0.20711	26.303	89.803	2.016	2.016
7	128	127.5	52.605	0.20711	52.812	180.312	2.008	2.008
8	256	255.5	105.624	0.20711	105.832	361.332	2.004	2.004
9	512	511.5	211.663	0.20711	211.870	723.370	2.002	2.002
10	1024	1023.5	423.740	0.20711	423.948	1447.448	2.001	2.001
		136.46667				136.467	136.467	136.467 136.467

	2	0.5	1.85975	0.92988	1.430	Octahedron Ratios		
1	2	1.5	1.86	0.92988	2.790	2.121	3.000	1.951
2	4	3.5	5.58	0.92988	6.509	4.950	2.333	2.333
3	8	7.5	13.02	0.92988	13.948	10.607	2.143	2.143
4	16	15.5	27.90	0.92988	28.826	21.920	2.067	2.067
5	32	31.5	57.65	0.92988	58.582	44.548	2.032	2.032
6	64	63.5	117.16	0.92988	118.094	89.803	2.016	2.016
7	128	127.5	236.19	0.92988	237.118	180.312	2.008	2.008
8	256	255.5	474.24	0.92988	475.166	361.332	2.004	2.004
9	512	511.5	950.33	0.92988	951.262	723.370	2.002	2.002
10	1024	1023.5	1902.52	0.92988	1903.454	1447.448	2.001	2.001
		136.46667				136.467	136.467	136.467 136.467

	2	0.5	15.68523	7.84262	8.343	Octahedron Ratios		
1	2	1.5	15.69	7.84262	23.528	2.121	3.000	2.820
2	4	3.5	47.06	7.84262	54.898	4.950	2.333	2.333
3	8	7.5	109.80	7.84262	117.639	10.607	2.143	2.143
4	16	15.5	235.28	7.84262	243.121	21.920	2.067	2.067
5	32	31.5	486.24	7.84262	494.085	44.548	2.032	2.032
6	64	63.5	988.17	7.84262	996.012	89.803	2.016	2.016
7	128	127.5	1992.02	7.84262	1999.867	180.312	2.008	2.008
8	256	255.5	3999.73	7.84262	4007.576	361.332	2.004	2.004
9	512	511.5	8015.15	7.84262	8022.995	723.370	2.002	2.002
10	1024	1023.5	16045.99	7.84262	16053.833	1447.448	2.001	2.001
		136.46667				136.467	136.467	136.467 136.467

Table 4-11 - Three Examples of the Octahedral Scaling Constant

Proton Charge

Although the Octahedron Mass Ratio Chart in Table 4-9 accurately predicts the proton and neutron to electron mass ratios, it still does not define the overall or the internal structure of either the proton or the neutron. However, proton charge and charge radius does offer some clues to the structure of the proton. The five Platonic Solids, along with thirteen each of the Archimedean and Catalan solids for a total of 31 possibilities, were evaluated for proton structure; however, none came anywhere close to defining either the proton or the neutron accurately. Next the torus was evaluated as shown in Fig. 4-42. However, the mathematics is more complicated since the structure has two variables, the ring radius R_t and the tube radius r_t. Therefore, the equations were first solved where its volume and surface area together exactly matched the volume and surface area of the already known values for both the sphere and octahedron for the electron developed earlier in the VPP section of this chapter. Thereby these calculated values must also yield the correct charge of plus one for the proton.

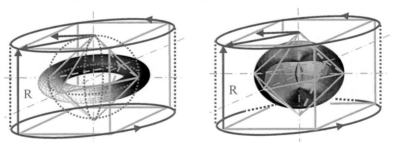

Fig. 4-42 - Ring Torus (left) & Spindle Torus (right)
within Lockyer's VPP Spinning Electron Cube

Solution of the equations for the sphere derived values of $R_t = 3R/4\pi$ or .238732414R and $r_t = R/3$ or .333333R, and solution of the equations for the octahedron derived values of $R_t = 3R/4\pi = .238732414R$ and $r_t = R/3\sqrt{2}$ or .23570226R. This immediately brings up the question as to how the values for R_t can be the same, while there are two different values for r_t, which are coincidentally only different by the square root of two. This question can be answered by solving the equations for all possible values, which show that the only variable that affects the calculations for charge is R_t, while r_t can be any value. This can be easily understood when realizing that the volume and surface area formulas for the torus are the same as a cylinder that is merely curved around in a circular pattern, and accordingly the surface area changes linearly with r_t times $2\pi R_t$ while the volume changes by the square of the r_t. times $2\pi R_t$. However, the rule derived earlier says that the change in the volume must equal the square of the change in the surface area; and accordingly, r_t drops out of the equation and R_t becomes the only variable that effects the calculations for the value of charge. Therefore, there would be a whole family of particles from the ring torus to the horn torus to the spindle torus that could be created as long as the ring radius $R_t = 3R/4\pi = .238732414R$. A comparison of Lockyer's VPP Electron Cube, the sphere, the octahedron and the torus equivalent to the sphere are shown below in Fig. 4-43.

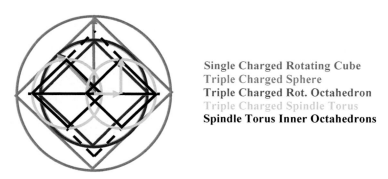

Single Charged Rotating Cube
Triple Charged Sphere
Triple Charged Rot. Octahedron
Triple Charged Spindle Torus
Spindle Torus Inner Octahedrons

Fig. 4-43 – Comparison of Unitary Charge Structures

Proton, Neutron and Nucleon Structure

Another significant clue in determining the internal structure of the proton and neutron comes from the following analysis. Earlier in this chapter in Table 4-2, the twist-loop fractal was presented as having odd and even numbers starting at six loops and then increasing in whole number values or fractional values above the number six. However, it is also possible to build fractals with numbers below the number six. Graphical representations for the whole numbers from three through six are shown in Fig. 4-44. Please note that fractals above six loops are equivalent to the ring torus, the six loop hexagonal fractal is equivalent to the horn torus, and less than six loops are equivalent to the spindle torus.

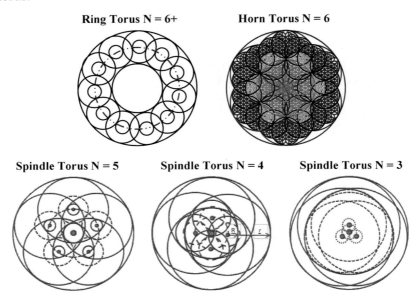

Fig. 4-44 – Fractal structures for numbers below six

Both multi-layered and surface-only octahedral hexagonal fractal structures were evaluated for the proton to electron mass ratio; however no correlation was found as both structures were not anywhere close to the correct mass ratio. I then realized that the internal proton structure must be an irregular fractal structure since it contains a mixture of up and down quarks; whereas electrons are made exclusively from all down quarks and positrons are made exclusively from all anti-down quarks, and therefore both are regular and isometric fractals. The problem is then finding an irregular fractal structure that matches both the correct proton to electron mass ratio, as well as, the shape of the spindle torus that was derived from the proton charge radius.

At this point in the evaluation, I jumped ahead and made the assumption that the spindle torus in Fig. 4-44 with N = 4 is a great candidate. First, the scaling ratio is the square root of 2, which occurs repetitively in both Lockyer's VPP electron cube and in the earlier proton charge radius evaluation. Furthermore, it fits rather well inside the spindle torus, and more importantly, it can be built from aetherons on 4D axes. Reviewing the theoretical mass ratios in Table 4-9, it is seen that the first layer has too much mass, while the second layer possesses insufficient mass. However, if you multiply the combined total of the next three layers that were originally removed to predict the correct proton to electron mass ratio, by four, and then add to that the two lowest layers of the same three layers times four again, you end up with a mass ratio that is within about ten parts per million of the accepted CODATA value for the proton to electron mass ratio. I have titled this structure the 488 Structure since it is four times the third layer, plus eight times both the fourth and fifth layers that adds up to the correct mass ratio as shown below.

	Proton	Neutron
Earlier Top-Down Method	1836.157	1838.689
Accepted CODATA Value	1836.153	1838.684
2112 Bottom-Up Method	1836.147	1838.507
712 Bottom-Up Method	1836.140	1838.409
488 Bottom-Up Method	1836.135	1838.312

As can be seen, the current accepted CODATA value falls perfectly within the upper and lower limits. Also, other potential theoretical structures, 712 and 2112, even narrows these limits. Further analysis will be required to reconcile the difference between these proposed theoretical values and the current accepted CODATA values. I have also obtained similar results for other subatomic particles, such as the pion, lambda, and delta particles, but have not completed a full analysis of all particles as the 488 structure was realized just recently. An illustration of a possible structure for the 488 proton is shown in Fig 4-45. Please note that the four secondary smaller structures interlock precisely with the same four primary inner structures within the four larger structures to create eight interlocked structures, which further interlock with the four larger structures creating a single interlocked irregular structure. I propose that torus structures are the form and shape for most particles, especially those with very short half lives; however, when the aetheron's axes are lined up properly within the torus, the 488 proton or equivalent is formed with extreme stability and an extremely long half life. Furthermore, the mass ratios listed in Table 4-9 indicate that the neutron is alpha times larger than the proton. Accordingly, the neutron may simply be a larger Compton version of the proton; may be an arbitrary neutral zone between plus and minus charges; and thereby may form an abstract nucleon when a proton is nestled inside it.

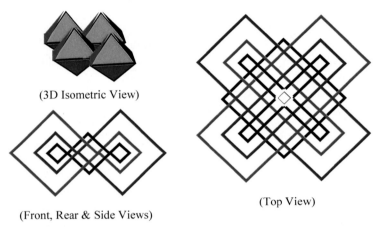

(3D Isometric View)

(Top View)

(Front, Rear & Side Views)

Fig. 4-45 – Proposed Irregular 488 Fractal Structure for the Proton
(with Interlocking Mass Structure Lines)

In addition to the 488 structure, there are many other similar structures that are theoretically possible for both the proton and the neutron, including the 558, 628, 635, 642, 705, 712, 2112 and many others, which all are within a few parts per million of the accepted CODATA value for both the proton and neutron mass ratios. There are also several different versions of the 488 structure, including changing the amount of overlap of the individual octahedrons, or rotating each octahedron 45 degrees and then shrinking the entire structure. However the correct structure must also meet the accepted CODATA value for the charge radius, which the 488 structure shown above does within a few parts per thousand. Verification of the exact structure will probably only be determined from still other criteria such as angular momentum or possibly Beta-Minus Decay as shown in the Feynman Diagram in Fig. 4-46. Not only is the nucleon made of one proton and one captured neutron; but also the half life for a free neutron is about 15 minutes, at which time it decays into both a proton and an electron. An alternate diagram illustrating an alternative process for Beta-Minus Decay is shown on the right in Fig 4-46, where a D quark from the neutron splits into a w+ and a w- boson wave, which both wobbly oscillate as separate halves of an electromagnetic wave. The U quark regenerates a D quark, and the U quark regenerates a D quark, thereby creating two new and complete waves. The w+ boson wave replaces the D quark with its own U quark thereby morphing the neutron into a proton, while simultaneously, the w- minus boson wave morphs into an electron. Any proposed proton and neutron structure must eventually include a mechanism for Beta-Minus decay.

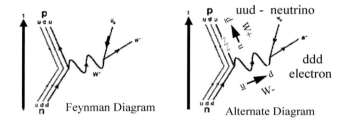

Fig. 4-46 – Beta-Minus Decay

Atomic Structure

The next consideration concerning the internal structure of the proton and the neutron is their synthesis into either nucleons or higher order and more complex nuclei structures that form the basic elements of the Periodic Table. It should be apparent by now that I do not believe in the current orbiting concept of particles like planets orbiting the sun in our solar system. Instead, a fractal concept similar to how snowflakes condense from the water vapor in the air is more appropriate. I believe that electrons, protons and neutrons all condense as fractals from the aethereal energy of the heavens. In other words, these particles are not rigid and do not orbit each other as mainstream science currently professes, instead they just provide the energy from which more complex fractals are formed. If you put a thousand drops of water into a glass, do you have a glass full of drops or a glass full of water? In other words, are the basic elements of the periodic table and their many isotopes made from electrons, protons and neutrons, or are they instead merely new composite fractals equivalent to the energy supplied by these fundamental particles. I would suggest that the latter is the case, since there are always variances and missing energy in all of our current scientific charts and mathematical equations.

One of my earlier evaluations, illustrating the nuclei of atoms as complex structures of various sized proton loops, may aid in solving this question. This method assumed that it is the nucleus that determines the structure of the electron shells and not vice versa; similar to a kaleidoscope where the structure of the glass colored beads determines the image that is seen on the screen at the end of the tube. Therefore, it is the nucleus that determines the size and the shape of the atom. The contemporary electron orbits and sub-orbits of an atom are therefore applied to the nucleus, under the assumption that the only way the nucleus could force the electrons into those shells is if the nucleus exhibited a similar structural variance, for structure is the only language of nature. In this analysis, protons were assumed to be loops of energy that could link or fuse together, as illustrated in Fig. 4-47. The 4-loop arrangement illustrated in the middle image met the above conditions. However, closer examination of this structure has shown that it is actually four sides or four spin axes of the octahedron as shown in the two right images. Accordingly, the first four loops correspond to the 1s and 2s orbits, and the six fused points correspond to one each of the six p orbits. This same process is then expanded to a final structure that correlates very closely to all electron orbits as illustrated in Figs. 4-48 thru 4-54, which are all proposed to be in reality fractal structures.

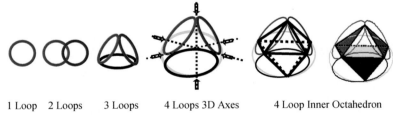

1 Loop   2 Loops   3 Loops   4 Loops 3D Axes   4 Loop Inner Octahedron

Fig. 4-47 - Fused Loops within the Nucleus of an Atom

Inside each of the circles in each of the figures on the following pages is listed the equivalent number of protons in that group, color-coded to match the same sequence number as on the sequence of groups in the periodic chart summary also shown. The figures then illustrate the equivalent number of protons in each group or cluster and the order in which each group or cluster of protons is added to the previous group or cluster. The interconnect lines are not real, but merely represent the point at which the two groups or clusters of protons are fused onto one of the polar axes. Definitions for the overall structure are then broken down into arms, bands, and groups. An arm is any number of protons along any one of the 3D spatial axes, a band is as any number of protons along at any one spatial location in all of the arms, and a group is any cluster of protons at any one location in any arm or band. Accordingly, groups are equivalent to orbits and bands are equivalent to suborbits. This structure then allows for clusters within nuclei to break off and to fuse with other clusters, and to thereby create other atoms. However, all combinations are not possible due to the structural arrangement of the protons in the various arms, groups and clusters.

There are three unresolved issues and one known conflict in the construction process. The first unresolved issue is the order that the arms are filled and there are two methods. The first fills one end of each arm in each axes and then fills the opposing ends of those same arms. The second method, as illustrated in the following figures, fills both ends of a single axis before it progress to the next axis. It works structurally either way, however this second option is more probable, since it would create more balance and hence more stability in the overall structure.

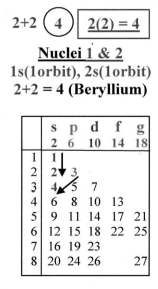

$2+2$ (4) | $2(2) = 4$ |

Nuclei 1 & 2
1s(1orbit), 2s(1orbit)
$2+2 = 4$ **(Beryllium)**

	s	p	d	f	g
	2	6	10	14	18
1	1				
2	2	3			
3	4	5	7		
4	6	8	10	13	
5	9	11	14	17	21
6	12	15	18	22	25
7	16	19	23		
8	20	24	26		27

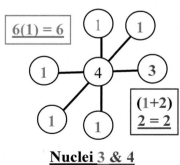

$6(1) = 6$

$(1+2)$
$2 = 2$

Nuclei 3 & 4
2p(3orbits), 3s(1orbit)
$4+6+2 = 12$ **(Magnesium)**

Fig. 4-48 - Fractal Structures for Nuclei 1 thru 4

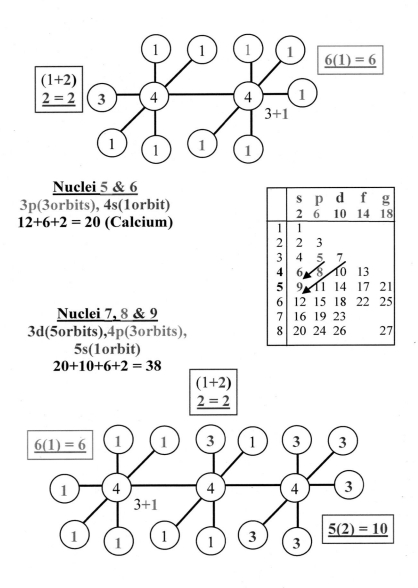

Nuclei 5 & 6
3p(3orbits), 4s(1orbit)
12+6+2 = 20 (Calcium)

	s	p	d	f	g
	2	6	10	14	18
1	1				
2	2	3			
3	4	5	7		
4	6	8	10	13	
5	9	11	14	17	21
6	12	15	18	22	25
7	16	19	23		
8	20	24	26		27

Nuclei 7, 8 & 9
3d(5orbits),4p(3orbits),
5s(1orbit)
20+10+6+2 = 38

Fig. 4-48a - Fractal Structures for Nuclei 5 thru 9

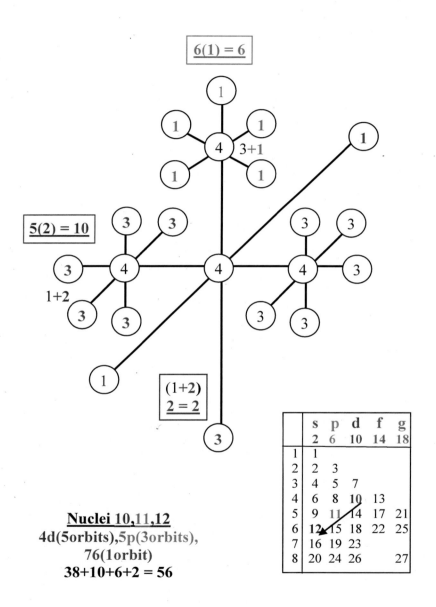

Nuclei 10,11,12
4d(5orbits),5p(3orbits),
76(1orbit)
38+10+6+2 = 56

Fig. 4-49 - Fractal Structures for Nuclei 10 thru 12

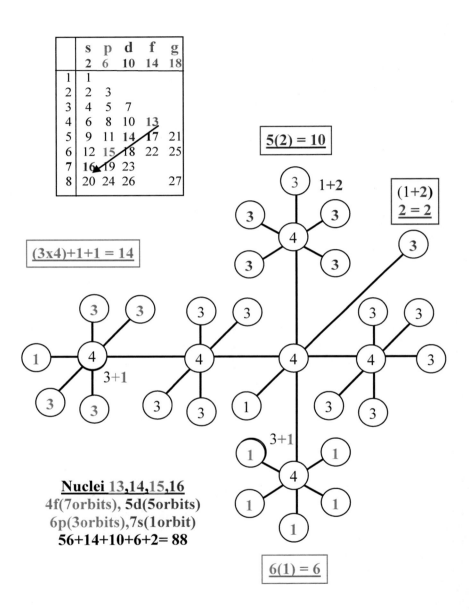

Fig. 4-50 - Fractal Structures for Nuclei 13 thru 16

	s	p	d	f	g
	2	6	10	14	18
1	1				
2	2	3			
3	4	5	7		
4	6	8	10	13	
5	9	11	14	17	21
6	12	15	18	22	25
7	16	19	23		
8	20	24	26		27

Nuclei 17,18,19,20
5f(7orbits), 6d(5orbits)
7p(3orbits), 8s(1orbit)
88+14+10+6+2 = 120

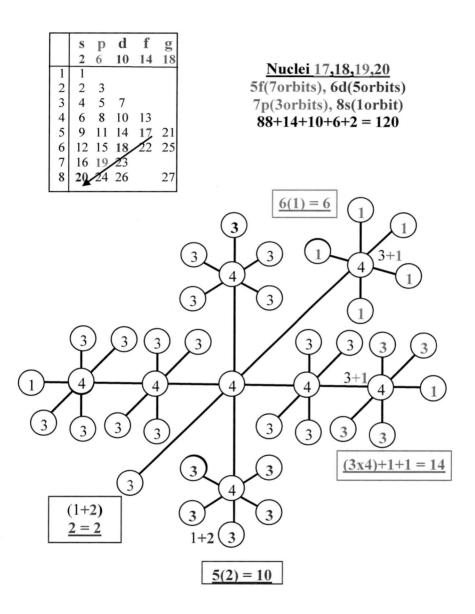

Fig. 4-51 - Fractal Structures for Nuclei 17 thru 20

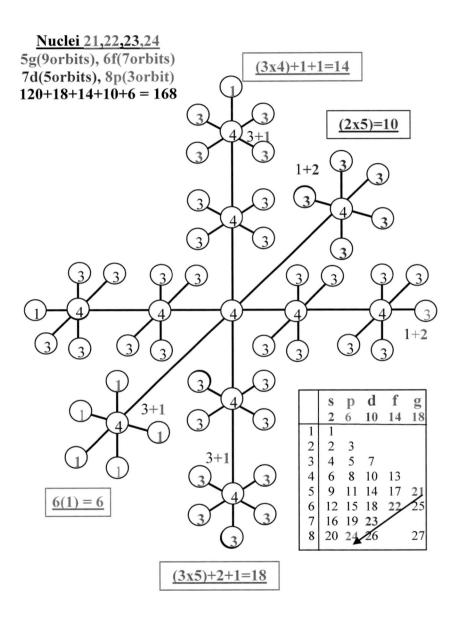

Nuclei 21,22,23,24
5g(9orbits), 6f(7orbits)
7d(5orbits), 8p(3orbit)
120+18+14+10+6 = 168

$(3x4)+1+1=14$

$(2x5)=10$

$6(1) = 6$

$(3x5)+2+1=18$

	s	p	d	f	g
	2	6	10	14	18
1	1				
2	2	3			
3	4	5	7		
4	6	8	10	13	
5	9	11	14	17	21
6	12	15	18	22	25
7	16	19	23		
8	20	24	26		27

Fig. 4-52 - Fractal Structures for Nuclei 21 thru 24

	s	p	d	f	g
	2	6	10	14	18
1	1				
2	2	3			
3	4	5	7		
4	6	8	10	13	
5	9	11	14	17	21
6	12	15	18	22	25
7	16	19	23		
8	20	24	26		27

Nuclei 25,26,27
6g(9orbits), 8d(5orbits)
8g(9orbits)
168+18+10+18 = 214

(3x5)+2+1=18

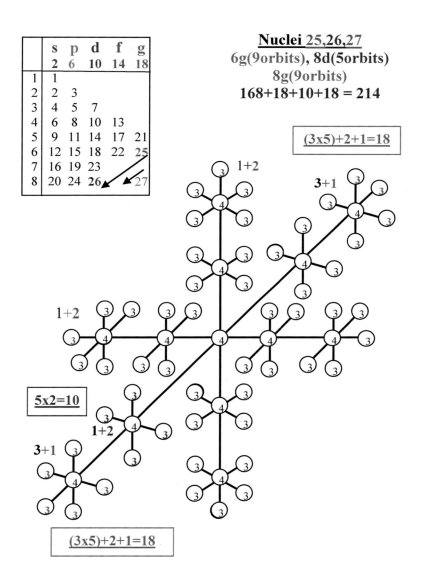

5x2=10

3+1

1+2

(3x5)+2+1=18

Fig. 4-53 - Fractal Structures for Nuclei 25 thru 27

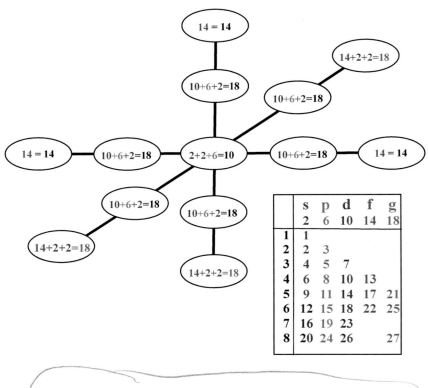

Fig. 4-54 - Summary of the Proposed Fractal Structures for the Nucleus

The second unresolved issue deals with the relationship between the F and G bands and the possibility that they could be combined into a single band, since the F band fills only three of the six outside arms, and the G band fills the other three of the six outside arms. Fig. 4-54 is a summary of the number of protons in each group or cluster of an arm of the 214 proton nucleus as illustrated in the previous construction process. Notice that there are 22 protons in the center band, there are 16 protons each in each of the six middle bands, and that there are also 16 protons each in each of the outside six bands for a total of 214 protons. This diagram clearly illustrates the relationship and sequence of the three groups of F bands with 14 protons and the three groups of G bands with 18 protons, and that two protons from each G group that are placed in the first three arms in order to finish their F group construct. It is another possibility that 4 protons in each group of 18 protons function as a subgroup. In any event this does not alter the validity or the functionality of the construction process but only further defines the process. Also, it is purely a theoretical problem and will probably only be solved by the mathematics involved.

The known conflict is in the combined P/D bands. There are thirty groups of protons (5 groups x 6 arms) while there are only spaces for twenty-six groups (a 3 x 3 x 3 cube minus the center), which means that each arm must rotate 45 degrees to leave space for the additional groups, or the groups must coexist or simply not exist at all. Although rotation works well for loops it may not work very well for rigid octahedral structures. Since coexistence seems to be impossible by definition, only combinations of rotation and early termination of the process are likely. Rotation of the arms would start to occur at about element 50 and full rotation of the arms would be completed by about element 86. Complete obstructions of the arms would begin to occur at about element 114, which probably accounts for why higher order nuclei are very difficult to make. This is because the last two arms require that all arms rotate 30 or 60 degrees, which makes it very unlikely that they could all fit into the allowed space within the nucleus. It will again require structural mathematics to prove the viable amount of rotation in each of the arms that are possible for each of the elements.

The final unresolved issue is the exact relationship between the neutron and the proton, although the mass ratio chart indicates that the neutrons may form a loose band around the proton nucleus, and which would then probably act as a buffer between the proton and the electron. I have completed some preliminary structural investigations of Hydrogen-3 decaying into Heliun-3, but nothing significant enough to present at this time. It is interesting to note that the differential between the top-down structure and the 488 bottom-up structure for the proton proposed earlier parallels very closely to the differential between Hydrogen-3 and Helium-3. Hopefully, recent papers submitted by others to the Chappell Natural Philosophy Society may be of some help in sorting out this conundrum. Of course, these issues must be resolved before there is any confirmation of this proposed sub-theory. There are no other known conflicts in the construction process, since the F/G bands exist far enough out in the arms of the nucleus so that no further obstructions will occur.

Also, the proposed construct does not preclude larger atoms with additional nuclei beyond the number of 214, since the sequence could theoretically continue on towards infinity. There must be a limit to the process, which may simply be the obstructions of arms noted above or the instability of larger nuclei where the nuclear binding forces are not strong enough to supersede those forces tearing the nuclei apart. Again, this construction process was based upon the idea that the nucleus is patterned after the electron shells, since it is the nucleus that gives rise to the electrons in the various electron shells. Also, since the electron shell system is well defined, it was just a matter of finding a structural sequence for protons, which mirrors the electron shell system. However, the inter-relationship between the nuclei and the electrons, and how the electrons form a fractal field or fractal cloud around the nucleus must still be determined, such that all effects have a true and reasonable cause.

Finally, the issue of dark energy and antimatter must be discussed. First, dark energy is not dark, since there is only energy and it is light. The word 'dark' in dark energy only reflects upon our lack of imagination and our inability to imagine and to visualize the true form of the invisible energy that actually exists within the cosmos of the universe. And the word antimatter is a misnomer, for something to be anti, it must be the exact opposite; and therefore exhibit reverse polarity for all of its parameters. Accordingly, to be true antimatter, particles must have anti mass or negative mass, as well as, negative or reverse charge. As Lockyer proposed, a much more accurate description is clockwise wound matter and counterclockwise wound matter. Then, it would be more than likely that the existing counter clockwise, reverse wound antimatter simply exists in reality right along with the clockwise, forward wound matter; and that we simply have not recognized it as yet. For example, the overall structure of the DQB ball indicates that electrons must also contain some of the same forces as antimatter and that positrons also contain some of the same forces as regular matter; and therefore, the only two differences between them are the direction of their field lines and their spin axis relative to the direction of travel.

These two subsets of matter could then be further interrelated and interlaced into virtual diatomic mirrored structures. For example, take electrolysis of water. If there are two kinds of water, forward wound (cw) water that is comprised of two forward wound (cw) hydrogen atoms and one forward wound (cw) oxygen atom; and (ccw) reverse wound water that is comprised of two reverse wound (ccw) hydrogen atoms and one reverse wound (ccw) oxygen atom. Then, the chemical equation for electrolysis would occur as follows:

$$4H_2 + 2O_2 = 2H_2\uparrow + O_2\uparrow + 2H_2\downarrow + O_2\downarrow = 2H_2O\uparrow + 2H_2O\downarrow + 2e^- + 2p^+$$

The electrical circuit that describes this process would be two cw hydrogen atoms that combine with one cw oxygen atom, while at the same time two ccw hydrogen atoms combine with one ccw oxygen atom. Furthermore, two electrons would travel down the negative side of the circuit, while two positrons travel down the positive side of the circuit. At this point, the electrons and positrons collide and annihilate each other producing energy, or they could simply be used in another chemical process. This description would then integrate the current philosophies and descriptions for regular electronic circuits with transmission lines. It may also explain why some gasses form molecules of two atoms that bond freely in the air, since one atom would be a cw wound atom and the other atom would be a ccw wound atom, thereby creating a binding force between them.

A New Model for the Universe & A New Paradigm for Physics

I have begun most of my physics papers by first describing a structure for the aether and then from that common structure trying to explain the various observed phenomena of the universe. Instead in this dissertation, I have saved the description for the aether for last, since the real structure for aether is actually the composite picture drawn from all of the individual descriptions for all the individual particles, matter and electromagnetic fields that exist within the aether. There are several key linear points along this combined electromagnetic wave and particle spectrum, of which the first is the saturation point of the aether where visible light or the photon forms; and the second is Plank's Length, which is the mathematical point where the electromagnetic wave spectrum ends. Electromagnetic waves exist at frequencies below the frequency of the photon, and are therefore larger in size than the photon; and x-rays, gamma rays, cosmic rays and sub-nuclear particles exist at frequencies above the frequency of the photon, and are therefore smaller in size than the photon. I propose that at the midpoint between the photon and Planck's length, the octahedral shaped aetheron forms from the internal energy of two dual-interlocking electromagnetic waves; and furthermore, that each aetheron is made from four dipole vortices proportional to the same forces that exist within a full cycle of the dual electromagnetic wave. I further propose that electromagnetic waves are fields of circular motions or eddy currents within the aether, which are amplified by the spin axes of the many free floating aetheron particles traveling throughout the aether.

Then at the midpoint between the photon and the aetheron, the forward wound octahedral shaped electron and the reverse wound octahedral shaped positron form. I further propose that the proton and the neutron are irregular octahedral structures that are more complex. and therefore heavier than the electron and positron, and which are in effect just higher order structural derivatives with the same identical unitary charge. All of these particles are held together by the fused vortices within their constituent aetherons. The periodic table of elements, molecules and physical matter as we know them, are yet more complex fractal structures formed from these same aethereal vortices within the aetherons. Furthermore, all of these structures are in constant flux, change and motion. Mainstream science has got a lot of things right about our world and has performed many miracles from this knowledge, even though it has started from a flawed foundation. Space is not empty but is instead filled with an array of the energy of aethereal light in multitudes of various forms, structures and shapes.

It has been extremely difficult for physicists to determine both the overall size, shape and form of the universe and its internal sub-nuclear structure, since it is both so incredibly large and has such an incredibly small fine structure. Therefore, we must first answer the critical question of whether the universe is filled with a single universal substance from which all things are made or whether it is for the most part empty and void. Second, we must determine an equally critical question of whether the universe is finite or infinite. I hope that the previous descriptions and explanations presented within the first four chapters of this book have clearly shown that the current empty and void postulate of mainstream science makes no sense, and that instead the universe is filled with a plethora of energetic structures of which we are but one. Moreover, there is no reasonable alternative to the realization that the images we perceive exist solely within our minds, and that there is instead both another world and a higher reality that exists outside of our minds and beyond our human perceived images. Furthermore, we must also realize that the physical matter of the physical universe is constructed from fractal structures that are condensed out of the energy of the aethereal heavens into the myriads of complex energy forms and physical structures found within the universe. Accordingly, fractals are a much better model for subatomic and atomic structures, mass and matter than a solar system of orbiting particles.

Secondly, I propose that the universe is finite and not infinite. For if the universe is infinite, then the darkness of the void or its equivalent of nothing must also be included by definition within the universe, and must also make sense. Accordingly, both the physics and the mathematics of the real stuff within the universe, as well as the real stuff itself, would thereby exist both into the realm of the infinitely large and into the realm of the infinitely small, along with the nothingness of nothing. This discourse is both illogical and irrational, in that, nothing can exist only when there is something around it to define it, for nothing by itself has no parameters. All parameters that are assigned to voids, holes or nothingness are assigned in error or simply for convenience; but are in fact, characteristics of the rest of the somethings of the universe. For example, nothing cannot spin, only the stuff around it can spin; nothing cannot possess charge, for only the stuff around it can possess charge; and nothing has no size, shape or form unless there is something around it to give it size, shape and form.

Accordingly, only in the Land of Oz can something come from nothing or can something disappear into nothing. Such is the case with those infinitely small and imaginary singularities proposed by some in the mainstream, which can both magically exist and magically not exist both at the same time. This would be a very difficult task since both voids and singularities by definition have no size, no shape, no dimensions and no form. Similarly, if the vacuum of space is proposed to be infinitely large, then there is nothing around it to define its unimaginable infinite boundary. These entire arguments of nothingness and its equivalent of the void within the vacuum of space are irrational, illogical and nonfunctional, in that everything breaks down and no congruent

or working model can be devised. Accordingly, everything else you try
to define makes no sense, and therefore everything becomes nonsense.
This obviously cannot be true, as the things and the true somethingness
of those things in the universal world of things, have to add up to something or its equivalent of something else or we could not exist. Moreover, if the world of things is infinite then there is chaos, but if the
world of things is finite then there is order. This whole discourse reasonably reflects the current state of both physics and science. That is,
since the idea of nothing and nothingness has been illogically deduced,
then the known parameters of the universe cannot be organized into an
integrated whole of common sense.

At this point, please allow me to digress into the meaning of the
three words, something, nothing and just things in general. The phrase
'ing' within the structure of our spoken language indicates the energy of
motion, such as running, playing, or working. It also infers that this
energy of motion is a singular and repetitive process. Accordingly,
'something or 'some-thing' indicates some kind of motion, whereas
nothing or 'no-thing' indicates no motion. The word thing can be further broken down into 'the - ing' or the motion itself, such that the motion of things is one unending self-contained internal process. Accordingly, existential things are any form of one unending self-contained
process of motion with an independent existence of its own. In contrast, nothing possesses no motion and has no existence whatsoever.
The things of the universe each have their own existence and are the
only forms of energy within the universe that have any real existence of
their own. Finally, something can only come from or dissolve into
something else, and can never come from or disappear into nothing.

However, again in the Land of Oz, nothing can be purported to have
very unique and imaginary properties. That is, it can be infinitely large
or infinitely small, and it can travel instantaneously, backwards in time,
and on to infinity, since its uniqueness is that it has no properties and
does not exist. Instead, when nothing disappears at one point in space
and time and then magically reappears instantaneously at another distant point in space and time, it is in fact, the holistic parameters of the
something else of the universe that has been transfigured from one
structure at one point in space and time, to another structure at a different point in space and time. Accordingly, neither the infinitely large
nor the infinitely small exist except in the land of fantasy, and therefore

any parameters assigned to the voids of the nothingness are assigned in error and should instead be assigned holistically to the rest of the some-thingness of the universe. If there is nothing or 'no thing' to detect then there is 'no thing' there; and therefore by direct inference, both the smallest and the largest increments of the universe are finite.

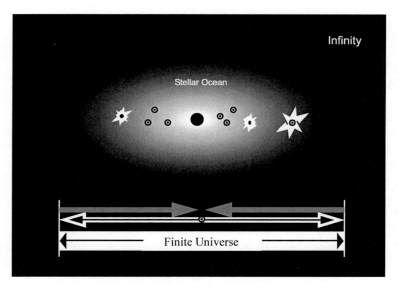

Fig. 4-55 – Our Universe

Accordingly, it is proposed that the universe is instead finite as illus-trated in Fig. 4-55. Furthermore, it is filled with an aethereal ocean of something, whether you call it luminous aether, stellar air, quantum foam, or whatever name you would like to apply to it, for it is the only way that energy can traverse the heavens. A finite universe simply can-not be both void and empty and yet meaningful. Secondly, any defini-tion or model of the universe must include everything that is measured, detected, heard and seen, or in other words all things that exist; and therefore outside of the universe is nothing. Moreover, nothing is per-mitted to continue on to infinity since it doesn't exist anyway. There-fore, infinity is an abstract concept that exists solely within the human mind, and it can therefore be any size, shape or quantity you wish it be, for it doesn't exist anyway. It is from this perspective, that I believe the exact mechanics of the universe will eventually be solved, including exact mathematical proofs for Planck's Length, the Fine Structure Constant, and a host of other mathematical and scientific parameters.

Finally, there must be a force and a method that holds the universe together, which I proposed much earlier in this chapter to be gravity, and which I believe is caused by an intense energy form, such as a three-dimensional gravitational hurricane circulating at its center. Accordingly, I believe that the descriptive words 'black hole' are another misnomer and that white storm or crystal dome may be a much more appropriate name. I propose that aetherons and aether are flowing from the heavens into the center of this universal storm, thereby creating a universal gravitational field of universal gravity, which thereby holds the universe together. Furthermore, I propose that periodically the universe burps or hiccups, ejecting a new wave of the energy of mass outward through this aethereal universe. This new wave of energy are the seeds for what we define as the physical universe; and accordingly it travels outward through the aethereal universe against the inflowing aethereal storm, and then explodes into stars, galaxies and more stars on its journey outward through the heavens. They each grow and expand, each on their own journey, and each with their own gravitational fields and their own life cycle throughout the heavens. The physical universe then dissolves back into the energy of waves near the edges of the heavens, as the energy of light of the aether and the aetherons begins their long journey back towards the center of the universe.

Again, back in the land of make-believe, the imaginary energy of darkness disappears outside of the aethereal universe of space and time into the imaginary darkness of infinity. Accordingly, infinity is a place of no substance, no borders, no size and no shape, and is simply represented as a square in the illustration in Fig 4-55. The only purpose for the concept of infinity is to permit the finite aethereal universe of space and time to have size, shape and meaning within the human mind; and therefore infinity is merely an abstract concept created by the human mind. In contrast; the aethereal universe is eternal without beginning and without end and contains all that there is. The physical universe that is expanding within the aethereal universe has its own life cycle consisting of birth, growth, expansion, and dissolution, and which thereby defines both the direction of time and the process of entropy. In this descriptive paradigm, both the concept makes sense and the model is functional. Accordingly, the energy of the finite universe is sourced by and within itself; and therefore, the infinite has become finite. When all of the concepts for the universe are complete, and when all of its equations and mathematics are finished, I sincerely believe that this concept will surely be the case.

In summary, the proposed universe is then comprised of two worlds, the physical world, which is carved from the energy of the liquid light and the heavenly world, which is carved from the aethereal energy of the stellar air; and both are defined and described by the perceptual and conceptual worlds, which exist solely within the human mind. Furthermore, it is proposed that the heavenly ocean of universal aether is an open plenum closed by the process of gravity, and which maintains a relatively constant size with its energy transformations occurring in both directions; and therefore, Dr. Hoyle's steady state universe is correct. Accordingly, aethereal space is eternal and is not expanding; however, the physical universe is expanding within aethereal space and has a definite life cycle and is not eternal.

The physical world of liquid light expands within the heavenly world, thereby establishing the effects of entropy within the physical universe and the direction of time. Within our world, the aetherons flow through our bodies and into the earth causing the sensation of gravity, and is then converted into mass or liquid light through the process of sub-nuclear fusion causing the earth to grow and to expand and the earth's continents to drift apart. This same process occurs within all of the planets, stars and galaxies within the universe, as well as, the universe itself. Moreover, there are absolute speeds in the universe, which must be by theory, by definition, and by empirical evidence, referenced to the center of the universe, which is the only static reference point available within the universe.

Accordingly, it is the instructions for the universe that were holistically present at the center of the universe, at the beginning of creation and at the beginning of time. Therefore, the big bang might be more appropriately named a universal hiecup, since most of the mass for the stars, planets and galaxies is created on its journey outward through the heavens. As the present physical universe expands throughout the heavens, a new instruction set is being developed at the center of the universe for the next cycle of universal creation, and therefore the process is repetitious but not reversible. However, multiple waves of creation are structurally possible, and therefore multiple concentric physical universes are possible within the one single heavenly universe. The expansion process of a growing earth, and its other growing cosmic cousins, and the processes of exploding stars, galaxies, and the big bang of the universe are all part of a continuous cycle, just as the water evaporates into our skies and then falls as rain to the earth.

There are many ideas and conclusions that can be generated from this paradigm. First, I would hope that this paper finally puts to bed the issue of whether there is an aether or not, yes Virginia, there is an aether. Second, the universe does not penetrate the infinitely small, but is instead limited by the fine structure of the aether. If there were no quantum limit to the smallest size in the aether, then fractals could not form and instead all energy would stay suspended within the aether as pure energy; and therefore, there would be no limit to the highest frequency electromagnetic wave or the smallest quanta of energy. Moreover, in an infinite non-quantum universe, even pure energy could not exist. Accordingly, fractals, particles, atoms, matter, planets, stars, and galaxies could not form and we would not be here. But since we are here, there must be a finite aethereal universe with a quantum limited fine structure. Moreover, when all of the mathematics is all complete, when all of its variables are all explained, and when our final concept is all complete, then that is all there is, and with that we must be satisfied. Again, when all of the mathematics is all complete, when all of its variables are all explained, and when our final concept is all complete, then that is all there is, and with that we must be satisfied.

Wouldn't it be interesting if we found out that the physical universe can only form by a separate, individual and discrete act of intelligence.

Summary

So what was this chapter all about – mathematics, waves, fractals, sub-nuclear particles, quantum limits, charge, atoms, the creation of matter, a growing and expanding earth, planets, galaxies or the universe? None of these, it is about psychology, point of view, attitudes, perception, surrendering the self to a higher view and a higher power, and a belief in a truth greater than ourselves. It is about developing a frame of mind that allows new ideas to flow through our minds, and the recognition that science is not king. It is about the realization that there must be a medium for energy to travel through and to travel in. It is about developing a viable theory that is worth the time for scientists to consider and to evaluate. Unfortunately, this chapter has also included lots of details, since without details any new theory has no chance of being considered by the mainstream, which by definition tends to be a closed and aloof institution. However, if we are not looking in the right places, we will never find the right answers. Accordingly, science has been looking in the wrong places for a long time now and keeps getting the wrong answers – space is a vacuum, the warped space time continuum, the duality of light, the sine-sine paradox, the twin paradox, which all end up as mystery, conflict, contradictions, confusion and conundrums. It seems as though one of the most difficult things for human kind to accept is another world existing beyond the physical world of our human perceptions. Many of our hearts believe, but our minds say no, as our greatest obstacle has been our own limited consciousness. We get so entrenched in this visual world that we see, that we don't realize that the things that we do not see also have their own existence, just as much as we do. Yet, until we accept this recognition, we continue the strange odyssey of misidentifying and misrepresenting the various occurrences of our physical world, through our misspoken vocabulary of euphemisms.

We misidentify matter as being held together by glueballs instead of fused energy cells. We misidentify the cause for the earth's continents drifting apart as plates floating on a moving mantel instead of a growing and expanding earth. We misidentify the ability of energy to travel at speeds other than the speed of light as a warped space time continuum instead of a variation in the speed of light. We misidentify light waves bent by the forces of gravity instead of light waves drifting laterally from the inflowing stellar air. We misidentify galaxies as interconnected with worm holes so the inflowing energy and matter has somewhere to go, instead of recognizing the internal growth of the galaxy; and we misidentify the weight of our bodies as an imaginary force instead of the energies of the aether flowing through our bodies and into our mother earth. Accordingly, the world we perceive is actually a grand illusion created within the boundaries of our minds, and there actually exists another world beyond our human perceptions that can only be accessed through the powers of our imagination, through the anecdotal stories of those among us who have had out-of-body and near

-death experiences, and finally through the real possibility of life beyond physical death.

I am not alone in these propositions, as I have met many scientists, physicists, philosophers, artists, engineers, lawyers, near-death survivors and healthcare providers among many others at the many conferences that I have attended who share similar perspectives and points of view. These are all sincere and caring people who have made significant sacrifices within their personal, professional and financial lives to further the deepest beliefs and convictions of their hearts. The Natural Philosophy Alliance and its successor the Chappell Natural Philosophy Society are blessed with an abundance of these people and has been a great blessing to me. I have never met so many intelligent people, with such open minds and a great abundance of common sense, in one place and at one time before in my life. Finally, we must remember those among us who have actually made that journey into the world beyond through near-death and out of body experiences, and have returned to this world to tell us of their experiences. If we would only listen.

Chapter Five

The Fourth Dimension of Life

*"For God so loved the world, that He gave
His only begotten Son, that whosoever
believeth in him should not perish,
but have everlasting life."*

- Jesus Christ, The Book of St. John

Introduction

It is by the metaphysical nature of the universe as outlined in the previous four chapters that spiritual beings can exist only within the fourth dimension of the collective forces of the universal domain. The only alternative is individual or disintegrated forces which are merely singular characteristics of the individual laws of science and nature, and therefore possess no spiritual content. Spiritual beings are instead composed of highly integrated forces carved from the OWS, and which reside only within the fourth dimension of the esoteric winds of universal change. This does not infer that there is not a spiritual content to the lower forms or dimensions of life, but only that there are quantum differences between each of these various levels of life. It seems that one of the more novel discrepancies of our human perspective of our self and of our surroundings, is our inability to clearly dissociate the feelings and meanings of our self from the other forms of life, within our surroundings. I have previously tried to enhance this process of discrimination by describing molecular life as robots or machines, and trying to dissuade the perception of spiritual life. However, this does not mean that we do not share some of our own characteristics with these lower forms of life.

For instance, it is obviously apparent when you see an animal suffer pain, or intuitively evident when you see it become lonely from the loss of its master, that we do share many common characteristics besides just our simple existence of being. So, it is not the emotional dimension of our human behavior, which describes our quantum differences, instead it, is our verbal, intellectual and conscious dimensions that describes those differences. Especially when realizing that those intellectual characteristics are highly integrated into the feelings, sensations, and emotions of our own self-awareness and of our own self being. Naively, we classify life by its physical form and then interpret its mental variations. From a physical perspective this makes sense; however, from a spiritual perspective we should classify life first by its mental form, and then subsequently interpret its physical variations. It is therefore proposed that life be classified into four distinct groups representing the four dimensions of being within life.

> One Dimensional Life (Existence) - What is the earth but a flower in bloom?
>
> Two Dimensional Life (Behavior) - What are the animals, but the instincts of motion?
>
> Three Dimensional Life (Language) - What is a dolphin, but an angel of the sea?
>
> Four Dimensional Life (Spirit) - What is a spirit, but the essence of you and me?

Existentialism is then indeed appropriate for the understanding of the materialistic aspects of life, whether we are talking about the existence of atoms, the earth, or the universe, or whether we are talking about the existence of a flower, or the body of an animal or a man. Behaviorism is also appropriate for understanding the motivational and instinctual aspects of life, since it is indeed our environment, which spurs and prods us along into the actions of being. Also, language is appropriate for understanding the intellectual aspects of life, since it is indeed the essence of that intellect. However, none of these endeavors are sufficient for the understanding of the spiritual aspect of life, for it is instead the holistic integration of our combined intellectual, behavioral, and existential dimensions of being.

It is then this highly individuated process of holistic integration, which represents the spirit of each individual living and growing within our societies. Likewise, this same integrative process also applies to the collective political, religious, and social groups functioning within each of our societies, reflecting upon the true nature of that group or society. Ultimately, it can also be applied to our entire world society, reflecting upon the true nature of our collective human race. The spirit, which develops in each of these cases can occur in two ways; that is, based upon absolute truths or limited truths. However, since truth by definition can only be absolute, anything less is a mere approximation of the truth, and therefore is a mistruth, or potentially even worse, a conscious or an unconscious lie.

This reasoning agrees with the theorem that the whole is greater than the sum of its parts. That is, as the collective man ascends to higher and higher levels of understanding, he also ascends closer and closer to the absolute truth, since that is only one of the two ways that each succeeding whole can be greater than the previous or lesser whole. However, there is a contradiction that occurs when the base knowledge that the higher levels are built upon is false or incorrect. Then he actually descends away from the absolute truth, eventually attaining an absolute lie, for this is the only other way that the whole can be greater than the sum of its parts. It is then by definition that we are each individually, as well as collectively, on a course towards good or evil, and it is the direction of that course which represents the spirit at work within us.

The Philosophy of Religion

Many of today's religions, including mystical far eastern religions as well as ancient tribal religions, have recognized the existence of these greater spirits within us, and some have even recognized them to exist outside of us. On the other hand, many other religions ask how we can be sure these spirits exist at all, and suggest they are merely feelings or concepts within our minds. Adding confusion to this controversy are many contemporary theologians and philosophers who refer to God as though God Himself is merely a concept, especially when realizing that any expressed ideology of God by its own nature can only be presented as a concept. This reasoning seems to infer that the highest realization for the identity of God can only be found through a highly integrated and intellectually devised concept.

For instance, a biological scientist may try to describe a human being as a cellular mass of microorganisms arranged into a body of flesh and bones; the bioengineer as a chemical-mechanical robotic machine; or the psychologist as a socially motivated behavioral animal. However, in fact, these abstract concepts merely represent a part of the collective self-knowledge of one's own self-being, for I am instead at any moment simply and holistically me. Likewise, through transcendent images as presented in Chapter One, and philosophical reasoning as presented in Chapters Two and Three, it is possible to develop a highly accurate conceptual awareness of the supernatural entity we think of as God. Just as the cause-and-effect relationships of our nerve impulses causing our muscles to contract, does not preclude the existence of our own higher level of consciousness controlling those very same nerve impulses. Likewise, our understanding of climatic or geological cause-and-effect relationships does not preclude the existence of a higher force controlling them.

This is not meant to infer the doctrine of pantheism, either. For I am not proposing that the individual forces are reflective of any corresponding supernatural deity, but only that they, as well as all of the forces within the supernatural energy continuum of the universe, eventually fall within the jurisdiction of a supremely holistic integrative process. For example, each of the various weather changes occurring on the surface of the earth can be individually described and retrospectively analyzed. However, they still function as a single whole with each individual change in our weather affecting each of the other potential changes to our weather, therefore acting together in a single integrative process. Likewise, this same integrated whole also becomes part of an even greater whole; and therefore, any single cause-and-effect relationship cannot preclude the existence of this greater whole.

Philosophy by its very nature constantly strives to group or to unite the lesser forces of both nature and man into more highly integrated concepts; for example, those social relationships described by the words justice, fairness, or equality. Each of these words describes a highly integrated word structure reflecting the nature of that spirit within us. Accordingly, just as the words describing our human nature can be organized, so also can the words describing earthly nature, or what is more commonly called mother nature, be organized. Furthermore, it is proposed that when these words are organized into the most highly integrated structure possible, they will become a part of a single supremely integrated word, called God. However, for this to be true, the integrative process must also combine and unite human nature with earthly nature, since man is a part of our physical earth. Therefore it is proposed that our physical world represents the extension of the manifested body of God from Heaven to Earth, that man represents the extension of the manifested intellect of God from Heaven on Earth, and that the Earth's lesser life forms represent the life support systems for the preservation of that intellect.

This proposal therefore represents the essence of the heart of the controversy between competing theories of evolution and creation. However, as I indicated earlier, I believe that within the honest remarks of honorable men can be found the essence of all truth, and therefore I accept them both as a part of the truth. For instance, there is much detailed information available today supporting evolution, while at the same time there are sincere convictions within the religious community of the knowledge of a supreme God. I suggest that these two perspectives are not as far apart as it seems. First of all, God does not perform magic nor is He magic, for that area of expertise belongs to the spirit of deception. He is instead a real spirit which lives within the body of the universe and is divinely manifested within the hearts and the minds of man. Although He is invisible to our carnal senses, He is just as real as we are, and instead of magic, performs miracles. The best definition that I have heard for a miracle is simply the right thing happening at the right time. In each and every instance, there must be an equally real process, either natural or supernatural, by which He accomplishes that miracle. Just as we move our hands to create our works, He moves mountains to create our lands. Creation comes from the creator, and evolution comes from the passing of time. The creator uses time just as we do to create His works.

Other examples supporting the theory of an intellectual creator are the highly sophisticated mechanisms functioning within animals and man. For example, as indicated earlier, some animals change color to protect themselves from their predators. But how does the animal know that his particular predator even sees in color, since color is a subjective phenomenon custom-tailored to the apparatus of the other's mind? Similarly, the complexity of our reflexes occurring independently of our conscious intellect and solely within our spinal cord implies a higher creative and transcendental power greater than our own conscious or unconscious intellect. Just as I am different from any concept that anyone may develop to describe me, God is also separate and different from any concept that may be developed to describe Him. He is, and becomes, the greatest manifestation of the perceptual and conceptual feeling arising from the phrase "I am."

Therefore, our collective knowledge of the individual forces of science and nature is not merely an abstract conceptual awareness of the world that surrounds us, but instead a part of the self-knowledge of the being of God Who is at any moment simply and holistically, Him. The personal feeling of His own self-being is a unique perspective of which only He can be directly aware. Accordingly, we can only truly relate to God's circumstantial feeling of being by first sharing equivalent experiential feelings within our own being. Therefore, whereas any concept of God exists solely within our minds, the person of God exists independently as a self-perceiving Being, and possesses His own self-identity supernaturally within the collective universal domain.

God and the Trinity

It is therefore by the metaphysical nature of the universe, or in other words, by the struggling of divine necessity that a species must develop, comprised of a similar four-dimensional nature to that of the spirit of the universe. That is, man becomes the incarnation of the collective intellect of God. Therefore, just as we are able to describe and to organize the words reflective of our own human psyche, God should similarly be able to organize the words reflective of His own psyche. We therefore add to the earlier descriptions for the intellect of God, the further human characterizations of the conscious self and the unconscious spirit.

God the Father becomes the conscious self of the being of the universe and the creator through His laws of absolute nature, and is incarnate within the collective minds of men as the law of the known. Accordingly, God the Holy Spirit is the unconscious spirit of that same living universe and reigns as the spirit of truth and the collective law of the unknown. Furthermore, it is the conscious intellect of God, through our own self-knowledge of His existence that adds self-identity to Himself, thereby establishing Him as a self-perceiving being with His own attributes of knowledge, understanding, and wisdom. It is further proposed that the story of Adam and Eve symbolizes the birth of His own Conscious Awareness into the self-identity of His own Self-Being. God the Father and God the Holy Spirit are one in the same, just as man is a part of that same. Man is therefore a part of God as an instrument of God, and God becomes a part of man as an extension of His own Being. God created man so that he could more fully actualize himself through us, just as we can more fully actualize ourselves through Him. He has always existed and through us only manifests that existence. We are the children of God: the temple of the Father, the essence of the Son, and Spirit of the Holy Ghost.

I offer one more piece of evidence in support of a self-perceiving, conscious God. That is, the precise timing of the many prophesies of both Judaism and Christianity. There is no other reasonable explanation for major religious historical events to occur in nearly exact multiples of 40-year, 100-year, or 1000-year increments. If the spirit of the universe were only an unconscious spirit, events would not unfold by this definite, prescribed time schedule. We sometimes get lulled into disbelief because of God's patience, for one day is to God as 1000 years is to us; but we must remember that it is exactly and precisely 1000 years. Remembering that an organized whole is always greater than the sum of its parts, and that we are the part and not the whole. It is then by definition alone that we can neither philosophically nor intellectually ever totally discover God, but can only theorize about His physical, psychological and spiritual attributes. On the other hand, the theorem requiring an equivalent discernible cause for each discernible effect requires that there be logical and rational understandings for the complexity of forces at work within our various cultures, and that they must also be discernible both on an individual and on a collective level.

The resulting paradox of these two theorems requires that we must first understand our cultural and philosophical selves before we can truly comprehend the personhood of God, while at the same time it is only through God that we can accomplish this task. Therefore, it is necessary for God to periodically intervene within the affairs of man in order to reveal both His existence and His truths to us, and thereby at the same time to establish a personal relationship with us. This is accomplished on an individual level through prayer and on the collective level through the prophecies of His prophets. The human race is therefore set on a course towards self-God realization, which we are still completing today. This process applies not only to our collective conscious intellect, but also to our individual unconscious intellect. This process must eventually include the knowledge of all of the various political, religious, and social forces within the cultures of our collective human race, thereby representing the completed manifestation of the conscious being of God within the entire human race. Therefore, all religions must eventually be united under one single banner of absolute truth, since there is only one God and only one absolute truth.

To complete this process, we must remember that there are actually two spirits living within this earthly kingdom: the spirit of truth and the spirit of evil. Likewise, there are two conscious selves, God the Father, and Satan. This becomes doubly evident when remembering that in the last chapter there were two halves to the Organized Word Structure, one for good words and the other for bad words. Therefore, just as the collective consciousness of truth becomes incarnate in man as God the Father, the collective consciousness of evil becomes incarnate in man as Satan. However, in the case of evil, there is no effective equivalent to the Holy Spirit, since evil is the spirit of destruction and hence, disintegration. Therefore, Satan's only hold on the earth is the limited integration by intentional deception of our instinctual behavior into his limited conscious intellect. The only other place that Satan exists is within the chaos of the underworld. In contrast, God the Father lives eternally within the substance of the heavens and by His own schedule will eventually manifest Himself within our collective human race.

Throughout Chapters One and Two, it was implied that since the images we perceive exist solely within our minds, almost anything is possible outside of our minds. This seemingly infinite range of possibilities now becomes severely limited by the premise that only those supernatural forces, which have the capability of actually manifesting themselves in meaningful and productive ways, really exist. This disallows spurious occurrences without justifiable continuity as simple accidents of chance, and instead defines only those highly integrated and evolved spiritual forces. It is therefore only the individual force of random chance that Satan can use in his fight against the Holy Spirit. Upon the face of this earth Satan has many faces, which can be described by words like atheism, agnosticism, communism, astrology, fascism, and war. He also can be seen on the more personal level as deceit, vindictiveness, revenge, or hate. Through these deceptive and destructive forces he has managed to infiltrate many of our religious, social and governmental institutions, and much of our human race.

There are then today many examples of social, religious, and political forces, which have arisen within the cultures of man and are, by their very own existence, real spiritual forces living within the collective anatomy of man. However, there is only one of these forces, which by its own definition is the single and most powerful force of the universal world. As this war of the spirits rages within the minds and cultures of humanity, it is this one spirit which by our own organized language can only be called the Holy Spirit; and which can, will, and must reign. For only when the Holy Spirit completely and totally manifests itself will the paradox finally be shattered and the world be at peace with itself and with God. This is not an easy task, either, because of the variety of our various cultural and religious differences creating a tremendous potential for jealousy, animosity, hatred, and vindictiveness, to proliferate.

The existence of a single God of the universe at first seems to contradict the existence of more than one religion, for either God is not capable of totally manifesting Himself, or He has multiple and divergent personalities. I therefore propose that none of today's religions are totally correct, but instead the real truth exists only within a highly integrative process of the best attributes of each religion. The solution to this proposition can only be found by first evaluating the evolution of each religion, which can only be accomplished when realizing that you judge the founder to determine the validity of the religion, and the followers to determine the effectiveness of the religion.

The Religions of Man

From this perspective it is proposed that six of the seven major contemporary religions represent the best possible mental integration of each of the six interconnected energy flow lines within the mind. For example, the ancient Chinese religions represent the predominant energy flow lines of understanding (Confucianism) and its complementary opposite of being (Taoism). The ancient Indian religions represent the predominant energy flow lines of deciding (Hinduism) and its complementary opposite of learning (Buddhism). And finally, the Middle East religions represent the predominant energy flow lines of thinking (Judaism) and its complementary opposite of knowing (Islam).

Each of these religions represents the cultural evolution of the predominant psychological types of their individual peoples based upon the individual knowledge and beliefs of their original founders. In the cases of Buddha, Lao Tzu (Taoism), and K'ung Tzu (Confucius), no claims were ever made by any of them as to their individual divinity; therefore, their corresponding religions must be accepted as great philosophies which are today only being misapplied as religions. In the case of Mohammed, his claim is to be a prophet of God, and therefore Islam is a great cultural religion. Likewise, many of the religions within Hinduism are led by gurus or prophets, and are likewise great cultural religions. In contrast, Judaism claims to be chosen personally by God through which He would reveal Himself to humanity. They along with other religions seem to have added the mistaken impression that this precludes other religions from being valid, or likewise elevates them above other people. However, each cultural religion was probably chosen for their own individual unique task, not because of the abundance of their righteous attributes but in spite of their need for those attributes. No matter how holistic religions are, each contains some mistakes and some errors.

There is one additional technique for organizing human nature, which sheds a little more light on the relevance of these basic religions, and that technique is known as the stages of life. The six energy flow lines and corresponding parameters can be listed by the order of the growth of our intellects, as shown in Table 3-1a in Chapter Three and as listed on the following page.

Dynamic Mental Processes	Predominant Static Memories	Religion	Energy Flow Lines
Being	Objective Instincts	Taoism	(10-17)
Learning	Subjective Concepts	Buddhism	(20-27)
Knowing	Conceptual Holism	Islam	(30-37)
Understanding	Perceptual Logic	Confucianism	(40-47)
Thinking	Logical Objectives	Judaism	(50-57)
Deciding	Rational Holism	Hinduism	(60-67)

It now becomes evident why God truly chose Abraham and the Jewish People to reveal Himself to human beings. That is that only the fifth psychological type of logical thinking, has the potential to generate the cultural and genetic instincts necessary to conclusively discover God. However, this does not imply that their religion is divine or perfect, since they, along with all of today's major religions, possess considerable negative cultural traits. Although many of today's religious sects claim to be founded on or based upon these basic fundamental religions, some have been almost completely lost to the forces of evil, others only partially lost, and still others instead mistakenly derived from the evil of satanic lies and deceptive tricks.

Christianity

As I indicated in Chapter Three when discussing psychological types, there is also a seventh category integrating all six functions above and that is holistic behavior. It can only be revealed by God and can further only be achieved by surrendering ourselves to God. It was, in fact, God Himself who in the body of His Son had to give His life on the cross "to save the lost from the tribe of David". And it was only Christ, Who came both revealing Himself and His truths as God and is today widely accepted by many to be God. It is difficult for me to imagine a God, which needed to intervene personally in the affairs of humanity more than once to accomplish His plan. Also, if He did, each time His personality, as a signature on a check, would always be unmistakably and identically the same. Therefore, Christ was not just another prophet of God but instead a perfect prophet, which can only mean that He, was God. Christ was the essence of the conscious Father and the being of the unconscious spirit. This should create great humility for each of us Christians since it only took philosophers and prophets to get the attention of the rest of the world, but it took the life of God's Son Himself to save us. There was then a dual purpose to His journey, and that was to reveal his true self to us while establishing a personal relationship with each of us.

Many are confused and unable to recognize what is meant by a personal relationship with the conscious being of a spirit, for they are only aware of their somewhat limited relationships with their fellow man. However, just as the more primitive aspects of our human relationships can be shared with life forms lesser than we, our nobler and more virtuous aspects can also be shared with spiritual life forms greater than ourselves. This, in fact, will be one of the greatest challenges of the Far Eastern religions, since they must learn to incorporate this personal relationship with God the Father into their predominantly spirit oriented religions and philosophies. Just as our fellow Christians are our brothers in Christ, the other major religions will become our cousins with Christ; and therefore, they must shed their dogmatic beliefs and principles, and instead, incorporate the teachings of Christ into their cultural relationship with God. Likewise, Christians must shed their own personal dogmas and recapture the true Spirit of Christ within their own hearts, for it is only through the lifelong development of personal integrity and character that we can hope to achieve the realization of His presence within us.

This process is not an easy process either, as it most usually requires much personal effort and sacrifice. First, we must be called as he gives to each of us the choice to follow Him. Although He intervenes in all lives, it is only through the choice of believing in His son, that we are guaranteed the promise of everlasting life. It is at this point that many can no longer follow the rationale of my logic. That is because this portion is not rooted in logic, but instead is based upon my personal relationship with the God manifested within me. You, too, must develop this relationship for God to be real within you. He has given to us a guide to help us along our path within the historical writings of the Bible. The destiny of the Bible was firmly established by the personal intercessions of God the Father with His chosen people, and its writers divinely inspired by His Holy Spirit. Although its translations and interpretations are only mostly true, its essence is absolute truth.

Adopting the teachings of Christ and the truths of the Bible as one's own beliefs does not make a person whole. Instead, it only writes God's laws into our minds and then in the uncomplimentary form of the self - righteous or superego, whereas God said He would write his laws into our hearts. The irony of this new Christian life is the intermingling of the memories of our past mistakes with the principles and philosophies of our new beliefs. We continue hurting both others and ourselves as we try to sort out our problems in search of the truth. One of our greatest difficulties is integrating our new beliefs with our past mistakes.

Generally, Christians at first do a fairly good job of following their new beliefs; however, the continued suppression of unwanted desires and needs eventually creates psychological, as well as physical ill-health. These maladies are actually the reflections of our past sins and ironically a potential for true spiritual healings. Whereas the conscious act of suppression creates a hypocritical or a lukewarm Christian, the unconscious act of letting-go after suppression is a method for writing God's truths into our hearts, through his divine ordering of the personal events of our lives. It should be noted that I am not proposing that sin is a viable method for growing and becoming, since it was an unconscious act of letting go and not a conscious act. Accordingly, it was not a conscious decision to sin but an unconscious act of surrender to sin, and an opportunity to learn right from wrong. This is what separates Christianity from the other religions of man. For instance, some of the Far Eastern religions of understanding and enlightenment purport a middle-of-the-road as the best way for advantageously living within the perplexities of this world; however, it is proposed that misunderstanding and delusion are more descriptive words for this philosophical pretext. Christianity instead demands the difficult road of self-sacrifice, as the only way for becoming within the perplexities of this world. Moreover, whereas the Far Eastern religions promise only the hopeless repetition of reincarnation, Christianity promises the personal reward of eternal life.

We came from the dust in the ground, by what forces we know not, and yet we believe that we are the world. Instead, we are the children of the world. We say that God is love, but yet we know not how to love. Instead, God loves, and yet we still do not know love. We say that we are like God, and yet we know not what God is like. We say that God is dead, yet we know not the secrets of life or death. Instead, we are like God, and must choose between life and death. We believe in our own Gods, yet we know not the source of our own beliefs.

As for my life, it has been a unique combination of both successes and failures. I grew up in the Christian Church, but gradually drifted away from those religious teachings during my teenage years. It was only during my twenties that I achieved some semblance of self aware-ness and a positive self-image. Unfortunately, it was accomplished by excelling at some of the less virtuous aspects of our being. There was then an uncommon week when I realized the stupidity of my dishon-esty, the existence of another world, and the belief in Jesus Christ. I could not absorb so many changes at one time, as I collapsed from the weight of my past mistakes. However, with my newly found friends of honesty and wholeness, I continued on with the process of building a soul within the body of my life. I have since failed many times and still have much growing ahead of me. However, my successes seem to in-variably develop when I am walking my closest to the truths of God; and likewise, my failures develop when I stray from those truths. How-ever, I know of no other way to grow or to become, except to do my best, and then to accept God's forgiveness.

I did not ask God to be born nor has the human race accepted its birth. I did not ask for the body I was given, nor has the human race accepted the body it was given. I did not ask for the teachers who taught me knowledge, nor does the human race comprehend its teach-ers. I did not ask for my family who taught me to love, nor does the human race love its family. I did not ask for my friends who taught me respect, nor does the human race respect its friends. I inflate my self-worth until I believe that my destiny is my own; and the human race, too, believes more in itself than to place worth on its destiny.

Whether heaven is on earth or high above the earth, and whether we arise now or generations from now, within our grasp today is the poten-tial for every person to live at a standard of living far above anyone's physical or psychological needs. Christ said that he came so that we could live more abundantly; however, he did not say extravagantly, wastefully, or disrespectfully. I personally believe God fully intends to extend His kingdom from Heaven onto Earth. And our only choice is to accept his eternal truths or through His judgment to perish from the Earth.

In the name of His Son, he listens to and answers prayers; however, sometimes with an emphatic no. Your life may be rewarding or distressing, exciting or depressing, gliding or struggling. He cares, He loves, He decides, and He judges. He creates, He marvels, He prophesies and He fulfills. His greatest unfulfilled prophecies are the great judgment of the tribulation and His Second Coming. Only when these two prophecies are fulfilled will the world finally know unquestionably an unequivocally that God is real.

"Hear ye therefore the parable of the sower.

He that soweth the good seed is the son of man; the field is the world; the good seed are the children of the kingdom; but the tares are the children of the wicked one;

The enemy that soweth them is the devil; the harvest is the end of the world, and the reapers are the angels.

As therefore the tares are gathered and burned in the fire; so shall it be in the end of this world.

The son of man shall send forth his angels, and they shall gather out of his kingdom all things that offend, and them which do iniquity;

And shall cast them into a furnace of fire."

Jesus Christ - The Book of St. Matthew

Chapter Six

God's Love

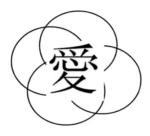

"Love knows not its own depth,
until the hour of separation."

- Kahlil Gibran

It is now thirty-two years since the death of my son in 1984, at the tender age of five and one-half years old. Only now do I begin to truly understand and to appreciate the depth of his and our individual and collective loss. The birthdays, the family vacations, religious holidays, his proms and his graduations, the sanctity of his marriage, the in-laws, the grandchildren that never were born and the unfathomable loss of all of these experiences. There is not a day that I do not think of him and his innocence, his beautiful smile, his intelligence and his wonderful personality. When he passed on, each of us experienced an avalanche of emotions and a complete change in our understanding of life and our personal priorities. When you have a child with a birth defect, you feel a special responsibility to care, love, teach, and provide for them in any way and in every way that you possibly can. A genuine and caring love grows beyond comprehension and with a special and eternal bond.

The loss of my son left me with an empty soul and a hole in the middle of my heart that you could drive a Mack truck through. I believed in God and was a Christian at the time, and therefore was taken completely by shock and surprise when he died. As Kahlil Gibran wrote in his book *The Prophet,* love knows not its own depth, until the hour of separation. Besides the immediacy of disbelief, anger and fear, I also felt a complete loss of purpose and struggled to find meaning in life. The agony and the despair seemed insurmountable and took years to work through. Writing this book has been part of that therapy in order to add some meaning and value to my life. It is a way to make up for my failures as a father, as maybe I should have gone to another doctor, another hospital or another something. The what if's menaced my life for years. These emotions required a complete internal reassessment in order to cope with the memories of his lost love. That must be how God feels about us, his children on Earth, for each and every one of us is born with character defects, if not physical defects. It is only through the grace of His help, the mercy of His guidance and the wisdom of His understanding that can we grow through our problems and our inadequacies, and thereby become the best of what we were meant to be. God loves all of us and wants us all to prosper. His love for us is probably one of the more misunderstood emotions of our human nature. God speaks of perfect love, while we speak of falling in love.

There are many different kinds of love, as well as depths of love. However, if we separate kinds of love from depths of love, we can begin to understand this seemingly uncontrollable urge. For instance, pretend love or puppy love is a projection of the fantasy of love upon another person. Physical love or sexual love is the association of a sex object, a body or a thing, with the feeling of self-gratification. This love is developed through our sexual escapades. Falling in love, or ideal love, is an illusion created by the mind. We idealize the perfect love within our mind, and then connect fantasies of self-gratification with these imaginations. When two people meet who respectively fit each other's ideals, they each play out their own self-induced fantasy role. This is coupled with a height of physical warmth and gratification, which perpetuates the attraction as a giant wave rolling in on a rocky beach. However, just as the wave is torn apart by the rocks on the beach, we, too, open our eyes and see through our ideal, and our love dissipates from our minds. We then have the choice of really loving.

Perfect love, or God's love, is then the voluntary choice of sacrificing one's own needs, desires, and wants for the betterment of another. This extraordinarily emotional aspect of God's love can be easily seen in the depth of love that mothers have for their children. However, love does not only include self sacrifice, but also includes fatherly love through exemplary acts of caring, continuity and self discipline. Only those people who have truly loved and lost that love, can begin to know the true essence of God's love. It is the unselfish choice of total commitment to the health and welfare of another person, and the deep sense of incomprehensible satisfaction, as the other person grows and becomes. God's love cannot be institutionalized, as some people for selfish reasons profess, since love can only be love when it is one's own individual choice without any outside persuasion or coercion.

When we share God's love with our neighbors, it is respect. When we share God's love with our friends, it is concern. When we share God's love with our parents, it is honor. When we share God's love with our children, it is pure love. And when we share God's love with a mate it is perfect love. All happiness is rooted in our human relationships whether at home, at work, or at play; and it is the sharing of our mutual goals, values, and ideals which generates our mutual love and its greater understanding. The following poem was written several weeks after the death of my son, and captures the many feelings and emotions, and the turmoil of my newly found circumstances; and hopefully captures both the lost love that I had and still have to this day for my son, and the deep abiding love and respect that I have for God.

Singing a
Song of Love

Birth and Love, Death and Love
Does anyone understand?
Human joy and happiness,
And then the fears of man.

The birth of a being,
God's most wonderful event.
Made from human bodies,
And from God the soul is sent.

Born to have emotions,
So that we can be like Him.
Hear to learn how to love,
And to be with Him again.

Feeling sorry for ourselves,
The pity of our soul.
Our burdens are so heavy;
We've lost our strength to go.

And sadness without hope,
Is the feeling of despair.
What's lost is gone forever;
What's left, love must repair.

And when we look at others,
And see them in disgust.
It's reflections of ourselves,
We really do not trust.

And jealousy and envy,
Are resentment of our soul;
Someone else forgot to love us,
Unfulfilled as we grew old.

And anger is a promise,
To make right a past wrong.
And rage is anger on the loose,
Singing loud our hurting song.

And the pain that's in our mind,
Is just to let us know,
That we still have so much to learn,
And still a ways to go.

Yet, our stubbornness abounds!
A commitment to ourselves,
That we are each much greater,
Than anybody else.

And from this lack of understanding,
Come the fears within our heart.
His love and knowledge, unaware,
Throughout our lives, we start.

What are these things that we feel?
A purpose, we must know.
They're learned by us as we grow,
To show the hurt within our soul.

Born to think about ourselves,
So that we can be like Him.
Hear to learn, to understand,
And to be with Him again.

Giving empty compliments,
Is a desire for support.
We feel so insecure inside,
And sell ourselves so short.

And manipulating others,
Is making life a game.
It's abusing God's knowledge
Without feeling any shame.

And to justify our only self,
We make naive decisions.
Not aware of whom we are,
Or of our limitations.

And then we give excuses,
Defending what we do.
Thinking those around us,
Will believe that they are true.

Pretending to believe in God,
A decision of the mind.
Not really thinking He is there,
But needing help of some kind.

Or believing not in anything
It makes no sense at all.
Marching on to nowhere,
Thinking we are big and tall.

Or believing in the worst,
The evil in our mind.
Thinking that bad is good,
And hurting all we find.

Thinking bad or thinking good,
He gave to us the choice.
Search the limits of your mind,
Until you hear His voice.

What are these things that we think?
A purpose we must find.
To learn to understand ourselves,
And the knowledge of our mind.

Born to resolve the differences
So that we can be like Him.
Hear to learn, to love ourselves,
And to be with Him again.

Half of us is reason,
The other half is love.
A marriage of two strangers,
Made in Heaven up above.

Knowing we should care and share,
The feeling of deceit.
Feeling that "I really care,"
And thinking of deceit.

Knowing we should love each other.
The feeling that we hate.
Feeling that "I love you, darling,"
And thinking about hate.

Feeling reasons in our heart,
And thinking wrong from right.
At times it's so confusing;
Why can't we see the light?

Will we ever understand
The purpose of this all?
The challenge that He gave to us,
To learn to live, to love us all.

Born to live together,
So that we can be like Him.
Hear to learn, to love each other,
And to be with Him again.

Cooperation with each other,
His chance to teach us from above.
Look beyond misunderstandings;
Base it on respect and love.

And when we care for others
And give freely of ourselves,
Time will build a friendship
That will outlast time itself.

A marriage of two persons,
Is a sharing of two souls.
We'll share the good part and the bad,
And help each other grow.

And giving love to another,
He gave to us the choice.
It's the total feeling of all feelings,
And selfless sacrifice.

Do you understand these things?
Do you feel them in your heart?
A love so special, just for us,
God's love that's in His heart.

Made by God to help each other,
Made to be like Him.
Hear to learn of His Church,
And to be with Him again.

The building of His Church,
His sacrifice is done.
He loved and cared for us to much,
That He gave His only Son.

They say the Church has hypocrites.
And how else can it be?
We all are imperfect souls,
Until the day we leave.

Our Baptism is a Holy Union,
By man and God, for all to see.
The Holy Spirit will guide us,
Down life's road through eternity.

God's Son, Himself, and the Holy Spirit,
Is His Holy Trinity.
The Body, His Soul, and the Spirit of Love,
All in one, for us all to see.

What is the reason for His Church?
Its purpose we should know.
To teach to us the knowledge,
Of God's Eternal Soul.

Made by God to be His friend,
Made to be like Him.
Hear to learn of His grace,
And to be with Him again.

Belief in God, Faith in God,
Just a step away.
The fulfillment of His promise,
Given freely every day.

We start by first believing,
That He is really there;
Then His Holy Spirit enters us,
Teaching us to care.

He is a God of Mercy.
His tools are love and wisdom.
He never uses punishment,
To teach us of His Kingdom.

He permits some things to happen,
That we can't comprehend.
But, be assured, if it's allowed,
It benefits His children.

What is the reason for His grace?
A purpose we should know.
To give us each some space and time,
So together we can grow.

Made by God to understand,
Made to be like Him.
Hear to learn how to live,
And to be with Him again.

We all will feel great sorrow,
For it teaches wrong from right.
And it's the only way to travel,
From great joy to great delight.

The intentions of our mind,
Only God and the intender know,
Judge not of life's happenings,
Unless you are one of those.

And trust is a commitment
To follow someone else.
Be sure that he who leads,
Walks with God, not by himself.

Mix caution with ambition;
It's the being of your soul,
Needing praise and recognition,
And help to reach your goal.

And showing pride in those you love,
Your hopes for all to see.
It's striving for your excellence,
Or what you wish to be.

But beware of foolish pride,
Reversing wrong and right.
You need to show your love, but fail,
To keep what's good in sight.

And confidence takes years to build,
It's what you know and understand.
When combined with faith in God,
It's courage, walking hand in hand.

And show concern for those you meet,
Search deep inside your soul.
It's the sharing of your total hurt,
And respect for those you know.

Have you gained the knowledge?
Its purpose must you know.
That God's love is the only way,
To become a perfect soul.

Made by God to share His love,
Made to be like Him.
Hear to learn how to see,
And to be with Him again.

Like those times of your life,
When you violate your own rule,
You display it on your face,
And no one can you fool.

Or your nervous habits,
Such childlike things to see.
Proclamations made to all,
Of your inadequacy.

Or friendly personalities,
It's liking those you see.
It's the very best in them,
Or what you wish to be.

Or the face of happiness,
Life's gift for a good deed.
Reflections of your inner soul,
The meeting of your need.

Or silence of your heart and mind,
When everything is calm;
A glimmer of His inner peace,
While He holds you in His palm.

Or when you dream, another,
A piece of Heaven sent.
A time to ponder and reflect,
And a time to be content.

So seek to know within
Your heart, your soul, your mind.
The act of love, the choice,
The gift of love, to find.

Use this knowledge with understanding,
And learn to love thyself.
Love thy neighbor and all God's children,
But love Thy God, above all else.

If you understand these things,
If you feel them in your heart,
Then you have a love so special;
His love is in your heart.

The death of a body,
The freedom of a soul,
A chance to be in Heaven,
If you could only know.

Birth and love, Death and love
Yet do you understand?
God's genuine concern,
and Eternal joy for man.

Chapter Seven

In Search of the Truth

*"For those who believe in God, no
explanation is necessary; and for those
who do not believe in God, no explanation
satisfies."*

Unknown

The evolution of science within the cultures of human kind is a living testament to the earnest desire within human beings to reach out and to grasp the real and absolute truth. It has been said that when scientists finally achieve their innate purpose and epoch goal of climbing that vast and gargantuan mountain of eternal truth, they will find the sages, the philosophers, the gurus and the poets already there, each anxiously awaiting for the scientist's arrival. With great tribute and respect, I have collected quotes and sayings from selected authors whom in their search for their own truth, helped to inspire me to continue on my path of finding my part of the real and absolute truth.

A Personal Commentary – W R Hohenberger

A Growing & Expanding Earth

"The Earth is Expanding and We Don't Know Why"

Geological evidence of the fit of the continents against one another in the distant past, together with patterns of ocean floor spreading, show that the earth must have been much smaller 200 million years ago.

Hugh Owen - *The New Scientist* (November 12, 1984)

The concept of an expanding earth has been a controversial issue because expansion does not seem to offer most earth scientists answers to pressing global problems of geology as they are conceived today. The expansion hypothesis generates strong opinions and sometimes heated discussions; but my paper was indeed intended to be serious.

J. Steiner - Geology Forum (June, 1978)

More than a century has passed since the promulgation of the first ideas on the possible expansion of the earth during the geologic past; ... however, even recently, such views, stated from time to time by individual scientists, have not attracted serious attention from large groups of investigators. . . . Recently, the position has changed significantly; the increasing amount of scientific publications in the Soviet and foreign literature . . . and the conduct of scientific conferences (the international symposium on the expansion of the earth organized by the University of Sydney, February, 1981) and the conference... (organized by the Geologic Faculty, Moscow University, and MOEP in November, 1981), serve as indicators of the increasing interest ... by a greater and greater number of natural scientists.

YeYe Milanousky -
International Geology Review (June, 1983)

Pangaea, Reconstructed on a globe of present Earth, occupies a little more than a hemisphere . . . So that the Pacific, far from reducing to zero, has greatly increased in area. This is impossible except on an expanding earth.

S. Warren Carey, University of Tasmania
The Expanding Earth Symposium, University of Sydney, 1981

Recent Updates for a Growing Earth based on Expansion Tectonics vs. Plate Tectonics

One of the most profound statements the late Professor Sam Warren Carey (Emeritus Professor of Geology from the University of Tasmania) said to me when I first started researching Expansion Tectonics was: If 50 million believe in a fallacy it is still a fallacy.

Dr. James Maxlow, Australian Geologist
www.jamesmaxlow.com

The most important outcomes of my Expansion Tectonic research to date are:
• *Modeling of continental plate assemblages has now been completed for 100% of geological Earth history, ranging from the early Archaean Era to the present day. These assemblages have demonstrated a high degree of crustal fit accuracy and, most notably, without the need to arbitrarily fragment continents or dispose of pre-existing crusts by subduction.*
• *A formula for rate of change in Earth radius has been established and modeling of physical data completed. This mathematical modeling demonstrates that Earth radius has been increasing exponentially throughout time, increasing to a current rate of 22mm/year.*
• *Ancient magnetic poles plus equator have been accurately located on all models constructed. Both poles plot as diametrically opposed north and south poles, enabling the ancient equators and climate zones to be precisely established.*
• *Geological, geographical and geophysical data have been investigated on all models. These data are shown to coincide precisely with expected polar and equatorial climatic and biotic constraints.*
• *Models have been animated in four dimensions, showing the increase in Earth radius throughout time along with global distribution of selected data sets.*

Dr. James Maxlow, Australian Geologist
www.jamesmaxlow.com

Many of my ideas may seem too extreme or too bizarre for many to believe, but that does not make them any less true. Accordingly, one of my first realizations in 1975 that led me on this odyssey of finding the absolute truth, was a growing and expanding earth. I spoke with Warren Carey in the mid 1980's about my beliefs and their metaphysical origins. Although he is considered by many to be the father of the Expanding Earth Theory, he saw no reason or need for any metaphysical cause, especially one with religious overtones. I then realized that it would take decades until irrefutable evidence was finally available, before those ideas would be scientifically accepted. However, the evidence is now in and yet the struggle continues.

Obviously, one of the greatest difficulties for even those geologists who believe, is the incomprehensibility of creating matter from nothing. However, when one realizes that energy is just as real as we are and that matter is merely a condensed form of that energy; it then only requires a mechanism as previously outlined in Chapter Four, and evidence such as the color coded sea floor age map below (0-180 million years ago), to firmly establish a viable theory for a growing and expanding earth

A Personal Commentary – W R Hohenberger

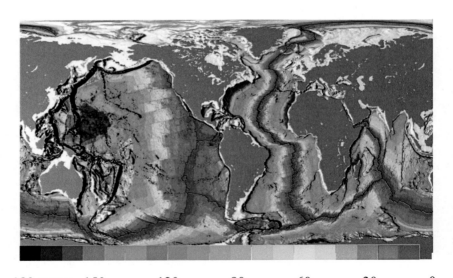

180 (MYA) 150   120   90   60   30   0

National Oceanic and Atmospheric Administration, US Dept. of Commerce, 1996

Figure 7-1 - Oceanic and Sea Floor Age Map

The Aether

Life, and all that lives, is conceived in the mist and not in the crystal. And who knows but a crystal is mist in decay?

Kahlil Gibran - *The Prophet* (1883-1931)

And before the throne was "a sea of glass like unto crystal..."
And I saw as it were a sea of glass mingled with fire.
And the building of the wall of it was jasper: And the city was pure gold, like unto clear glass.
And the street of the city was pure gold, as it were transparent glass.

St. John the Divine – *Revelation*

I am certain of nothing but the holiness of the heart's affections, the truth of imagination. What the imagination seizes as beauty must be truth....

John Keats, English Poet (1795-1821)

It is the hyper-dynamic qualities and supernatural capabilities of the aether that has not been previously or fully recognized by scientists, and that has been just outside of the grasp of their imagination and their belief structure. Granted, some physicists have somewhat dismissively discussed the possible existence of the aether; but then most just return to their own preconceived idea of reality, and moreover just continue on with their current endeavors. Kahlil Gibran nailed it by plainly naming the aether, the aetherons and the stellar air as the mist and naming matter as the crystal. Likewise, St. John the Divine clearly had a vision of his own divine revelations into the supernatural world of the mist and the crystal that lays just beyond our human perceptions. I sincerely hope that the many vivid pictures described in Chapter One along with the mathematical physical structures delineated in Chapter Four, will help those who are not aware or who do not believe, to understand that there is another world beyond our human perceived world that is just as real, if not even more real than our own human perceived world.

A Personal Commentary – W R Hohenberger

The Organized Word Structure

In the beginning was the Word, and the Word was with God, and the Word was God.

John Verse 1.1

And round about the throne were four and twenty seats: and upon the seats I saw four and twenty elders sitting, clothed in white raiment; and they had on their heads crowns of gold.

And out of the throne proceeded lightnings and thunderings and voices: and there were seven lamps of fire burning before the throne, which are the seven Spirits of God.

And before the throne there was a sea of glass like unto crystal: and in the midst of the throne, and round about the throne, were four beasts full of eyes before and behind.

And the first beast was like a lion, and the second beast like a calf, and the third beast had a face as a man, and the fourth beast was like a flying eagle.

And the four beasts had each of them six wings about him; and they were full of eyes within: and they rest not day and night, saying, Holy, holy, holy, Lord God Almighty, which was, and is, and is to come.

Revelation Verse 4.4 thru 4.8

The structure for our spoken words is the same structure that is the foundation for all things that exist. The positive attributes of our spoken word is just one form of God. The essence of the Word is God. Furthermore, the four beasts are the four corners and the six wings are the six dynamic processes within the four point diagram of the Organized Word Structure. The seven spirits of God are the seven of the eight points in the eight point diagram, excluding instincts for it is God's instinct only to be Holy. The twenty-four seats for the twenty-four elders are the twenty-four basic words in the matrix of the Organized Word Structure.

A Personal Commentary – W R Hohenberger

Truth

Science and religion are "sisters" and need each other for enlight-

ened understanding and truth. While science tries to learn more about the creation, religion tries to better understand the creator. While through science man tries to harness the forces of nature around him, through religion he tries to harness the forces of nature within him.

Dr. Werhner Von Braun, Scientist

Nor do I seek to understand that I may believe, but I believe that I may understand. For this I too believe, that unless I first believe, I shall not understand.

St. Anselm (1033-1109)

If a man begins with certainties, he shall end in doubts, but if he will be content to begin with doubts, he shall end in certainties.

Francis Bacon (1561-1626)

All men by nature desire to know.

Aristotle (384-322)

Nature has planted in our minds an insatiable longing to see the truth.

Marcus Tullios Cicero (106-43 B.C.)

Human salvation demands the divine disclosure of truths surpassing reason.

St. Thomas Aquinas (1225-1274)

All truth is a species of revelation.

Samuel Taylor Coleridge (1772-1834)

From a perspective of being as listed in Table 3-2 in Chapter Three, beliefs precede understanding. At times in the evolution of the Organized Word Structure, I lived with so many word definitions left hanging in the air, that I would lose my footing as well as my direction. This is exactly the vessel that the Kabbalah both missed and omitted in the Tree of Life. That is, when you hold that thought, you have to be holding it somewhere. Finally, our curiosity represents God's desire to know the truth through us, while revelation represents His self-realization of the truth within us. It is therefore our search for the truth within us, which represents the process of divine struggling within Him.

A Personal Commentary – W R Hohenberger

The Nature of Man

The unconscious is not just evil by nature, it is also the source of the highest good; not only dark but also light, not only bestial, semi-human, and demonic but super human, spiritual, and in the classical sense of the word, "Divine."

Carl Jung, Psychologist (1875-1961)

For to sin, indeed is human; but to persevere in sin is not human, but altogether satanic.

St. Joannes Chrysostomus (345-407)

Ignorance of good and evil is the most upsetting fact of human life.

Marcus T'ullius Cicero (106-43 B.C.)

The chief cause of human error is to be found in prejudices picked up in childhood.

Rene Descartes (1596-1650)

Understanding does not cure evil, but is a definite help, inasmuch as one can cope with comprehensible darkness.

Carl Jung, Psychologist

It is only the very wisest and the very stupidest which cannot change.

Confucius (551-479 B.C.)

The foundation of morality is to have done, once and for all, with lying.

Thomas Henry Huxley (1825-1895)

It is my sincere conviction that the completed Organized Word Structure will ultimately prove that lying is the cause of all evil, including those little white lies that abound among us. However, I am not

inferring that we should be brutally honest, but instead sincerely honest. For I also believe that honesty exists somewhere between truth and sincerity, whereas lying exists somewhere between selfishness and cruelty. Our greatest obstacle in finding the real truth is the conscious deception by those who have learned to fake honesty and sincerity. Therefore, the process of determining the truth must involve both our hearts and our minds, and then requires great skill and prudence. Even though the sincere truth may hurt both our selves and others at times, it is only because of that hurt that we are able to psychologically grow and become, through the integral processes of internal change.

A Personal Commentary – W R Hohenberger

The Body of God

And if you would know God be not therefore a solver of riddles.
Rather look about you and you shall see
Him playing with your children.
And look into space; you shall see him
Walking in the cloud, outstretching his arms
In the lightning and descending in rain.
You shall see him smiling in flowers,
Then rising and waving his hands in trees.

Kahlil Gibran - The Prophet (1883-1931)

Nature is the art of God.

Dante Alighieri (1265-1321)

Called or not called, God is present.

Carl Jung

All things were made by Him; and without Him was not anything
made that was made.

The Book of St. John (70 A.D.)

To hear God speak, we must listen to the birds singing in the trees and to the wind ruffling the leaves.

A Personal Commentary – W R Hohenberger

The Intellect of God

In the beginning was the Word and the Word was with God, and the Word was God.

The Book of St. John

The first thought of God was an angel and the first Word of God was a man.

Kahlil Gibran (1883-1931)

Conscience is God's Presence in Man.

Emanuel Swedenborg (1688-1772)

If it is true that God became man, it's also true that man became God.

Johannes Eckhard (1260-1327)

Don't oppose forces; use them. God is a verb, not a noun.

R. Buckminster Fuller (1895-1983)

The symbol is not a sign that veils something everybody knows. Such is not its significance; on the contrary, it represents an attempt to elucidate, by means of analogy, something that still belongs entirely to the domain of the unknown or something has yet to be.

Carl Jung

The Divinity of Christ

The difference between Socrates and Jesus Christ? The great conscious; the immeasurably great unconscious.

Thomas Carlyle (1795-1881)

Everyone in the world is Christ and they are all crucified.

Sherwood Anderson (1876-1941)

Miracles

The standing miracle of the visible world is little thought of, because always before us-for man himself is a greater miracle than any miracle done through his instrumentality.

St. Augustine (350-430)

The Religions of Man

I believe in the fundamental truth of all the great religions of the world. I believe that they are all God given .... I came to the conclusion long ago - that all religions were true, and also that all had some error in them.

Mohamdes Karamchand Gandhi (1869-1948)

A religion that requires persecution to sustain it is of the devil's propagation.

Hosea Ballou (1771-1852)

Truths for a new day.
1. *The oneness of mankind.*
2. *The foundation of all religion is one.*
3. *Religion must be in accord with science and nature.*

Baha"U"Llah (1817-1892)

It is the way of Tao not to act from any personal motive, to conduct affairs without feeling the trouble of them, to taste without being aware of flavor, to account the great as small, and the small as great, to recompense injury with kindness.

Lao Tzu (565 B.C.)

The Teachings of Christ

I am the way, the truth, and the life, no man cometh unto the Father, but by me.

John 14: 6

It is my sincere belief that Jesus Christ was God himself, incarnate in the body of his son. If you listen to the words that he spoke, there is a spiritual content that implies self-awareness of a greater truth than was known then or that is even known yet today.

A Personal Commentary – W R Hohenberger

And ye shall know the truth, and the truth shall set you free.

John 8:32

Self-awareness comes only from our experiential base of spoken words. It is through self-awareness that we achieve higher levels of consciousness, and it is through higher levels of consciousness that we find truth.

A Personal Commentary – W R Hohenberger

For nothing is secret which shall not be manifested; neither anything hid, that shall not be known and come abroad.

Luke 8:17

God not only has absolute knowledge of man, but also absolute knowledge of life itself. God is omniscient and possesses a depth of understanding which penetrates understanding itself

A Personal Commentary – W R Hohenberger

For by thy words thou shalt be justified, and by thy words thou shalt be condemned.

Matthew 12:37

Whereas man constantly struggles to establish absolutes with his spoken words; God, from the beginning has always known the absolute nature of each spoken word.

A Personal Commentary – W R Hohenberger

And the light shineth in the darkness; and the darkness comprehended it not.

John 1:5

As simple as it may sound to open our minds and to listen to each other, our egos and superegos absolutely refuse to let in the message. Truth is the highest level of awareness attainable by man, and cannot be found within our language or within our books - but first, within our heart, and then, within our mind.

A Personal Commentary – W R Hohenberger

Therefore, speak I to them in parables: because they seeing see not; and hearing they hear not, neither do they understand.

Matthew 13:13

If we are to truly understand the message that Christ offered us, we must be willing to listen to the convictions of our fellow man. Words spoken from the mind are mere words; however, words spoken from the heart, are God's words.

A Personal Commentary – W R Hohenberger

He that findeth his life shall lose it: and he that loseth his life for my sake shall find it.

Matthew 10:39

Change is the only method for growing and becoming. If we try to hold on to what we are, we will still change, but uncontrollably. However, if we adopt change as a way of life, we can then use change as a tool for becoming.

A Personal Commentary – W R Hohenberger

Enter ye in at the strait gate: for wide is the gate, and broad is the way, that leadeth to destruction, and many there be which go in thereat."

Matthew 7:13

Our only hope to sort out the confusions and misunderstandings, which we have interwoven in our complex psyche, is through the power of the Holy Spirit. This path is not an easy path, and therefore many will choose not to take it. For those who do choose the straight and narrow way is given his promise of eternal life.

A Personal Commentary – W R Hohenberger

Therefore, I say unto you, what things so ever you desire, when ye pray, believe that ye receive them, and ye shall have them.

Mark 11:24

It is the uniting of both our mind's convictions and our heart's desires, with God's spirit, which answers prayers.

A Personal Commentary – W R Hohenberger

For everyone that asketh receiveth; and he that seeketh findeth; and to him that knocketh it shall be opened.

Luke 11:10

It is only through the power of the Holy Spirit that we can hope to achieve truth within us. All we need to do is to invite this greater spirit in, and allow it to manifest itself within us.

A Personal Commentary – W R Hohenberger

Behold, I send you forth as sheep in the midst of wolves: be ye therefore wise as serpents, and harmless as doves.

Matthew 10: 16

The spirit of the apostles is still alive today. It is kind but firm, courteous but steady, and open-minded but strong.

A Personal Commentary – W R Hohenberger

For verily I say unto you, that whosoever shall say unto this mountain, "Be thou removed, and then be thou cast into the sea," and shall not doubt in his heart, but shall believe that these things he saith shall come to pass, he shall have whatsoever he saith.

Mark 11:23

It is through the sincerity of our convictions that our words become truth; and our aspirations become possible. As we continue to reach out for the helping hand of God's eternal truths, it is only with His helping hand that we will accomplish our greatest hopes, realize our greatest virtues, and become our greatest ideals.

A Personal Commentary – W R Hohenberger

About the Author

 W. R. Hohenberger was born in northwest Ohio, holds an engineering degree (BSEE - 1968) from Indiana Institute of Technology in Fort Wayne, Indiana, and has dedicated much of his life to searching for answers to the unknown. This book represents the culmination of that search, and thereby establishes a firm foundation for a better understanding of ourselves, the world that surrounds us and our relationship to that world. He considers himself to be a philosopher of the heart and the mind, and even though writing this book was an arduous process at times, requiring much dedication, sacrifice and hard work, he has enjoyed contemplating the mysteries of the universe and the intricacies of human nature. However, it is now time to let others finish this task and to appreciate and to enjoy life at its most and at its best.

Made in the USA
San Bernardino, CA
04 June 2016